At a time when some of the world has begun to question the importance of environmental friendly, sustainable, and corporate responsibility, Peter Krull delivers the antidote to this wrong-headed view. Peter explains in clear terms the why and how to invest in a manner that not only enriches your portfolio but also enriches the world at large.

—**Ron Insana**, *CNBC contributor*

Peter's financial expertise, engaging storytelling, and data-driven case studies succeed in bringing sustainable investing to the forefront. This book is a timely read for financial advisors and retail investors interested in understanding and addressing financially material risks and unlocking investment opportunities in our rapidly changing world.

—**Maria Lettini**, *Chief executive officer at US Sustainable Investment Forum*

In a world drowning in greenwashed funds and "less bad" ESG nonsense, Peter Krull cuts through the noise with refreshing clarity and zero patience for Wall Street's sustainability charade. Drawing from 20 years in the trenches, he delivers what financial advisors desperately need: practical, no-BS strategies for building truly sustainable portfolios that actually align with client values. Ignore this book at your peril—unless you're fine watching trillions in assets walk out the door to advisors who get it.

—**Garvin Jabusch**, *Chief investment officer at Green Alpha Investments*

This is the book that the fossil fuel industry does not want you to read. It dispels the myths about investing with your values and provides you with the information and resources you need to invest in an environmentally responsible way.

—**Leslie Samuelrich**, *President of Green Century Funds*

A well-researched book on sustainable, resilient, and innovative investing that is structured for a broad audience and well suited for both professional and novice investors. For those interested in a deeper dive into sustainable investing, this book serves as a solid foundation, offering both clarity and depth on the subject.

—**Matthew Patsky**, *CEO and portfolio manager at Trillium Asset Management*

The Sustainable Investor is a timely and essential guide for financial professionals navigating the evolving landscape of sustainable investing. Through insightful storytelling—shaped in part by his firsthand experience of Hurricane Helene's devastation—Peter provides advisors with the tools and narratives needed to engage clients in meaningful conversations about impact. This book is a must-read for those looking to align their investments with a deeper purpose.

—**Jennifer N. Coombs**, *Head of content and development at the US Forum for Sustainable and Responsible Investment*

The Sustainable Investor is an excellent capsule history and analysis of sustainable investing over the decades while also providing thoughtful guidance for financial advisors seeking to be responsive to clients wishing to invest consistent with their values.

—**Tim Smith**, *Founder and senior policy advisor of Interfaith Center on Corporate Responsibility (ICCR)*

Peter Krull has written an up-to-date primer on the state of sustainable and resilient investing that will educate both the advisors who are already working in this space as well as the advisors who should at least understand it, which is all of them.

—**George Gay**, *CEO of First Affirmative Financial Network*

THE
SUSTAINABLE
INVESTOR

THE
SUSTAINABLE
INVESTOR

RESPONSIBLE, IMPACTFUL, AND
VALUES-DRIVEN INVESTING STRATEGIES
FOR FINANCIAL PROFESSIONALS

PETER KRULL

FOREWORD BY **ED BEGLEY JR.**

WILEY

For general information on our other products and services or for technical support, please contact our Customer Care Department within the United States at (800) 762-2974, outside the United States at (317) 572-3993 or fax (317) 572-4002.

Wiley also publishes its books in a variety of electronic formats. Some content that appears in print may not be available in electronic formats. For more information about Wiley products, visit our web site at www.wiley.com.

Library of Congress Cataloging-in-Publication Data is Available:

ISBN 9781394253517 (Cloth)
ISBN 9781394253524 (ePDF)
ISBN 9781394253531 (ePub)

Cover Design : Wiley
Cover Image : © Ivan Bajic/Getty Images
Author Photo: Courtesy of Reggie Tidwell
Printed and bound by CPI Group (UK) Ltd, Croydon, CR0 4YY

C9781394253517_100925

For Melissa, my muse, my cheerleader, my love — this journey wouldn't exist without you.

And for all the advisors out there who see the opportunity in helping clients align their investments with their values. This is for you.

CONTENTS

CONTENTS

CONTENTS

FOREWORD

I've been an environmental advocate for well over 50 years – my advocacy started back in 1970. I had been living in smoggy Los Angeles for two decades at that point, and I was tired of it. You couldn't spend any time outside for 150 or more days a year because the air quality was so bad. People wondered why they called it the San Fernando Valley because you couldn't see the mountains surrounding us.

In addition to the horrible air in Los Angeles, I had also seen the 1969 Santa Barbara oil spill up close. That disaster dumped about four million gallons of crude oil into the water and onto the Santa Barbara beaches and even parts of the pristine Channel Islands. The effect on marine life was profound as it killed thousands of sea birds, and countless dolphins, seals, and sea lions.

And then in June of that same year, the Cuyahoga River in Cleveland caught fire and made national news. I would later learn that it wasn't the first time the highly polluted river had burned and that the locals had become used to it. With the Los Angeles smog, the Santa Barbara oil spill, and the Cuyahoga River catching fire, I thought to myself, what are we doing to this place we call home?

Since I was a child, my dad had a huge impact on me. He was a conservative Republican, back when conservative meant conservation. The son of Irish immigrants, he lived through the Great Depression and all the hardships that came along with it. Because of this, we turned off the lights, turned off the water, and reused string and tin foil. When I complained about the smog as a young man, he'd tell me, "I know what you're *against*, but tell me what you are *for*? What are *you* doing to make the world a better place?"

One day in 1970, I heard through the grapevine that they were going to do this thing called *Earth Day*, and I was immediately interested. My friend Dennis Hayes was involved, and he asked if I wanted to be a part of it. I replied, "Sure, but what do you want to do and what is the goal?"

He said, "Well, many things, but we want to clean up the air and clean up the water." At that point, I said sign me up, as I thought about the Los Angeles smog and the water pollution from the previous year.

My dad died within a few days of that first Earth Day. After the celebration had ended, and all the speeches had been made about what we *might* do, I made the decision to make a list of things I *could* do and started that very week. I started riding my bike, taking public transportation, recycling, composting, and eating lower on the food chain. And I did all of this on the very modest budget of a broke and struggling actor. I quickly realized that everything I was doing was not only green but also saving a lot of green! In another sign of good things to come, later that year the Environmental Protection Agency was created.

My dedication to environmental advocacy honors my dad and his legacy. He believed that one of the most patriotic things we can do is conserve energy, and because of this, so much of my work has been based on finding ways to decrease my footprint and be an example for others.

Over the years, we were able to make a difference in that Los Angeles smog. Today, despite there being four times as many cars on the road than in 1970, and millions more people, the air quality has improved exponentially. In 2024, a team of conservationists released lake sturgeon back into the Cuyahoga River. This release is a sign that the river cleanup has succeeded because lake sturgeon needs clean water to reproduce. All of this happened because people acted.

I've learned that action happens through what I call the *three pillars of advocacy*:

1. **Personal actions.** Actions such as riding your bicycle or taking public transportation, installing solar panels, replacing your bulbs with energy efficient LEDs, and recycling water fall into this category

2. **Corporate responsibility.** Holding corporations to a higher standard, demand products and services that are sustainable and environmentally friendly, and invest in those that take their responsibility seriously

3. **Legislative action.** Legislation like the Clean Air Act, and the Clean Water Act, which came about in the early 1970s as a direct result of the issues I described, combined with politicians who worked for the people instead of corporate interests

Climate change is now our biggest threat, and we are seeing the impacts in our everyday lives now. The Los Angeles fires in early 2025, Hurricane Helene hitting the North Carolina mountains, droughts, crop failures, and climate migrations are the new reality. Now, in addition to reducing our emissions and being more sustainable, we also need to be more resilient and adaptive to this climate reality. That will take innovation and resources and all of us working together using the three pillars of advocacy.

I like to talk about the importance of investing in the world that you want to live in. I started this practice back in the 1970s by investing in choices like riding my bike or using public transportation, switching out my light bulbs with energy efficient ones, and installing an energy-saving thermostat and then built on those decisions. They helped me to save money. With the savings, I bought a rain barrel to collect rainwater.

By 1985, I saved enough to put solar hot water on the roof of my house, and in 1990, I proudly installed solar electric on my roof and never looked back.

My current house is a LEED Platinum home, which is the most energy efficient and environmentally friendly rating you can get. From its small footprint to solar panels, rainwater harvesting, airtight insulation, and nontoxic materials, our home exemplifies just about everything you can do to live in harmony with nature.

Of course, investing isn't just about the lifestyle choices you make but also about the actual investments you own. You can't say that you care about people, the environment, sustainability, and climate change and own stock in big oil, tobacco, or defense contractors at the same time. All too often there is a disconnect between how we invest our money and how we live our lives. When I invest, I want to know that the companies I own are making a difference, that they are providing products and solutions to move us forward, not hold us back. That's what this book is all about, and why I was excited when Pete asked me to write the foreword.

I've known Pete Krull for many years now, and he exemplifies what it means to be a true advocate for the environment, sustainability, and sustainable investing. His concept of sustainable, resilient, and innovative (SRI) investing is an advancement from what I used to know as socially responsible investing back in the day.

This book will offer you a glimpse into Pete's world as the 2024 *Investment News* ESG/Responsible Investing Advisor of the Year.[1] You'll learn how he started in the business and pivoted from traditional investing at Merrill Lynch to hanging up his shingle and starting an SRI firm from scratch. You'll understand what the difference is between environmental, social, and governance (ESG) and sustainable investing and how to

---

[1] Awarded June 2024 for the 2023–2024 year period by *Investment News*. No compensation was provided.

communicate that difference to the public. You will hear a cautionary tale of greenwashing and how to avoid the worst of this deadly sin.

And then he'll walk you through the steps he takes to construct the sustainable portfolios that Earth Equity manages for its clients. You'll learn that financial planning should also include the effects of climate change and how to talk with clients about it. And finally, Pete will give you advice on how to build your own sustainable investing practice and deal with the realities of the politics surrounding ESG and SRI.

I wish you luck on your journey as you learn about what I believe is one of the most important tools we must use to create positive change: investing with your values.

—Ed Begley Jr.
Actor and environmental advocate

INTRODUCTION
WHY I'M QUALIFIED TO WRITE ABOUT SRI

I wrote the original introduction to the book back in 2023, and that part is still here, following what I'm now calling the *second introduction*. This second introduction was inspired by the events of September 27, 2024. On that date, my town of Asheville, North Carolina, was devastated by Hurricane Helene, showing the world the awesome power of a fossil-fuel-charged hurricane. As of this writing, there is no official monetary cost of the disaster, but it will likely be in the tens of billions of dollars. Strap in – this is just the beginning.

Only a few days later, on October 9, 2024, Hurricane Milton slammed into the west coast of Florida. Milton, which was a tropical storm on October 5, rapidly intensified over the ensuing 24 hours, developing into a full category 5 storm on October 7. This is one of the shortest periods that a hurricane has ever increased in intensity from tropical storm to category 5. The reason for this explosive intensification was sea surface temperatures in the Gulf of Mexico of almost 90° Fahrenheit. And the reason for the elevated water temperature: climate change.

And in January 2025, the Los Angeles region was rocked by a series of wildfires that destroyed thousands of homes. The climate change–driven whiplash effect of intense rains and vegetation growth, followed by severe drought, left the area ripe for this "perfect storm" event.

Since Dr. James Hansen's testimony before the Senate Committee on Energy and Natural Resources in June 1988, scientists have been warning us that unregulated growth in greenhouse gas emissions was going to drastically alter our climate and produce more intense storms, as we've seen with Hurricanes Helene and Milton. In his testimony, Dr. Hansen said, "I would like to draw three main conclusions. Number one, the earth is warmer in 1988 than at any time in the history of instrumental measurements. Number two, the global warming is now large enough that we can ascribe with a high degree of confidence a cause-and-effect relationship to the greenhouse effect. And number three, our computer climate simulations indicate that the greenhouse effect is already large enough to begin to affect the probability of extreme events such as summer heat waves."

As I was thinking about writing an additional introduction, I knew that I wanted to start the book off with an urgent call to action. Dr. Hansen knew in 1988 that continuing the current pace of emissions at the time would lead to exactly where we are now. We can no longer look at climate change as something in the future – a belief that has allowed us to maintain our "kick the can down the road" strategy for so long. While major corporations and governments have set 2050 goals for becoming carbon neutral, mostly for supposedly economic reasons, the climate has ignored their intention and continued to warm. The reality is that the climate has changed, and it is going to continue to change if we insist on maintaining the status quo and using fossil fuels as our main energy source.

Because of this, I've decided to change the way I describe climate change to *the changed climate*. This phrase more accurately describes the current state of this phenomena and changes the time from an undefined future event to what is happening in the here and now. Climate change is happening now, and we are feeling the effects of the changed climate every day. The question is, are we going to do something about it?

I've also changed how I define SRI. As I talk about in Chapter 2, *SRI* used to stand for *socially responsible investing*. It evolved into *sustainable and responsible investing* over the years. I'm now beginning to call it *sustainable, resilient, and innovative investing*, integrating the need to not only transition to a more sustainable economy but also to a more resilient one that uses innovation to help address our challenges. The hurricane damage in Asheville more than exemplified the need for more resilient infrastructure, and for more adaptive systems.

As I was finishing this book, we also had a major election in the United States where we moved from an administration that actively worked to promote climate solutions to one that is a self-described climate change skeptic. We have been through this cycle before and came out stronger on the other side. The demand for a cleaner economy persists, irrespective of the political party in charge in Washington. Many corporations have made environmental, climate, and social pledges and risk a consumer backlash if they were to step away from those values.

While we will likely see some legislative and executive actions that may not favor the next economy, the reality is that the train has already left the station. Instead of relying on the government to be the driver of change, we must work as individuals and groups to be advocates. We must vote with our dollars. We need to hold corporations accountable and figure out how to keep improving this experiment we call democracy. But at the end of the day, just like climate change, the next economy is moving forward, whether we like it or not.

And so, these factors make this book much timelier. The time to transition our investment strategies from the legacy economy to a new, cleaner, more resource efficient, more resilient, and more equitable economy is now. It's also the time to transition your financial advisory practice to focus on sustainable, resilient, and innovative investing.

I've gone back and made edits to many of the chapters that I had already written. Although this was a time-consuming process with my deadline looming, I felt it made sense to go back and reassess how I may have worded things and if there were any changes necessary considering new circumstances. Thanks for indulging me!

Original Introduction

I've always had an interest in investing. Growing up in the Buffalo, New York, area, I thought it was interesting and exciting that Berkshire Hathaway owned *The Buffalo News* – the Warren Buffet conglomerate bought the paper back in 1977. In the 1980s, when I began to take notice, Berkshire Hathaway[1] shares were trading about $3,000, which was ridiculously expensive for a single share of stock at the time (it still is).

I didn't have the money to buy any shares then, and I couldn't convince my dad to buy the three shares that I wanted either. Supposedly my parents had been burned in the 1970s when they lost their entire investment in commodities. Unfortunately, I never got the full story on that one. But even more unfortunate is that the $9,000 I wanted to invest in Berkshire Hathaway back then would be worth about $1.35 million today.

In fact, from 1965 through 2021, Berkshire Hathaway had a compound annual return of 20.1%, nearly double the 10.5% for the S&P 500. A remarkable feat considering all the upheaval over that time and Buffet's

---

[1] Specific investments described herein do not represent all investment decisions made by Peter Krull. The reader should not assume that investment decisions identified and discussed were or will be profitable. Specific investment advice references provided herein are for illustrative purposes only and are not necessarily representative of investments that will be made in the future.

aversion to most technology names. For me, it was a lesson learned about the return potential of the stock market as well as learning to be comfortable with missing out on an opportunity.

Growing up, my family had a small piece of land in the woods south of Buffalo that we would visit often. I spent a lot of time there in my teens, hiking and learning to appreciate nature. I attribute my love of nature to my older brother, who helped me to understand what I was seeing and experiencing as we walked and hunted in the woods. I have since given up hunting but cherish the opportunity to learn as much as I did over the years. It helped me to be the person I am today.

When I was in school at Bethany College in West Virginia, I studied communication, not business. Ultimately, I believe having a communication degree has been a big advantage for me. Sustainable investing requires you to educate prospective clients and the public on its differences and advantages in a way that isn't always necessary with traditional investing.

One unique feature of Bethany College's curriculum is its annual J-Term (or January Term) classes. In between semesters, you could take a short, one-credit-hour class on an interesting topic that was outside of your course of study. I took a class on investing and was further hooked.

We learned the basics, such as what is a stock and bond, how mutual funds work, and concepts like asset allocation. Not long afterward, I took a couple of hundred dollars and invested in my first mutual fund.

Fast-forward a few years, and I found myself working in management for a regional electronics retailer. I had continued investing what little I could (I was in my twenties and basically living hand-to-mouth) and saved up a few thousand dollars in a brokerage account at Merrill Lynch. At the time, Merrill Lynch was a leader in the investment world. I was lucky enough to have a customer who was a Merrill advisor, and he opened a small account for me.

When I learned that my employer was about to file for Chapter 11 bankruptcy, I immediately knew what my next step was going to be – I wanted to get into the investment world. I called my advisor and asked if he could help get me an interview at the local Merrill Lynch office in Roanoke, Virginia, where I was living at the time. He did so, I got the job, and I started the process of becoming a financial advisor.

It was the end of 1998, and I was about to take my Series 7 exam and jump into the deep end. The internet boom was just starting, CNBC had gotten considerable traction in homes and offices, and there was a world of opportunity ahead of me!

Merrill Lynch had a great training program, including multiple trips to the "mothership" in Princeton, New Jersey, for weeklong sessions on prospecting, investing, and communicating. While in Roanoke, new advisors gathered regularly with a senior mentor who had responsibility for our success.

It was during this time that I had my first taste of socially responsible investing, or at least the concept of it. Our mentor mentioned, more than once, after a visit from the Calvert Investments representative (Calvert is one of the legacy SRI fund families), how he was considering specializing in SRI as he saw it as a future market opportunity. He never followed through, and part of the reason for this, I believe, is that it was merely a marketing opportunity for him and not driven by his values. At the time, it seemed the only folks who specialized in SRI were the hard-core tree huggers that you could easily stereotype. That was not him.

Over the next few years, I grew my business and met Melissa Booth, the woman who would eventually become my wife. She happened to have PhDs in microbiology and molecular genetics, and we were having long conversations about the environment, sustainability, climate change, and social issues. These conversations were ultimately the genesis of Earth Equity Advisors and my career in sustainable investing.

At about the same time, I brought on a new client who was installing rainwater catchment systems at houses and businesses. He also was focused on environmental issues, specifically the growing concern about freshwater availability and drought.

This new client also happened to be installing a rainwater catchment system at the home of Bill McDonough, the renowned green architect and author of the sustainability and circular economy tome *Cradle to Cradle*. I was lucky enough to be invited to a meeting at Bill's office with my new client. That meeting sealed the deal for me that there was a future in investing sustainably!

In June 2004, I officially hung up my shingle at my little home in Roanoke, Virginia. The name of the new firm was Krull & Company, and my intention was to focus only on socially responsible investing from the start. Most of my clients at the time came over with me to the new firm, so I started out with a fair amount of assets.

At the time, my choices for SRI funds were quite limited. Calvert, PaxWorld, Domini, Green Century, and only a couple of other fund families had options. Some were good, most were, well, let's just say they could have used some work. But we made it through and created fund portfolios for clients that were good enough to continually bring on new assets and keep my current clients happy.

Over the years, an evolution took place. I saw an explosion of investment options, mutual funds, exchange-traded funds (ETFs), and many more individual stocks that I would consider sustainable. As with investment options, I also saw SRI evolve from socially responsible investing to sustainable, responsible, and impact investing. I saw the advent of the ESG (environment, social, governance) movement and the intention to quantify companies' impact. There's now an alphabet soup of acronyms (as there is with everything), and sometimes it feels like you need a sherpa just to navigate it all.

For a long time, I bought into the rhetoric that investing in fossil fuels helped to maintain a seat at the table for proxy voting. The rationale being that these companies could be changed by working with them instead of simply divesting. At the end of the day, however, I decided that divesting from fossil fuels was the better choice because the funds invested in the main driver of our existential climate crisis could be reallocated to companies making a sustainable difference. This played out in real time after an activist investor got environmental advocates on the ExxonMobil board. Since they were elected, no progress has been made in making ExxonMobil a more sustainable or environmentally friendly company. The disconnect between shareholder advocacy with fossil fuel companies and actual impact and change is disappointing.

Over the years, I've applied my communication training by writing articles, providing expert commentary in publications, including the *New York Times,* the *Wall Street Journal, Bloomberg Businessweek,* and *Barron's,* and making appearances on podcasts and financial news television. I host a podcast, *Dollars & Change: The Expert's Guide to Sustainable & Responsible Investing,* showcasing discussions with leading experts in sustainable investing from across the country. I provide training to both individual investors and financial advisors and have traveled to Washington, DC, to advocate for more sustainable and responsible policies and legislation. I've also proudly been named the 2024 *Investment News* ESG/Responsible Investing Advisor of the Year,[2] as well as receiving several other awards and honors over the years. Change doesn't happen on its own; we need to make it happen.

I believe that it is supremely important for leaders to lead, speak their minds, and work to make positive change. The current course we find ourselves on very well may lead us to a lower standard of living for our children and grandchildren, and what will we reply when they ask us why we didn't do anything to shift course? Sustainable investing is about intentionality; it

---

[2] Awarded June 2024 for the 2023–2024 year period by *Investment News.* No compensation was provided. https://awards.investmentnews.com/ina24-featureprofile-winner-peter-krull/p/1

is about seeing the opportunities in sustainability, adaptation, and resilience; it is about reducing systemic risks, and it is about fostering diversity, inclusion, and equity. Ultimately, it is about doing the right thing for our clients, our families, and the world at large.

Thank you for joining me on this journey. This book is intended to be more of a practical guide to integrating sustainable investing into your practice. You won't find a lot of technical details on how to evaluate company A versus company B. What you will find is 20-plus years of observations and on-the-ground experience creating and growing a firm that has become recognized for its expertise and thought leadership. My intention is to help set you up for success as the financial services industry, economy, and culture continues to evolve. I look forward to sharing insights that will empower you to integrate sustainable investing into your practice.

"Yes, the planet got destroyed, but for a beautiful moment in time we created a lot of value for shareholders."

Source: Peter Krull / CartoonStock

SECTION I

THE BASICS

CHAPTER ONE

WHY YOU NEED TO KNOW ABOUT SRI NOW

OVERVIEW

Sustainable investing continues to gather steam (and assets) across the investment industry. Virtually every major investment firm on Wall Street now has some sort of sustainable, resilient, and innovative (SRI) or environmental, social, and governance (ESG) offering. There's a sense across the industry of FOMO, or fear of missing out, if you don't at least have a basic responsible portfolio for your clients. This is encouraging as we continue to build a movement that embraces responsible investing.

US SIF – The Sustainable Investment Forum, our SRI industry trade group, publishes a biennial report on the state of the industry called the "US Sustainable Investing Trends Report."[1] The latest report released in December 2024, showed that 12% of the US invested assets are self-declared as "sustainable." That's the equivalent of $6.5 trillion. In addition, about 80% of the $52.5 trillion US market indicated that there is a stewardship policy or guideline in place and that 60% provide regular reporting on stewardship efforts.

Morgan Stanley also released their "Sustainable Signals"[2] report in December of 2024. This report details the attitudes of institutional investors on sustainable investing. The report says, "More than three-quarters (78%) of asset managers expect Assets Under Management (AUM) in sustainable funds to increase over the next two years, driven by a combination of new mandates and higher allocations from existing asset owner clients. This is consistent with responses from asset owners, where 80% expect the proportion of their assets allocated to sustainable investment options to increase over the same period. Notably, only 3% of asset owners and asset managers expect a decline in asset allocation or AUM."

The report goes on to say, "For both groups, the exposure to growth opportunities that sustainable investments offer is the top reason for this expected increase, followed by a more established track record for sustainable investing as a strategy. For more than 70% of both asset owners and asset managers, sustainable investments make up less than half of assets or AUM today, suggesting there is indeed room for growth."

---

[1] US SIF, "US Sustainable Investing Trends 2024/2025 Report," December 18, 2024, https://www.ussif .org/research/trends-reports.

[2] Morgan Stanley Institute for Sustainable Investing," Sustainable Signals: Institutional Investors," December 2024, https://www.morganstanley.com/content/dam/msdotcom/en/assets/pdfs/CRC_3923864-2024_ Sustainable_Signals_Institutional_Investors-PDF_Report-FINAL.pdf.

In addition to the survey's motivations, there are multiple additional reasons why this momentum continues to build:

- Climate change hitting home
- Income inequality and social justice in the headlines
- Corporate greed and malfeasance
- More information available
- Demographic shifts
- The great wealth transfer
- The changing economy

Let's break each of these down.

CLIMATE CHANGE HITTING HOME

The impacts of the changed climate are everywhere. From more intense storms to droughts to wildfires, there's not an individual in the United States who hasn't felt at least a small impact. And it may not necessarily be a direct impact, like a hurricane washing away your home. It could be the cost of a food commodity that is now more expensive because of drought across the country or across the world.

But on September 27, 2024, I personally felt the direct impact of Hurricane Helene on my home city of Asheville, North Carolina. A rainstorm had dropped as much as seven inches of rain on our region two days before, so the ground was already saturated. Then Helene moved up from the Gulf of Mexico with massive amounts of water stored up and ready to release. And release she did!

Reports are that as much as 31 inches of rain were dropped in the region. Scientists say that for every degree Celsius of warming, the atmosphere can hold 7% more moisture. It has been calculated that Helene, plus the storms preceding it, dropped forty trillion gallons of water on the southeast. An easier-to-understand analogy shows that if concentrated on North Carolina alone, the forty trillion gallons would cover the entire state with over one meter of water. According to AccuWeather, that would also be equivalent to the flow of Niagara Falls for 1.75 years![3]

World Weather Attribution is an initiative to analyze weather events rapidly following major storms. They can determine if and how much of a storm's intensity is attributed to climate change by running multiple computer models. Yale Climate Connections summarized some of their Hurricane Helene findings in an article:

- Hurricanes as intense as Hurricane Helene are today about 2.5 times more likely in the region: They would be expected to occur on average every 130 years in a preindustrial climate but now have a one-in-53 chance in any given year.
- Hurricane Helene's wind speeds on the coast of Florida were about 13 miles per hour or 11% more intense due to climate change.
- Climate change increased Hurricane Helene's rainfall by about 10%. This level of rainfall that led to catastrophic flooding in the Appalachians has shifted from a once-in-115-year event to a once-in-70-year event today as a result of climate change.
- The high sea temperatures that fueled Hurricane Helene were made 200–500 times more likely by climate change.[4]

[3] Seth Borenstein, "Heavy Rainfall Is Growing More Intense, and Climate Change Is to Blame," Associated Press, January 18, 2025, https://apnews.com/article/rainfall-helene-carolina-tennessee-georgia-climate-change-flood-fcba634e14a0ffa1a8e1fa85d7e2b390.

[4] Daisy Simmons, "Climate Change Made Hurricane Helene and Other 2024 Disasters More Damaging, Scientists Find," *Yale Climate Connections*, October 2024, https://yaleclimateconnections.org/2024/10/climate-change-made-hurricane-helene-and-other-2024-disasters-more-damaging-scientists-find/.

At the time of this writing, AccuWeather estimates that the total damage from Hurricane Helene will be between $225 billion and $250 billion. The estimate includes "the horrific loss of life, the immediate and long-term costs of healthcare for storm survivors and injured first responders, extended power outages, major infrastructure reconstruction projects for utilities, highways, bridges, and railroad tracks, major business and travel disruptions, as well as long-term losses to tourism, technology, renewable energy and other industries across the southern Appalachians and south-eastern U.S."[5]

In addition to Helene, a week later we saw Hurricane Milton form in the Gulf of Mexico. Milton intensified from a tropical storm to a category 5 hurricane in about two days – one of the fastest intensifications ever recorded.

These intensified storms and other climate impacts are setting us up for an insurance crisis. In a number of states, including Florida and California, many large, regulated insurance companies are either pulling out or greatly reducing the properties they cover. This has left a gap that is being filled by "lightly regulated" insurers who come in as an insurer of last resort. Unfortunately, they don't have the same capital requirements as the large, fully regulated insurers.

According to NASA, 2024 was the warmest year on record. The agency said, "For more than half of 2024, average temperatures were more than 1.5 degrees Celsius above the baseline, and the annual average, with mathematical uncertainties, may have exceeded the level for the first time."[6] A benchmark of 1.5 degrees Celsius was set by the Paris Agreement as a level that should not be exceeded knowing that 2 degrees Celsius increase

---

[5] Kevin Byrne, "Helene Is 2nd Deadliest U.S. Hurricane in 50 Years, Could Cost $250 Billion," AccuWeather, https://www.accuweather.com/en/hurricane/helene-is-2nd-deadliest-u-s-hurricane-in-50-years-could-cost-250-billion/1698452.
[6] NASA Earth Observatory, "2024 Was the Warmest Year on Record," NASA Earth Observatory, https://earthobservatory.nasa.gov/images/153806/2024-was-the-warmest-year-on-record.

could very well result in catastrophic consequences. It appears those consequences are here.

Early in 2025, the Los Angeles region was ravaged by wildfires caused by climate change. The area has experienced what is called a whiplash effect. Basically, there are periods of heavy rains, often associated with atmospheric rivers, which causes rapid vegetation growth. For every 1 degree Celsius increase in temperature, the atmosphere can hold approximately 7% more water vapor.

These rains are then followed by prolonged drought where the excessive vegetation that grew in the wake of the heavy rains then dries out and becomes extremely combustible. Combine this with extreme Santa Ana winds of 80 miles per hour or more, and you have a perfect storm – one that is turning people's lives upside down. Just like we saw in Asheville.

Asheville could also experience a similar fate. According to the North Carolina Forest Service, approximately 40% of Buncombe County's trees were damaged or destroyed in the storm. Just like the dried vegetation in Southern California, those damaged and destroyed trees could serve as kindling for a future fire as climate risks continue to mount.

The unprecedented amount of destruction wrought by these two climate-fueled events has left those affected reeling. Pacific Palisades has been all but burned off the map, and Asheville will take years to clean up and rebuild.

And these events are prompting many Americans to uproot their lives and move to what they consider to be "safer" areas to live. The reality is that there is no such thing as a climate haven. A 2022 report from the First Street Foundation entitled "Climate Abandonment Areas" estimated that there had been $2.65 trillion in damage from billion-dollar disasters alone since 1980. The most widespread of these disasters has been drought, causing over $345 billion during that time, and the impacts were felt in all states, but concentrated in about half. The report showed that some of the fastest growing states also had some of the highest risks, including Florida, California, and Texas.[7]

But when informed about climate risks, homeowners tend to pay heed. As reported in "Climate Abandonment Areas," the real estate website Zillow found that 80% of home buyers consider climate risks when looking for a home. A climate migration is happening whether it is reported by the media or not. The report goes on to say that between 2000 and 2020, 3.2 million people have left what they call "climate abandonment" areas due to high flood risk. They expect more than seven million people to migrate over the next 30 years, and I believe they are underestimating the potential number.

Investors are also becoming more aware that environmental risks are often economic risks. The example I often use is Utah's Great Salt Lake. In 2022, politicians were up in arms because S&P Global Ratings had given the state a negative environmental risk rating for its debt. The politicians argued that this ESG rating was "politicized," and that ratings should be based on material information and be a purely financial decision. What the politicians missed is that the decision to give the negative rating *was* a financial one.

In a paper published in January 2023, Brigham Young University researchers cautioned of the unprecedented danger that the Great Salt Lake is facing, and "without a dramatic increase in water flow to the lake in 2023 and 2024, its disappearance could cause immense damage to Utah's public health, environment, and economy." They warned that excessive water use is destroying the lake, and that the lake is on track to disappear in five years.[8]

The report goes on to say that the lake provides nearly $2 billion in total economic value and supports nearly 9,000 jobs. Based on this information, the S&P rating doesn't look so bad. But there's more.

---

[7] First Street Foundation, "Climate Abandonment Areas: National Risk Assessment."
[8] Brigham Young University, "Great Salt Lake," Physical and Mathematical Sciences, https://pws.byu.edu/great-salt-lake.

The dry lake bed would harbor untold quantities of toxic substances, which would then be picked up by winds and carried into Salt Lake City, the state's largest population center with approximately 3.3 million residents. It's highly likely that there would be an exodus from the city because of the health concerns brought about by these toxic winds. But that's not the only economic impact.

The lake helps to provide lake-effect snowfall on Utah's prized slopes. It creates the wonderful powder that blankets each run on a regular basis. Without a lake to help create this powder, the state's $1.5 billion ski industry is at risk.

You can quickly see the importance and advantages of looking beyond the current financials of a municipality or corporation with this real-world example. Environmental impacts can be, and often are, material impacts. As a portfolio manager, I might decide to pass over Utah's bonds and buy another state's bonds with a more stable environmental outlook, which is what S&P's ratings are meant to do: inform the investor. As a fiduciary, it's not only prudent to gather as much information as possible but it's also your responsibility.

Morgan Stanley regularly publishes their "Sustainable Signals" research report, which takes a deep dive into the ESG/sustainable investing industry. The latest report from April 2024 showed that "More than 80% of investors believe companies should address environmental issues, and two-thirds say social issues should also be tackled." Additionally, over 80% of investors see renewable energy and energy efficiency as an opportunity to generate returns. We'll discuss more about changing demographics in the pages ahead.[9]

---

[9] Morgan Stanley Institute for Sustainable Investing, "Sustainable Signals: Individual Investors 2025," https://www.morganstanley.com/content/dam/msdotcom/en/assets/pdfs/2025_Sustainable_Signals_Individual_Investors_2025_report.pdf.

INCOME INEQUALITY AND SOCIAL JUSTICE IN THE HEADLINES

Investors interested in responsible investing are typically very socially aware as well. They understand the grave problems caused by income inequality globally and environmental injustices such as placing industrial facilities near low-income neighborhoods. When they see a school shooting in the news, they want something to be done – and coincidentally, they would be mortified to learn that they own a weapons manufacturer in their investment portfolio.

One often overlooked aspect of responsible investing is gender lens investing. Gender lens investing adds a layer of due diligence to the research process, including a company's overall gender diversity, its leadership and board makeup, gender pay disparities, and gender-friendly employee policies.

This aspect of investing is being actively attacked by politicians, and many corporations are scaling back their DEI or diversity, equity, and inclusion efforts. Despite the political attacks and corporate backsliding, there is a strong foundation underpinning the adoption of gender lens investing. A May 2020 McKinsey report entitled "Diversity Wins – How Inclusion Matters," details the financial advantages of having a diverse workforce. It starts out by saying, "Our latest analysis reaffirms the strong business case for both gender diversity and ethnic and cultural diversity in corporate leadership – and shows that this business case continues to strengthen. The most diverse companies are now more likely than ever to outperform non-diverse companies on profitability." The report found that "companies in the top quartile of gender diversity on executive teams were

25% more likely to experience above-average profitability than peer companies in the fourth quartile."[10]

It only makes sense that employing a diversity of opinions, backgrounds, and expertise makes for stronger teams and, ultimately, companies. For too long, our economy has been stuck in a rut of "that's how we've always done it," run by clones of guys who have always run these companies. This is especially true in industries such as energy, transportation, and utilities, where their argument of "why fix what isn't broken" doesn't fly in an increasingly diverse and carbon-constrained world. We need diverse leaders and out-of-the-box thinking to break us out of this rut.

There is much work to do when it comes to diversity – especially on corporate boards. According to 50/50 Women on Boards, as of 2022, women hold only 28% of board seats at Russell 3000 companies. In Q4 2022, 28.4% of directors reported their race and ethnicity, nearly a 1 percentage point increase from Q3 2022. The percentage of people of color on boards is nearly 17%, with women of color holding 7% of the seats and men of color holding 10% of the seats.[11] There is considerable business risk when a board is not representative of employees and the public. This lack of inclusion is a red flag for investors.

The changed climate also contributes to social justice issues. *Consumer Reports* commissioned an analysis of the impact of climate change on each American born in 2024. What they found was shocking – they estimated that climate change will cost everyone at least $500,000 over that child's lifetime.[12]

---

[10] McKinsey & Company, "Diversity Wins: How Inclusion Matters," May 2020, https://www.mckinsey.com/business-functions/organization/our-insights/diversity-wins-how-inclusion-matters.

[11] 50/50 Women on Boards, "Q4 2022 Infographic," https://5050wob.com/wp-content/uploads/pdf/5050WOB-2022-Q4-Infographic-FINAL.pdf.

[12] Jeff Blyskal, "The Per-Person Financial Cost of Climate Change," *Consumer Reports*, February 14, 2024, https://www.consumerreports.org/home-garden/climate-change/the-per-person-financial-cost-of-climate-change-a6081217358/.

The estimate includes increased housing costs – due to increased maintenance, operating, and insurance costs. Additional costs include energy, taxes, and health care. Food costs will increase because "warmer temperatures, extreme weather events, and changes in precipitation patterns are expected to challenge farmers, interrupt food supplies, and increase retail prices. Although some food-producing regions could benefit from warming temperatures, climate models consistently predict an overall negative effect on food production."

CORPORATE GREED AND MALFEASANCE

In many circles, the corporate world has a rather negative connotation associated with it. You can harken back to the robber barons of the last century and to Rich Uncle Pennybags, the mascot of the board game Monopoly, as examples of corporatism and capitalism gone awry. More recently, industrialists like Elon Musk continue to perpetuate this association.

Even though we have many more regulations than we did in the robber baron days, that doesn't mean that corporations don't try to take advantage of every opportunity they can to make a buck. Legally, that is what they are required to do, right? Maximize shareholder returns.

But many companies build in fines as a cost of doing business. Leadership can rationalize that being compliant and changing processes and operations can be more expensive than the potential fines to be paid, so it's simply about the numbers. Unfortunately, noncompliance often ends up hitting the bottom line much more than anticipated and sometimes costing people their lives.

In December 1984, a Union Carbide pesticide plant in Bhopal, India, released over 40 tons of methyl isocyanate (MIC), an extremely toxic and hazardous substance, into the atmosphere. The release immediately killed more than 2,000 people. But, because MIC is a gas, it spread to the surrounding areas and eventually killed over 20,000 people and injured well over 550,000.

Unfortunately, when industrial disasters take place, there are usually warning signs, and the Union Carbide incident was not an exception. There were official complaints of various chemical leaks going back to 1976. A worker died in 1981 after inhaling the chemical phosgene, followed by multiple accidents and injuries in the years leading up to the December 1984 incident. Many of these were the result of malfunctioning safety systems and valves and pipes that were in poor condition – all deferred maintenance that would have cost the company money.

Litigation from this disaster ultimately cost Union Carbide $470 million in a 1989 settlement (about $1 billion today). Corporate management had the choice to complete the necessary maintenance but chose not to. They also had the choice to use less toxic substances than MIC, as the chemical giant Bayer was doing. However, those processes were more expensive and would have eaten into Union Carbide's profits.

The Union Carbide incident exemplifies all three ESG components: an environmental disaster caused by using unnecessarily toxic ingredients in a process; social disaster affecting hundreds of thousands of residents of Bhopal, India (many industrial facilities are sited in poor areas); and a governance disaster where corporate management chose profit over safety.

Beyond the $470 million settlement, how much was Union Carbide's corporate reputation harmed? Perhaps not much back in 1984, but today, with the proliferation of readily available news sources, it would be major. ExxonMobil is still saddled with the Valdez oil spill stigma, and Facebook and other social media companies are viewed as having been complicit in spreading political and vaccine-related misinformation.

MORE INFORMATION AVAILABLE

When I started Krull & Company back in 2004, there was no such thing as ESG data. SRI fund families mostly focused on exclusion/inclusion strategies. Is it a fossil fuel company, a mining company, or a tobacco company? Let's exclude them. There weren't the shades of gray we now have with the reams of ESG data.

Over the years, the industry has realized that more data is better. It certainly assists investment advisors as we uphold our fiduciary duty to do what is in the client's best interests. With more advanced data gathering and management technology, we can now pull just about any metric that we want, from fundamental data to market opinion to ESG. Integrating all this information has never been easier, and with AI quickly maturing, gathering data and analysis will only become more efficient.

We now have data on gender diversity in both the boardroom and senior management. Racial and LGBTQ+ data is still lacking, but I foresee this information being available soon. Likewise, we continue to get better data on a company's greenhouse gas emissions, especially scope one and two. Scope three, or end-user data, is somewhat harder to gauge, but is coming along as well.

Beyond information, there are also more companies that qualify as "sustainable" now. When I started our Green Sage Sustainability Portfolio in 2012, there were no publicly traded battery companies, Tesla was only a couple of years old, and our choices for solar were limited. Now, I must decide which battery company to add to the portfolio, the level of crazy that Elon Musk is during the rebalancing period, and which solar company treats its employees best. These are good choices to have!

There are also many more fund and exchange-traded fund options available, some good, some not so good. We'll review the importance of looking under the hood to judge the different sustainable fund options later in the book. But for now, know that the explosion of funds has given us tremendous choice when it comes to creating diversified, fund-based portfolios.

DEMOGRAPHIC SHIFTS

I love the phrase, "The only constant is change." This could not be more appropriate when it comes to shifting investment attitudes. The hippy boomers of the 1970s brought us Birkenstocks, the green revolution, and socially responsible investing. Gen Xers watched in horror as Michael Douglas's character, Gordon Gekko raided corporate pension funds in the 1987 film, *Wall Street*. Millennials brought a strong sense of doing right by people and planet, and Gen Z amplified that message on TikTok.

In the early days of Krull & Company, and for several years afterward, women were most of my client base. There's no other way to explain it other than they just "got it." They understood that you can't separate out your values from how you allocate and use your money. Often, men can insulate the two concepts from each other. This has led to the traditional Wall Street talking point regarding SRI: "Make money investing in any way possible and donate any extra profits to do good."

This statement reinforces the fallacy that sustainable and responsible investing will earn you a substandard return (we'll talk more about returns in Chapter 9). Based on conversations with my female clients, this serves to build a wall between the advisor (usually a guy) and the client. It's that patriarchal attitude of "Let me take care of this, honey. You don't know what you're talking about."

Well, it turns out those early adopters did know what they were talking about, and their children and grandchildren have followed suit. Referencing the 2025 Morgan Stanley *Sustainable Signals* report again, 97% of millennials and 99% of Gen Z investors are either somewhat or very interested in sustainable investing.[13] Let's stop and think about that for a moment: 99% and 97%. If you ever had any reason as an advisor to at least begin to understand sustainable investing, this statistic should light a fire for you. These are your future clients!

And that's not all. The report also showed that 84% of the general population were either somewhat or very interested in sustainable investing. Most investors have an interest in investing responsibly. This is not a fad that's going away anytime soon. This is the future of investing.

This data is supported by an additional 2022 survey by Morningstar. In that survey, 62% of respondents believed that sustainable investing "would help them achieve their financial goals more than other investments." Also, 76% also want to understand how their investments manage risk related to environmental and social issues. That same percentage also stressed the importance of evaluating "the real-world tangible impacts their investments are having."[14]

Basically, investors want to be aware of their investments' positive and negative impacts on people and the planet. They want to do everything they can to positively influence the world around them, including their consumer choices, where and how they live, and how they invest their money.

And you need to ask them about it. The 2021 Morgan Stanley "Sustainable Signals" survey showed that a small majority, only 56% of advisors, have bothered to ask their clients about their nonfinancial priorities, and half reported receiving no information related to their portfolio's sustainability performance.[15] Clients want you, their advisor, to engage with them on the impact of their portfolio. They want information, and they want choice.

---

[13] Morgan Stanley Institute for Sustainable Investing, *Sustainable Signals: Understanding Individual Investors' Interests and Priorities.*
[14] Morningstar Inc., "ESG Market Research: A Quantitative Study on Investing Trends," 2023.
[15] Morgan Stanley Institute for Sustainable Investing, "Sustainable Signals and the COVID-19 Pandemic," https://www.morganstanley.com/assets/pdfs/2021-Sustainable_Signals_Individual_Investor.pdf.

The Morningstar survey shows that 56% of investors expect you to inform them about sustainable investing – a greater percentage than your corporate website, internet searches, their accountant, or friends and family. You are responsible for bringing up the subject, educating the client, and implementing the strategy that meets their needs and goals.

Outside of the wealth management industry, retirement plans are prime opportunities to offer sustainable options. A 2022 Vanguard study shows that only 13% of defined contribution plans offer a "socially responsible fund" option.[16] When you consider the statistics offered up by Morgan Stanley in which 97% of millennials, 86% of Gen X, and 99% of Gen Z are interested in responsible investing, and the fact that these groups currently make up the majority of the workforce, there is a serious disconnect between investment options in retirement plans and the demands of employees.

Again, this is your responsibility to meet this need. I understand that there has been political turmoil regarding ESG options in retirement plans over the past few years, but this appears to have been resolved. There is no excuse not to have at least one option for employees to choose sustainable investing in their retirement plan.

THE GREAT WEALTH TRANSFER

Millennials are the largest demographic in the United States, accounting for nearly one-quarter of the entire population. They also make up 30% of the voting age population, as well as almost 40% of the working age population.

---

[16] Vanguard, "How America Saves 2022: Insights to Action," June 2022.

They will be the primary recipients of the assets being passed down from the baby boom generation – a number estimated to be between $30 and $60 trillion. This "Great Wealth Transfer" will occur over the next two decades or so, bringing monumental change to the investment industry.

Typically, millennials have a different value set than their aging parents and grandparents. They tend to be more socially and environmentally aware and active in movements for diversity and equality. Many even blame prior generations for not doing enough to transition away from fossil fuels and ignoring the warnings of scientists on climate change.

A 2020 Ernst & Young article said, "Given the imminent intergenerational wealth transfer, we see an opportunity ahead for wealth and asset management firms to redefine the standard for investment options in an industry that will soon be dominated by the socially responsible millennial investor."[17]

This is where you come in. You need to be laying the groundwork for this transition by not only communicating with the parents and grandparents but also with their millennial and Gen Z heirs. (Gen X is important as well, but to a smaller degree.) If you are not starting this communication now, you run the risk of losing those assets post-transfer.

An Ernst & Young study showed that investment firms typically lose 70–80% of assets when changing generations. This is a tremendous opportunity to position yourself as an authority on sustainable and responsible investing, retain those transferring assets, and attract new ones.

THE CHANGING ECONOMY

The economy of today is not your parents' and grandparents' economy. In 1980, 7 of the top 10 holdings in the S&P 500 were oil companies,

---

[17] Ernst & Young LLP, "Sustainable Investing: The Millennial Investor," 2017.

with IBM, AT&T, and General Electric rounding out the list. As of today, none of those companies crack the top 10.

The top 10 of today is vastly different from just 40 or even 20 years ago:

1980	2000	2024
IBM	General Electric	Apple
AT&T	ExxonMobil	NVIDIA
Exxon	Pfizer	Microsoft
Standard Oil, Indiana	Citigroup	Amazon.com
Schlumberger	Cisco	Meta Platforms
Shell Oil	Wal-Mart Stores	Alphabet[a]
Mobil	Microsoft	Tesla
Standard Oil of California	American Int'l Group	Broadcom
Atlantic Richfield	Merck	Berkshire Hathaway
General Electric	Intel	JPMorgan

[a]Alphabet ranking is created by combining both Class A and Class C share valuations.

In 2024, we see a lot of technology or tech-related companies. More traditional companies such as Berkshire Hathaway, Eli Lilly, and JPMorgan are the outliers – companies that would have felt "normal" back in 1980, or 2000. The economy is shifting, and our way of investing needs to change as well.

Tesla has made appearances in and out of the top 10 over the past several years. It's simply being included is a glaring indicator of this change. You can argue all you want about Elon Musk and his public persona, but Tesla as a company has had a profound impact on the clean economy. They weren't the first company to market a fully electric vehicle (EV), but they were the first to sell them at scale successfully. In 2022, the company sold over 1.3 million EVs globally. In the United States, they sold over eight times as many EVs as its closest competitor, Ford. Combine this EV dominance with the vast opportunity available in solar and battery storage and other services, and you can see the shifting economy in action.

All the major automobile manufacturers are following in Tesla's footsteps. GM CEO Mary Barra has said, "Climate change is real, and we want to be part of the solution by putting everyone in an electric vehicle."[18] Ford has scaled back some of its EV plans, but still sees the clean drivetrain being the future. Even Toyota, which has been reluctant to make the shift to a majority-EV product line, plans to produce multiple new electric models by 2026. The economy is shifting.

And consider what goes into this new means of transportation. The industries supplying drivetrains and other complementary electronics are going to grow, for example, companies focused on fast and convenient charging solutions, both at home and on the road. And, of course, batteries.

In 2022, over \$73 billion was invested in battery plants in the United States.[19] Much of that investment could be attributed to new legislation pushing manufacturers to source components domestically. But ultimately, that investment was necessary to meet the demand coming from the transition to an electric transportation system.

Consumers are also tired of the lies and misinformation spread by the fossil fuel industry and are ready for change. According to the Yale Program on Climate Change Communication, 65% of Americans are worried about global warming, and 70% believe corporations should do more to address global warming.[20] These opinions will be reflected in their buying habits.

And what will they be buying? EVs and solar panels. Organic foods and sustainable real estate. And a host of other conscious choices, including shopping local and shopping less.

[18] *The CEO Magazine*, "Mary Barra: Leading General Motors into the Future," https://www.theceomagazine.com/business/coverstory/mary-barra-general-motors/.

[19] Mark Kane, "EV Battery Investments Skyrocketed in 2022 to \$73 Billion," *InsideEVs*, January 9, 2023, https://insideevs.com/news/651713/ev-battery-investments-skyrocketed-2022-73-billion/.

[20] Yale Program on Climate Change Communication, "Yale Climate Opinion Maps 2021."

According to the US Energy Information Administration, residential solar installation reached 3.9 gigawatts in 2021, a 34% increase over 2020.[21] And the Solar Energy Industry Association says that 500 gigawatts will be installed over the next decade, which is four times greater than the total amount installed through 2022.[22] In the European Union, solar and wind generated more electricity than fossil fuels for the first half of 2024 – the first time this has ever happened.[23] And 96% of all new grid capacity in the United States was clean energy in 2024 (solar, wind, and batteries) – about 37 gigawatts of utility-scale solar and 15 gigawatts of battery storage.[24]

The USDA reports that certified organic farms increased by over 90% over the decade ending in 2021. The *Nutrition Business Journal* estimates that organic food sales have doubled over the same period, with sales more than $52 billion.[25] Estimates of future growth vary widely, but it is safe to say that this market will continue its march forward as more consumers become aware of the health benefits of organic foods.

Leadership in Energy and Environmental Design (LEED) certified buildings are the standard for sustainable real estate. The certification covers several aspects of building design, from energy and water use to protecting and even enhancing biodiversity and ecosystem services at the building site. According to the US Green Building Council, the administrator of LEED certification, LEED buildings are responsible for contributing

[21] Kristen Bialik, "Home Solar Panel Adoption Continues to Rise in the U.S.," Pew Research Center, October 14, 2022, https://www.pewresearch.org/short-reads/2022/10/14/home-solar-panel-adoption-continues-to-rise-in-the-u-s/.
[22] Solar Energy Industries Association, "Solar Manufacturing Factsheet," June 2021, https://seia.org/wp-content/uploads/2021/03/SEIA-Manufacturing-Factsheet-June-2021-1.pdf.
[23] Ember, "EU Wind and Solar Overtake Fossil Fuels," https://ember-energy.org/latest-insights/eu-wind-and-solar-overtake-fossil-fuels/.
[24] Julian Spector, "Chart: 96 Percent of New US Power Capacity Was Carbon-Free in 2024," Canary Media, 2025, https://www.canarymedia.com/articles/clean-energy/chart-96-percent-of-new-us-power-capacity-was-carbon-free-in-2024.
[25] US Department of Agriculture, Economic Research Service, "Organic Agriculture," https://www.ers.usda.gov/topics/natural-resources-environment/organic-agriculture.

to a 25% decrease in energy use, a 34% reduction in carbon dioxide emissions, and an 11% decrease in water consumption.[26]

But an additional benefit of more intentional building designs is that they enhance their users' healthy lifestyles and the community's quality of life. Combined with the positive environmental benefits, LEED-certified buildings often command higher lease rates, leading to a better return on investment for investors.

CONCLUSION

I like to say, "The sustainable investing train has left the station." Uninformed politicians and other opponents who deride the investing style by calling it "woke investing" or other derogatory terms are missing the fact that it's here and it's not going away. Millennials, who comprise 96% of the largest demographic in the history of the United States, are interested in investing with their values. This is the same group that will be inheriting over $30 trillion over the next couple of decades.

Like sustainable investing, the climate change train has also left the station. We are now living in a *changed climate*, and we need to transition our economy as fast as possible – much faster than we currently are. Many industries are making major investments to transform the economy, from transportation to real estate, food systems to clean energy. This is the new economy: an economy focused on making a positive impact on the world, one that doesn't mortgage the future to maintain the injustices of the past.

Sustainable investing is the future of investing. It is growth investing in its purest form. It is where the economy is going and will transform how you do business and interact with your clients and prospects. In Chapter 2, we'll take a step back to find out how we got here and learn a little about the history of SRI.

---

[26] U.S. Green Building Council, "Benefits of Green Building," https://www.usgbc.org/articles/benefits-green-building.

CHAPTER TWO

THE HISTORY OF SRI, ESG, AND WHATEVER THE NEXT ACRONYM MIGHT BE

OVERVIEW

Long before the acronym ESG (environmental, social, and governance) was thrown around, and before SRI evolved to mean sustainable, resilient, and innovative, there was the original SRI: socially responsible investing.

It was a simpler time when your socially responsible portfolio most likely underperformed the market. I can't tell you how many times I've had people say to me, "I bought a Calvert fund 30 years ago, and it didn't make any money."

Calvert is a great organization that was founded back in 1976. As an industry pioneer, they unfortunately bear the brunt of the industry's long-ago growing pains. At the time, their options were limited in terms of the kinds of companies they could invest in (no battery or electric vehicles [EVs] back then), a lack of data (ESG didn't exist then), and a strategy that mostly focused on exclusion.

While many financial advisors in the space tend to be solo practitioners, there are a few examples such as George Gay's First Affirmative Financial Network that really laid the groundwork for many of us who came later. His SRI in the Rockies conferences are legendary gatherings that brought together industry veterans and newbies alike to learn and be better SRI advisors.

In this chapter, we'll look at the history of responsible investing. From faith leaders of the 18th century to modern ESG data, as they say, we've come a long way (and we have a long way to go). As with any movement, there have been great victories and regrettable losses, but the momentum continues to move forward. Let's start at the beginning.

FAITH-BASED INVESTING

SRI goes back much farther than Calvert's beginning in 1976. In 1760, John Wesley, the founder of the Methodist movement, gave a sermon entitled "The Use of Money." In this sermon, Wesley espoused the concept of ethical gains. He says one should "gain all we can without hurting our neighbor in his body."[1] In saying this, he is referring to alcohol and is specifically recommending against being a purveyor of spirits and the downward spiral that drinking may induce.

This concept led to the term *sin stocks*, which became one of the first exclusionary tactics in SRI and is still a tactic used in the faith-based subset of SRI. Sin stocks have traditionally included alcohol, gambling, pornography, tobacco, and sometimes weapons companies.

It's easy to see how SRI has its roots in faith-based investing. From the Bible to the Talmud to the Quran, these ancient texts preached the importance of ethical behavior. In an article on the Talmud and socially responsible investing, Rabbi Dr. Asher Meir of the Business Ethics Center of Jerusalem wrote, "Any economic activity that has special social value can be considered a preferred investment."[2] The Jewish concept of Tzedek, which focuses on justice and equity, has the intention of correcting imbalances that humans tend to create. Ownership has rights and responsibilities, including the prevention of any immediate or future harm.

In terms of the Quran and Islamic investing, Umar Moghul has some interesting insight in his article "Islamic Finance and Social Responsibility" in *The Stanford Social Innovation Review*. He says, "Islamic commercial principles are rooted in the Shari'ah, the faith's scriptural foundations. Their objectives are to bring about welfare and prevent harm, particularly in the preservation of religion, life, intellect, property, and posterity. Islamic ethics have been interpreted to require risk-sharing, rather than risk-shifting, in business and finance."[3] This concept of risk-sharing

---

[1] Christian History Institute, "Wesley's Sermon: The Use of Money," https://christianhistoryinstitute .org/magazine/article/wesleys-sermon-use-of-money.

[2] Aish.com, "The Jewish View on Charity," https://aish.com/48966911/.

[3] Adnan Ahmed Yousif, "Islamic Finance and Social Responsibility: A Necessary Conversation," *Stanford Social Innovation Review*, https://ssir.org/articles/entry/islamic_finance_and_social_ responsibility_a_necessary_conversation.

aligns well with modern responsible business and especially Benefit Corporations. B Corps, as they are called, gauge a business based not on shareholder value but on stakeholder values. The idea that multiple entities have a stake in the success and impact of a business makes sense but unfortunately runs contrary to modern business principles of profit above all.

And finally, back to the Christian roots of SRI. There are many other examples besides Wesley's sermon. The father of the Reformation, Martin Luther, had a lot to say about ethics in business. In a pamphlet entitled *On Trade and Usury*, published in 1524, Luther says,

> the merchants have a common rule among them, it is their motto and bottom of all their practices: I shall sell my ware as dear as I can. This they hold to be their right. But it means making room for greed and opening the door and window for hell. What else is this than saying: I will give no heed to my neighbor if only I may have my profit and greed full; what do I care if it brings my neighbor ten ills at once? So, you see how this motto goes so straight and shamelessly against not only Christian love, but against natural law as well.

The Quakers, long a socially responsible group, passed a resolution in 1759 prohibiting their members from participating in any aspect of the slave trade. This act ultimately contributed to the abolitionist movement and the end of slavery.

The first widely recognized socially responsible fund, called the Fidelity Mutual Trust, was launched in 1928 by World War I aviator Philip Carret. This fund was originally created for evangelical Protestants who wanted to avoid the sin stocks of alcohol and tobacco. It is still available and is the longest-running screened fund, now run by Amundi Asset Management.

PEACE, LOVE, AND ENVIRONMENTALISM

The hippies of the 1960s and 1970s made a lot of statements. From their clothing choices to their intoxicants to their love for the earth, this generation got the ball rolling on environmentalism and the modern version of responsible investing. An estimated 20 million people celebrated the first Earth Day in the United States on April 22, 1970.

Wisconsin Senator Gaylord Nelson's speech summarized the vision for Earth Day going forward, "Earth Day can – and it must – lend a new urgency and a new support to solving the problems that still threaten to tear the fabric of this society ... the problems of race, of war, of poverty, of modern-day institutions." He continued, "Our goal is not just an environment of clean air and water and scenic beauty. The objective is an environment of decency, quality, and mutual respect for all other human beings and all other living creatures."[4]

The momentum for the modern socially responsible investing movement gets its roots from the war protesters, civil rights, and labor activists of the 1960s. War protesters boycotted companies that provided weapons, chemicals, and other related products and services while students pushed university endowments to divest from these companies.

The community development financial system established its roots in the early 1960s as people finally realized the tremendous inequity caused by the readily accepted practice of redlining. Banks literally drew red lines around areas that they considered unacceptable for lending – usually areas with high minority populations.

---

[4] Door County Pulse, "Sen. Gaylord Nelson's Earth Day Speech," https://doorcountypulse.com/sen-gaylord-nelsons-earth-day-speech/.

Michael Harrington's book, *The Other America*, which was published in 1962, laid bare the assumption that the post–World War II boom was inclusive. This ultimately led to the Community Reinvestment Act of 1977, which requires banks to serve all communities in which they do business.

Of course, this all aligns with the work of Dr. Martin Luther King Jr. and others who were driving the civil rights movement at the time. Racial justice means equal access to financial services and ties in with environmental justice. The unfortunate reality then, as it still is now, is that many of the most polluting industrial facilities are located where poverty is the greatest.

SOUTH AFRICAN APARTHEID

Apartheid means apart or separateness. This philosophy of racial division and discrimination extends back to the early European colonization of Africa in the 17th century. While the United Kingdom abolished slavery in its colonies in 1833, this practice of oppression by separating whites from blacks extended well into the 20th century, especially in South Africa, where it was policy.

Like many protest movements, the anti-apartheid movement began on college campuses back in the 1960s. And, as with other protests, the results were rather limited. Having an impact on a country halfway around the world with local demonstrations is highly unlikely, as was the case in South African apartheid. The US government wasn't interested in getting involved either.

With this in mind, attorney Paul Neuhauser filed a shareholder resolution with General Motors (GM) on behalf of the Episcopal Church in March 1971. The resolution asked GM to pull its business from South Africa until apartheid was abolished. This shareholder advocacy action turned out to be the founding of the Interfaith Center on Corporate Responsibility, which continues its advocacy work today.

Later in the 1970s, Ramon Sevilla, a student at the University of California at Berkeley, began organizing to do more than protest on college campuses – he wanted college endowments to completely divest from companies doing business in South Africa. The intention of this divestment movement would be to have a negative economic impact on the country and use multinational corporations as the lever for change.

From 1977, when Hampshire College divested, through the fall of apartheid in 1991, over 150 institutions divested from companies doing business in South Africa. Cities and states also joined the movement. The state of Nebraska was the first to divest, ultimately followed by 26 states, 22 counties, and over 90 cities.

The US Congress eventually passed the Anti-Apartheid Act of 1986, overriding a Ronald Reagan veto. (It should be noted that a Republican majority in Congress overrode the president's veto – a sign that SRI has historically not been a partisan issue.) Among other initiatives, the act banned new investment in South Africa as well as police and military sales and new bank loans. The United Kingdom reluctantly join the United States, and 23 other nations in imposing various sanctions on the regime.

These combined efforts of shareholder advocacy, divestment, sanctions, and "capital flight" from South Africa ultimately contributed to the fall of apartheid. At the time of the fall, it is estimated that $625 billion was being screened to exclude South African investment.

The government released political prisoner Nelson Mandela in 1990 after 27 years in prison for his involvement with the African National Congress, a resistance organization dating back to the early 1950s. In a remarkable turn of events, Mandela was awarded the Nobel Peace Prize in 1993 and elected president of South Africa in 1994.

THE DIFFERENT ITERATIONS OF SRI

When I started in the business back in 1998, SRI stood for socially responsible investing, and it had meant that for decades. Some advisors and clients still call it that, and they're certainly not wrong in continuing to do so. But there is much more to SRI than simply being socially responsible.

Now, many advisors and companies have transitioned to calling SRI, sustainable, responsible, and impact investing. This newer definition expands on the original idea to include both sustainability and impact, themes that have seen increased popularity over the past several years.

Let's do a basic breakdown of the three components:

Sustainable. This is the concept that the current generation can meet its needs without compromising the ability of future generations to meet theirs. In an ideal world, all generations have the opportunity to thrive. Sustainable companies focus on resource efficiency, health, and equity. From clean energy and EVs to green real estate, electrification, and the circular economy, sustainable investments promote a new economy concept.

Responsible. How does a company interact with the world? Does it focus only on shareholders, or does it incorporate all stakeholders in its decision-making processes like B Corps? Is it a good corporate citizen? As with sustainability, we will look more into what makes a company responsible in an Chapter 4.

Impact. I define impact investing as the ability of an investor to see the direct impact of one's investments on the earth and society. This is typically done using private investments but can occasionally be seen with publicly traded securities. For instance, an impact investment could include low-income housing or a community solar project, where you can see your dollars having a direct impact. One great way that we've included impact investing in our client's portfolios is by using Calvert Impact Community Investment Notes – fixed-income instruments that are designed to support community development projects both domestically and internationally.

A continuing theme throughout this book will be understanding what SRI retail and high-net-worth clients want. As you probably already know, the wants and needs of institutional investors are very different from retail and high-net-worth clients. We will spend most of our time focusing on the latter two demographics. For simplicity, from here on out, when I say retail clients, I mean both retail and high-net-worth clients.

Retail clients want to own solutions-based portfolios. We'll dive deeper into this when we discuss the differences between ESG and sustainable investing. But for now, know that when you're talking with clients and prospective clients, owning a less-bad ESG portfolio probably won't be enough.

AND SPEAKING OF ESG ...

The acronym (or now term) *ESG*, or environmental, social, and governance, has been around for a relatively short period. It was originally attributed to a 2004 United Nations whitepaper entitled "Who Cares Wins: Connecting Financial Markets to a Changing World." The paper was written to help encourage financial professionals and organizations to integrate ESG analysis into their systems and processes. The report states, "Endorsing institutions are convinced that a better consideration of environmental, social, and governance factors will ultimately contribute to stronger and more resilient investment markets, as well as contribute to the sustainable development of societies."[5]

Up until this point, there was very little actual data related to ESG metrics. Companies had no real reason to release this type of information, and analysts didn't demand it. However, increasing pressure to better understand the risks associated with a company's negative impact forced this systemic change.

Investors realized that there was considerable risk associated with companies in all sectors of the economy, from energy to industrials to consumer discretionary. The 1989 Exxon Valdez disaster that spilled 11 million gallons of crude oil in Prince William Sound in Alaska was one such risk. The spill cost over $4 billion to clean up, and Exxon's reputation has never fully recovered.

In 2001, women made up 67% of Walmart's hourly workers but only 14% of store managers. Equally qualified men were three to four times more likely to be promoted, and women were paid less across the board for similar responsibilities. This company-wide failure to provide an equitable workplace led to a class action lawsuit alleging massive discrimination. And while the Supreme Court ultimately ruled against certifying the class, the negative publicity has hounded the company, which continues to see gender discrimination lawsuits to this day.

Risks such as those at ExxonMobil and Walmart exemplify the need for more data specific to a company's ESG metrics. The industry has, for the most part, embraced the reality of risks beyond the traditional metrics of price/earnings ratios and sales projections. There still is a lack of standardization when it comes to ESG metrics that continues to dog the industry but there is momentum building, both regulatorily and within

---

[5] International Finance Corporation, "Who Cares Wins: Connecting Financial Markets to a Changing World," *2005 Conference Report*, 2005, https://www.ifc.org/content/dam/ifc/doc/mgrt/whocareswins-2005conferencereport.pdf.

the industry, to create these standards. When that happens, I predict there will be widespread adoption and integration of ESG metrics in all securities analysis, and ESG investing will simply be investing.

WHERE WE'RE GOING

As I mentioned in the Introduction, I'm actively transitioning our firm's definition of SRI to sustainable, resilient, and innovative investing. The SRI industry needs to do two things: first, distinguish itself from the risk-management investment style of ESG that has been co-opted by large investment managers such as Blackrock. Second, it needs to evolve to address the demands of our changed climate, ensure the ability of future generations to thrive, be resilient in the face of climate impacts, and lead the way in science and innovation. Thus, my new definition of SRI is sustainable, resilient, and innovative investing.

Considering our changed climate, having a focus on resilience and adaptation will be vital. Storms will increase in intensity, droughts and fires will spread, floods will wash away cities and towns, and communications will be interrupted by all these events. Building in resiliency and adaptation, as well as hardening systems against these extreme events, will be vital to maintaining order in the face of change. Sustainable, resilient, and impact investing might just be the next evolution of the industry.

Innovation defines our generation. Over the past few decades, we've seen technologies such as smartphones, magnetic resonance imaging, and global positioning systems change our lives and solve some of the world's greatest challenges. With the advent of artificial intelligence (AI) and iterative learning, the pace of innovation is likely to continue growing exponentially. The timing couldn't be better, because without serious innovation, facing the existential challenge of the climate crisis will be very difficult.

Investment in this next level of innovation offers an opportunity to fund technologies that will reduce emissions, transition financial and energy systems, and develop cutting-edge medicines. We're likely to see game-changing technologies such as fusion power, advanced materials, and maybe even a cure for cancer.

As I said, standardization is key to the widespread adoption of ESG metrics across the investment industry. There need to be corporate disclosures, with accountability for accuracy and timeliness. Analytics providers need to show greater transparency in creating their rating algorithms.

AI will also play an important role, with the ability to monitor corporate actions, news, and operations and report and analyze them in real time. This AI-generated data will help investment managers better gauge risks and opportunities in the marketplace in a much timelier fashion. What else will AI provide? That has yet to be determined, but it likely will be considerable.

But mostly, financial advisors need to be communicating with their clients about the opportunities and risk mitigation inherent in sustainable, resilient, and innovative investing.

As we move forward as an industry, there will ultimately be a crossover point where investing responsibly is the norm, and those who ignore ESG risks will be the outliers. We will transition from a rear-view mirror form of investing in yesterday's indexes to a forward-looking strategy that addresses the need for resource efficiency, resilience, and equity in a new economy. My goal with this book is to help you prepare and be on the leading edge as this transition occurs. Let's start by digging into the *E*, the *S*, and the *G*.

CHAPTER THREE

ESG

A SET OF METRICS

OVERVIEW

ESG: environmental, social, governance. As I'm writing this, it is possible that there is no more disliked acronym. Companies dislike it because the reporting can be difficult, it requires transparency, and they could possibly get a negative score. Some politicians dislike it because they believe the practice equals "woke investing," and they don't like the idea of companies dictating social (and sometimes moral) policy. And most retail investors are just confused by another acronym.

Good or bad, it's the reality of today's investing environment: environmental, social, and governance data will continue to be incorporated more and more into security analysis. Currently, Europe is much further down the ESG road than the United States in terms of use, acceptance, and regulatory frameworks. I recently heard a quip that said, "What do they call ESG investing in Europe? They call it investing."

As fiduciaries, we have an obligation to know as much about a current or potential investment opportunity as possible. Sometimes, that information is beyond the traditional fundamental metrics analysts have used forever. And just because it's different and new, there is resistance. It is just human nature to have a fear of the unknown – it doesn't make it wrong; it just makes it different.

In this chapter, we'll provide an overview of ESG, address its advantages and disadvantages, make the case for more robust and accurate disclosures, and explain why simply using an ESG overlay on a traditional index isn't sustainable investing. Let's get started.

WHAT IS ESG?

As I said in Chapter 1, the term *ESG* (environmental, social, and governance) is originally attributed to the 2004 United Nations white paper, "Who Cares Wins: Connecting Financial Markets to a Changing World." The authors of the paper understood that the more data financial professionals had at their disposal, the better the quality of analysis.

All too often ESG critics contend that ESG data is not material and completely subjective. That there is an agenda behind the practice. Having been in this industry for over 20 years, I can say that there is an agenda: to make the world a better place. In that, the critics are correct. However, when it comes to materiality, they are increasingly wrong.

From data regarding greenhouse gas emissions, water and energy use (and sourcing), board, upper-level management, rank-and-file diversity, and many more, there is most definitely critical material data available, and more is being monitored regularly. The example I gave in Chapter 1 regarding the Great Salt Lake in Utah and its potentially devastating effects on the Utah economy, should misuse of the lake lead to its disappearance, is evidence enough of the materiality of real-world environmental data.

The example of Union Carbide's inexcusable release of toxic chemicals in Bhopal, India, is a lesson on mitigating risk – not just operational risk but also investment risk. In 1984, we didn't have the social and news networks that we do now. An incident of this type happening now could completely bankrupt the company simply by exposure of its misdeeds. Their negligence in not fixing and upgrading systems and processes lead to the deaths of over 20,000 people. And while companies still do just about anything they can to save a buck, with ESG reporting and oversight, and the potential for immediate worldwide bad press, they are less likely to allow such egregious errors to happen.

The Union Carbide example does hit on all the ESG metrics: unnecessarily toxic chemicals and the release of them into the environment, the deaths and other social impacts in the poverty-stricken areas where they chose to manufacture their products, and the lack of governance when it came to monitoring internal processes.

ESG IS ABOUT RISK

The bottom line is that ESG is about risk. Pure and simple. How do we evaluate a company beyond the basic monetary fundamentals of price/earnings ratio, debt, and cash flow metrics. Many people equate ESG with sustainable investing, but the two are quite different. ESG is simply a set of metrics that analysts can integrate into their analytical process, in whatever way they deem to be valuable. They use the data to assess the ESG risks on the company. ESG is not the end result portfolio, but data to help craft a more responsible portfolio with less risk.

The CFA Institute publishes a piece entitled "Definitions for Responsible Investment Approaches," where the authors describe what ESG is and what it isn't very well. They say, "Consideration of ESG factors means that these are part of the mosaic of information used to inform investment analysis and decisions and that they are given thought and weight proportionate to their relevance. ESG integration does not presume which, if any, ESG factors are material to an investment decision, although guidelines, standards, or recommendations may be used as an input."[1]

The piece goes on to say, "Consideration of ESG factors does not imply

- that there are restrictions on the investment universe,
- that ESG factors are given more or less consideration than other types of factors,
- that all ESG factors are given equal consideration, or
- that the resulting portfolio will have any particular characteristics."

MSCI is a leader in ESG data. And while they have in the past equated sustainable investing with ESG (and I called them out on it), they have done a better job of communicating what their ESG data can and cannot do. From their website: "MSCI's ESG ratings are designed for one purpose: to measure a company's resilience to financially material environmental, societal and governance risks. Our ESG ratings provide a window into one facet of risk to financial performance. They are not a general measure of corporate 'goodness', a barometer on any single issue, or a synonym for sustainable investing."[2] This transparency and clarity are refreshing, even though I had to dig to find the disclosure.

Likewise, Sustainalytics is also a provider of ESG data – in fact, they've been focused on responsible investing for over 30 years. In 2024, the firm published a report entitled "Fundamentals of ESG Materiality." In this report, the writers further define the purpose of ESG analysis when they say, "incorporating environmental, social, and corporate governance (ESG) considerations into modern investment strategies gives financial market

---

[1] CFA Institute, "Definitions for Responsible Investment Approaches," https://rpc.cfainstitute.org/sites/default/files/-/media/documents/article/industry-research/definitions-for-responsible-investment-approaches.pdf.

[2] MSCI, "What ESG Ratings Are and Are Not," https://www.msci.com/our-solutions/esg-investing/esg-ratings/what-esg-ratings-are-and-are-not.

participants a more holistic view of the risks and opportunities that their investments are exposed to. Analyzing businesses' exposure to ESG issues and how they manage them can be a window into their potential for long-term value."[3] Again, there's nothing about "being good" – it is about analyzing risk and opportunities for capital appreciation.

So, there you have it straight from a couple of the largest ESG data providers: ESG is not about how good a company is; it is about the potential risks posed *on* the company by ESG factors. There's nothing wrong with this at all – it's just important to realize that ESG is simply a *tool* of security analysis that is becoming more widely used.

ESG REPORTING AND ITS ADVANTAGES

When it comes to reporting, more companies are recognizing that they need to take reporting seriously. According to a 2022 Deloitte survey, 99% of companies surveyed have either already established an ESG working group or are in the process of establishing one. That same report listed numerous advantages that the respondents anticipated receiving from their enhanced ESG reporting including the following:

- Talent attraction and retention
- Increased efficiencies and return on investment
- Enhanced trust with stakeholders
- Brand/reputation enhancement
- Premium pricing of products
- Reduced risk[4]

---

[3] Morningstar Sustainalytics, "Fundamentals of ESG Materiality," 2024, https://connect.sustainalytics .com/fundamentals-of-esg-materiality.

[4] Deloitte, "Survey Findings on ESG Disclosure and Preparedness," https://www2.deloitte.com/content/ dam/Deloitte/us/Documents/audit/us-survey-findings-on-esg-disclosure-and-preparedness.pdf.

Betsy Atkins, an expert on corporate governance and veteran board member makes the argument that ESG initiatives can unlock competitive value within a corporation. She says, "Companies that recognize the importance of adapting to changing socio-economic and environmental conditions are better able to identify strategic opportunities and meet competitive challenges. Proactive and integrated ESG policies can widen a company's competitive moat relative to other industry players."[5]

Over my 20+ years as a financial advisor, I've seen a monumental shift in how investors judge corporate performance. Over that time, investors have shortened their time frame from focusing on long-term business-building to short-term performance and profits.

A perfect example of this is NRG Energy. In the mid-2010s, CEO David Crane had a vision of transforming the company from a fossil fuel–based utility to a leader in the next economy. From diversifying its generation mix to investing in electric vehicle chargers, the CEO saw where the economy was eventually going. An activist investor, however, didn't like how long the process was taking (and possibly didn't like the renewable energy strategy) and pushed Crane out. At the time, Crane said, "We have to be mindful that industry logic and investor logic do not always coincide."[6]

His successor also had next economy aspirations when he bought Vivint Smart Home Systems, a move that would put the utility on the cutting edge of smart metering and energy efficiency. That same activist investor forced him out as well for trying to create long-term business value instead of making immediate profits. This short-sighted strategy ultimately pushes companies to make bad decisions to satisfy short-term speculators at the expense of long-term investors.

---

[5] VentureBeat, "Achieving Sustainability Through Modernization," https://venturebeat.com/enterprise-analytics/achieving-sustainability-through-modernization/.

[6] Cassandra Sweet, "NRG Energy CEO David Crane Resigns," *The Wall Street Journal*, December 3, 2015, https://www.wsj.com/articles/nrg-energy-ceo-david-crane-resigns-1449151435.

Atkins makes the point that ESG investors tend to be "stickier." By that she means that ESG investors are more interested in a company's performance over the next decade instead of the next quarter. They know that change doesn't happen overnight. She says, "Investors incorporating ESG into their mandate often work alongside a company to strengthen it, as they are more interested in building long-term value over a multi-year period than in flipping the stock in the near term for a 'sugar high.'" I couldn't agree more.

REGULATION

For a long time, ESG reporting really has been the wild west. Sometimes, the information provided by companies was accurate, and sometimes it was a best guess – that is, if they provided any information at all. As I said, more companies are taking ESG seriously and releasing information, but regulation has finally caught up.

The EU's Corporate Sustainability Reporting Directive (CSRD) went into effect in January 2024. This directive requires companies to disclose information about their climate and sustainability risks and impacts. It will likely affect an estimated 50,000 companies over the following four years, including over 3,000 US companies.[7]

The reporting categories were outlined in the European Sustainability Reporting Standards and include the following:

- Climate
- Pollution
- Water and marine resources

---

[7] European Commission, "Corporate Sustainability Reporting," https://finance.ec.europa.eu/capital-markets-union-and-financial-markets/company-reporting-and-auditing/company-reporting/corporate-sustainability-reporting_en.

- Biodiversity and ecosystems
- Resource use and circular economy
- Company workforce
- Workers in the value chain
- Affected communities
- Consumers and end users
- Business conduct

This reporting requirement is important because, despite the ESG pushback in the United States by some politicians and business leaders, the European Union (EU) reporting is now law. For the most part, any company doing over €150 million in business in the EU will have to comply – and this would apply to virtually all the multinationals headquartered in the United States.

In addition, in March 2024, the US Securities and Exchange Commission (SEC) finalized a rule requiring climate disclosures. In addition to simple transparency, an intention of the rule is to create standardization and eliminate the "wild west" nature of ESG disclosures in the United States. SEC Chair Gary Gensler noted that the rule will provide "investors with consistent, comparable, decision-useful information, and issuers with clear reporting requirements."[8]

According to Deloitte, the key components of the rule include the following:

- Severe weather and other natural condition financial statement impacts
- Carbon offset and renewable energy credit information
- Material greenhouse gas emission metrics
- Governance info

---

[8] US Securities and Exchange Commission, "SEC Adopts Rules to Enhance Climate-Related Disclosures," https://www.sec.gov/newsroom/press-releases/2024-31.

- Strategy, business model, and outlook
- Risk management
- Targets and goals
- Material expenditures and impacts[9]

Unsurprisingly, this rule has been challenged in court, and considering the Supreme Court decision overturning the Chevron Rule, it remains to be seen whether it will take effect. This is only compounded by a new administration in Washington as of January 2025, which will likely not pursue the case. Nonetheless, between the EU rule and the desire for the SEC to standardize reporting in some manner, companies need to take ESG risks and disclosures seriously.

Now, let's break down each of the *E*, *S*, and *G* factors.

E IS FOR ENVIRONMENT

Historically, the environmental element of ESG has had the most focus. Much of the demand for ESG is rooted in concern for the environment, climate change, and sustainability. It has also been the element with the most quantifiable metrics, from carbon emissions to toxic waste to water use.

Environmental metrics include both positive and negative attributes. For example, how much of a company's electricity needs are being met from verified clean energy sources, such as solar, wind, or geothermal? How does the company handle toxic emissions, resource use, and waste, and are they making efforts to clean up their operations?

The example I used in Chapter 1 about the Great Salt Lake is a prime example of a situation in which an environmental factor could have a

---

[9] Deloitte, "SEC Climate Disclosure Guidance," https://www2.deloitte.com/us/en/pages/audit/articles/sec-climate-disclosure-guidance.html.

huge material financial impact on a municipality. The $4 billion in economic impact that the lake provides could, no pun intended, dry up rather quickly. The cascading effects on the Utah state economy would be devastating – and potentially have a negative impact on the state's debt securities.

A 2020 McKinsey report addressed the potential climate change impacts on supply chains – the lifeblood of many businesses. The report said, "Greater frequency and severity of climate hazards can create more disruptions in global supply chains – interrupting production, raising costs and prices, and hurting corporate revenues." The report goes on to say that the probability of an intense hurricane disrupting semiconductor supply chains may increase by two to four times by 2040 and that rare earth production may be disrupted by extreme rainfall increases two to three times by 2030.[10]

To further stress this point, Sustainalytics released a report in June 2024 entitled "Navigating Climate Risks in the Global Equities Market." In it they say, "Scientists, political representatives and civil society groups have dubbed climate change as a 'threat multiplier' because it can intensify the impacts of a wide range of hazards facing people's occupation, livelihoods, and asset portfolios."[11]

Climate change metrics are the largest contributor to ESG scores. However, as more data is being generated across a variety of factors, we are seeing more energy being dedicated to issues such as biodiversity, circular economy and water among others.

MSCI publishes the company's ESG materiality map online for transparency.[12] Sustainalytics does as well, and its materiality list is

---

[10] McKinsey & Company, "Could Climate Become the Weak Link in Your Supply Chain?" https://www .mckinsey.com/capabilities/sustainability/our-insights/could-climate-become-the-weak-link-in-your- supply-chain.

[11] Morningstar Sustainalytics, *"Navigating Material Climate Risks in the Global Equities Market,"* June 2024, https://www.sustainalytics.com.

[12] MSCI, "ESG Industry Materiality Map," https://www.msci.com/our-solutions/esg-investing/esg-industry- materiality-map.

very similar.[13] Many of the metrics include both company-owned and those in the supply chain:

- Carbon emissions
- Product carbon footprint
- Environmental and social impact of products and services
- Climate change vulnerability and resilience
- Water use
- Biodiversity and land use
- Raw material sourcing and use
- Toxic emissions and waste
- Packaging material and waste
- Electronic waste
- Opportunities in clean tech, green building, and renewable energy

S IS FOR SOCIAL

Probably the most controversial of the ESG triumvirate – social issues like politics, continues to divide. Using investments and corporate policy to promote social change is at the root of the ESG critics' term, "woke investing."

But the reality is that social issues have a tremendous impact on companies, from diversity in the workplace to employee safety to community involvement. They all can help to enhance or detract from a company's culture, which, oftentimes, can affect profitability.

Part of the difficulty with *S* is that there are fewer quantifiable, material metrics – but make no mistake, there are material metrics. According to

[13] Sustainalytics, "Material ESG Issues Resource Center," https://www.sustainalytics.com/material-esg-issues-resource-center.

Juliet Bourke of Deloitte, diversity can enhance innovation by about 20%.[14] In a separate study, the Boston Consulting Group confirmed that companies with above-average diversity scores have more revenue from innovation. This may not be a direct path to the bottom line, but some of the most innovative companies are also some of the most profitable.

Diversity also can be a risk management tool, bringing individuals from different backgrounds to the table. According to Bourke, "it also enables groups to spot risks, reducing these by up to 30%. And it smooths the implementation of decisions by creating buy-in and trust." The Boston Consulting Group study says diversity "can also strengthen resilience – the capacity to survive the unexpected ... . Diverse companies are better than their more homogenous counterparts at withstanding unanticipated changes and adapting to external threats."[15]

But you also need to partner up inclusion with diversity to really see the benefits. According to the Deloitte report, organizations with inclusive cultures are twice as likely to meet or exceed financial targets and eight times more likely to achieve better business outcomes.

Another social issue is supply chains. Global companies typically have complex supply chains, and with price being a driving factor so often, outsourcing often happens in countries with lax labor laws. A Boston Consulting Group report on supply chains says, "As supply chains become deeper, visibility becomes poorer, and the likelihood of violations rises."[16] Responsibility ultimately lies at the top of the chain to ensure that components and products are sourced ethically.

Companies such as Apple have faced scrutiny over the years for issues in their supply chains. Issues such as unsafe working conditions, child and

---

[14] Deloitte, "Diversity and Inclusion at Work: Eight Powerful Truths," https://www2.deloitte.com/us/en/insights/deloitte-review/issue-22/diversity-and-inclusion-at-work-eight-powerful-truths.html.

[15] Boston Consulting Group, "How Diverse Leadership Teams Boost Innovation," 2018, https://www.bcg.com/publications/2018/how-diverse-leadership-teams-boost-innovation.

[16] Boston Consulting Group, "Managing ESG Issues in Global Supply Chains," 2023, https://www.bcg.com/publications/2023/managing-esg-issues-in-global-supply-chains.

forced labor, and employee contract fees are a constant battle for the company as it continues to produce millions of devices every year. To keep costs as low as possible, manufacturing operations are sited on different continents, thousands of miles away, making monitoring difficult. Audits are performed regularly, but still issues continue to persist.

Some of the metrics that MSCI[17] and Sustainalytics[18] include in social materiality are as follows (again, many of these apply to both the company and its supply chain):

- Labor management
- Health and safety
- Human capital development
- Human rights
- Supply chain labor standards
- Product safety and quality
- Chemical safety
- Consumer financial protection
- Privacy and data security
- Community relations
- Controversial sourcing

G IS FOR GOVERNANCE

I often say that governance shouldn't even be included in ESG. Why? Because governance should already be a part of the due diligence process – it's not like environmental and social metrics are relatively new. Analysts should have been looking at governance metrics all along: does the company follow generally accepted accounting principles? Are there enough independent members of the board? And is the business a real business?

---

[17] MSCI, "ESG Industry Materiality Map."
[18] Sustainalytics, "Material ESG Issues Resource Center."

I ask the last question because you may have heard of a company called Enron. Enron was supposedly an energy trader, but once the veil was lifted, all we saw was a shell game. Enron is the poster child for why governance is so important to security analytics and why governance should have been a part of fundamental analysis all along.

There are also the examples of Adelphia Communications and Tyco International. Like Enron, both were Wall Street darlings in the early 2000s but fell from grace when it was disclosed that executives were using the companies as their personal piggy banks. Again, governance analysis is vital, and not just glossing over filings but also taking a deep dive into a company's governance operations.

There are a couple of other aspects of governance due diligence that do go hand in hand with responsible investing, though. The first is diversity on boards and in the C-suite. We've discussed diversity in the rank and file under social, but diversity in management is just as important and considered a governance metric.

S&P Global's Dr. Daniel Sandberg conducted a study entitled "When Women Lead, Firms Win." In the study, Sandberg looked at leadership data from Russell 3,000 companies from 2003 through 2019. What he found was very interesting and leads one to ask why aren't more women leading companies:

- Firms with female chief financial officers (CFOs) were more profitable and generated excess profits of $1.8 trillion.
- In the 24 months post-appointment, female CEOs saw a 20% increase in stock price momentum, while female CFOs saw a 6% increase in profitability and 8% larger stock returns.
- Firms with female CEOs have twice the number of female board members versus the average (23% versus 11%).[19]

---

[19] S&P Global, "When Women Lead, Firms Win," https://www.spglobal.com/content/dam/spglobal/corporate/en/images/general/special-editorial/whenwomenlead_.pdf.

The numbers don't lie. Yet companies continue to choose male leadership. As of 2018, the male-to-female ratio for CEOs was 19:1 and 6.5:1 for CFOs. Yet, in many companies, the rank-and-file mix tends to be 50-50. ESG investors often look for female leadership, both in the C-suite and on the board, because they understand the advantages.

Along those same lines, governance also looks at CEO pay. A report from the Economic Policy Institute showed that of the 350 largest public companies in the United States, CEOs were paid 344 times as much as the typical worker in 2022. This number has soared over 1,200% since 1978. During that same period, typical worker pay increased only 15.3%.[20] This has contributed to the tremendous wealth inequality that we see in the country.

Some ESG investors attempt to use shareholder resolutions to push for more equitable compensation within companies. However, many CEOs have leverage over their corporate boards, who ultimately have the final say on executive pay. Plus, shareholder resolutions are not binding, so this oftentimes turns into a public relations battle.

From an investment perspective, a study by MSCI Research in 2017 showed that there was very little correlation between a CEO's pay and stock performance. The report stated, "We find that CEO realized pay over the past 10 years was poorly aligned with long-term investment returns at a majority of large-cap US companies, and in some cases severely so."[21] Again, looking at nontraditional corporate metrics, such as CEO pay levels, as many ESG analysts do, appears to be a research advantage.

MSCI[22] and Sustainalytics[23] governance metrics include the following:

- Ownership and control
- Stakeholder governance
- Board

---

[20] Economic Policy Institute, "CEO Pay in 2022," https://www.epi.org/publication/ceo-pay-in-2022/.
[21] MSCI, "CEO Pay," https://www.msci.com/ceo-pay.
[22] MSCI, "ESG Industry Materiality Map."
[23] Sustainalytics, "Material ESG Issues Resource Center."

- Pay
- Accounting and financials
- Business ethics
- Tax transparency

WHY TRANSPARENCY MATTERS

All the ESG information in the world won't do any good if the data is bad. As I discussed, the SEC has finalized rule changes for climate-related metrics, but not for other environmental or social issues. It's a start, but there is so much more that needs to be done. The EU's CSRD reporting does address data beyond climate and will apply to some US companies, which is a win.

The one ESG area that has an advantage is governance, as there is already considerable SEC and other regulatory reporting that is necessary, including executive pay and accounting standards.

But more transparency is needed. And for that transparency to be meaningful, there also needs to be reporting standards, just like there are for some governance metrics. Much of the data that the large ESG research firms use is self-reported by the individual companies, and while useful, the information really needs to be looked on with some skepticism. A 2022 global investment survey from PwC found that 56% of institutional investors and 76% of asset managers support strengthening ESG disclosure rules for listed companies.[24]

Ultimately, it's in a company's best interest to be as transparent as possible and to provide robust and accurate disclosures of their ESG risks. It would make sense that companies resisting full disclosure and

---

[24] PwC, "AWM Revolution 2022 Report," 2022, https://www.pwc.com/gx/en/news-room/press-releases/2022/awm-revolution-2022-report.html.

transparency have something to hide or are behind their peers in addressing ESG issues. These are the companies that you would want to exclude from your portfolio anyway.

Companies that publish detailed sustainability reports, and many now do, will have an advantage over those that don't, or those that provide only rudimentary information. Companies that set meaningful targets for issues such as greenhouse gas reductions, supply chain standards, and board diversity, and subsequently show their progress, are companies that have a much better chance of being in one of our sustainable portfolios.

ESG IS THE FUTURE OF INVESTING

Ultimately, environmental, social, and governance data only helps with stock selection and monitoring. As I said, as fiduciaries, we are bound to do what is in the client's best interest. And that includes using as much data as possible when we're putting together their investment portfolios. The PwC survey referenced earlier found that "three-quarters of investors now consider ESG to be part of their fiduciary duties." The times they are a-changin'.

In that same PwC survey, the researchers found that 9 in 10 asset managers surveyed believed that integrating ESG into their investment strategy would improve returns. And according to the Russell Investments 2023 Manager ESG Survey, "only 7% said that ESG factors do not drive investment decisions, markedly down from 22% recorded in 2022." Investment managers across the industry know the importance of ESG, that it helps with security selection and reduces portfolio risk. Welcome to the future of investing.

In Chapter 4, I'll define sustainable investing and the opportunities that come with investing in what Garvin Jabusch of Green Alpha Advisors calls the *next economy*.

CHAPTER FOUR

SUSTAINABLE INVESTING

MAKING THE WORLD A BETTER PLACE

SUSTAINABLE INVESTING AND THE CLEAN, RESILIENT ECONOMY

In 1987, the United Nations defined sustainability as "meeting the needs of the present without compromising the ability of future generations to meet their own needs."[1] Alexandra Spiliakos of the Harvard Business School

Online expands on that definition by claiming sustainability as "doing business without negatively impacting the environment, community, or society as a whole."[2]

While, in general, sustainability is a noble goal, simply maintaining current standards of living seems to be an underachievement to me. Parents and grandparents want to see their families thrive in the future. If I were to ask you how your relationship was with your spouse or partner, and you replied, "sustainable," they would likely punch you! It reminds me of the character Data from the Star Trek Next Generation television series. When asked how he was performing, he regularly replied with "nominal."

And so, to me, sustainable investing is beyond just maintaining the status quo for future generations. It's setting future generations up to thrive. It's about investing in companies that are working hard to solve humanity's biggest challenges. It's about fostering a cleaner, healthier, more resource-efficient, and more equitable economy. It's about being resilient and adaptable in the face of the changed climate. It's about picking tomorrow's business leaders and visionaries and letting them take us into the future.

WHAT DOES POSITIVE, SOLUTIONS-BASED INVESTING MEAN?

Most companies provide solutions. Fossil fuel companies provide energy solutions. Hospital corporations provide health care, and financial firms provide the banking and capital necessary to maintain a working economy.

---

[1] United Nations, "Sustainability," https://www.un.org/en/academic-impact/sustainability.
[2] Harvard Business School, "What Is Sustainability in Business?" https://online.hbs.edu/blog/post/what-is-sustainability-in-business.

However, just because they provide solutions doesn't make them positive or good for society.

There must be context. For example, fossil fuels provided a positive solution at the time they were discovered and made commercially available. According to an article by Hannah Ritchie and Pablo Rosado in *Our World in Data*, fossil fuels have been "a fundamental driver of the technological, social, economic, and development progress that has followed."[3] We transitioned from horse and buggy to the automobile, from whale oil lamps to electric light bulbs, and from cow poop to chemical fertilizers.

The problem is that we enjoyed too much of a good (and easy) thing. The resource that afforded us so much energy and flexible solutions is also a resource that has saddled us with the existential crisis we're facing in climate change.

And so, the context has changed. Fossil fuels enabled generations to thrive but is not the resource that is going to allow future generations to thrive as well. The paradigm needs to shift to newer, cleaner ways of doing business and providing solutions and products to a growing population. Herein lies the ultimate value proposition for sustainable investing and the clean economy.

This description aligns nicely with my definition of growth investing. Growth investing is about investing in companies that are innovating solutions for the future and are continuously investing in themselves to produce more and greater breakthroughs. It is about seeing tomorrow's opportunities instead of simply today's profits.

By contrast, legacy industries, like fossil fuels, rely on yesterday's ways of doing business. The analogy I use is that investing in legacy companies is like rearview mirror investing, while sustainable investing is investing in

---

[3] Hannah Ritchie and Max Roser, "Fossil Fuels," *Our World in Data*, https://ourworldindata.org/fossil-fuels.

the road ahead (of course, while you're driving your solar-charged electric vehicle down the road).

In my talks and training sessions, I make the statement that the only constant is change, and that humans have a hard time accepting change. I then show a picture of a rotary phone like the one I grew up with and follow it up with a picture of an iPhone for contrast. We've come a long way over just 40 or so years.

To further prove my point, I show a picture of a strange physician performing a bloodletting on a patient, followed up by a picture of a magnetic resonance imaging machine. Change in the extreme has led to thousands if not millions of lives saved by the technological innovation of computerized imaging.

Sustainable investing in the clean economy is no different. We're moving from the legacy industry of burning rocks in the form of coal to boil water to make steam to turn a turbine to generate electricity to the new economy powered by windmills and solar panels. Brute force legacy economy to elegant technology of the future.

This is not to say that legacy companies can't change and be drivers of the next economy, but it is much more difficult. The example of David Crane at NRG Energy from Chapter 3 is an example of traditional investors being resistant to change and long-term investing versus short term profiteering.

When constructing our Green Sage Sustainability Portfolio, I actively look at several sectors and industries that I consider to be positive, solutions providers. They include but are not limited to the following:

- Clean energy
- Energy efficiency
- Battery technologies

- Infrastructure, resilience, and adaptation
- Water distribution, filtration, and efficiency technologies
- Green transportation
- Natural and organic products and services
- Sustainable real estate
- Information technology, big data, and the internet of things
- Green finance, insurance, and community investments
- Recycling and circular economy
- Scientific instruments and supplies
- Green building technology
- Cutting-edge biotechnology
- Organic and regenerative agriculture

This list is by no means complete, as it is constantly evolving as technology and innovation advance. In Chapter 11 on constructing portfolios, we will explore each of these a little more deeply.

One of the best definitions of sustainable investing comes from my friend and colleague Garvin Jabusch. Garvin is the cofounder and chief investment officer at Green Alpha Advisors. His firm is the only firm licensed to manage the Sierra Club portfolio.

Garvin coined the term *next economy* to describe sustainable investing, and the description addresses several of the industries that I've listed but does so quite eloquently:

The Next Economy™ is the emerging, de-risked, solutions-driven way goods and services are produced and consumed. As systemic risks – the climate crisis, resource degradation, disease burdens, and eroding social cohesion – continue to manifest, demand for solutions is accelerating. As a result, innovative companies addressing these systemic risks are leading long-term economic growth. Investing in them is our best opportunity to preserve and create wealth. By directing capital to the most competitive solutions creators, investors can both catalyze and benefit from the highly efficient, sustainable Next Economy.[4]

What Garvin has known for a long time is that "a rapidly evolving economy requires an equally adaptive approach to investment management." Innovation, both in how we invest and what we invest in, is vital.

Steve Jobs was known for innovation. From the Apple II computer that I learned to type on back in high school to the Mac, iPod, and iPhone, Jobs was constantly looking forward to what's next. But he wasn't asking customers what they wanted, he was showing them what they didn't know they needed. He said, "It's really hard to design products by focus groups. A lot of times, people don't know what they want until you show it to them."[5] This goes hand in hand with a line that is attributed to Henry Ford who said, "If I had asked my customers what they wanted, they would have said a faster horse."[6]

The same is true with sustainable investing. Many companies that we would include in a sustainable portfolio would likely not be included in the many traditional indexes that investors are using – either because they are too small, domiciled outside the United States, or don't meet traditional sector definitions. They are missing out on innovation that will likely be powering the next economy. Don't wait to discuss sustainable investing with your clients because it's possible, and even likely, that they haven't heard of the concept. It's your job to help them see the future.

---

[4] Green Alpha Advisors, "Investing in the Next Economy: A New Definition of Portfolio Risk" (white paper), https://greenalphaadvisors.com/investing-in-the-next-economy-a-new-definition-of-portfolio-risk-white-paper-2/.

[5] Innovation Observer, "On Steve Jobs, Henry Ford, and Fast Horses," March 6, 2020, https://innovationobserver.com/2020/03/06/on-steve-jobs-henry-ford-and-fast-horses/.

[6] Innovation Observer, "On Steve Jobs, Henry Ford, and Fast Horses."

WHAT IS DECARBONIZATION?

The term *decarbonization* gets thrown around a lot in climate change mitigation circles, so it's worth taking a moment to address it. Decarbonization gained traction from its use in international climate agreements such as the Kyoto Protocol in 1997 and the Paris Agreement in 2015. Basically, decarbonization is the process of reducing carbon dioxide (CO_2) and other greenhouse gas emissions to combat climate change and transition toward a low-carbon or carbon-neutral economy.

This process involves phasing out the use of fossil fuels like coal, oil, and natural gas in favor of renewable energy sources such as wind, solar, geothermal, batteries, and hydropower. It also includes electrifying transportation, heating, and household systems, and improving energy efficiency.

Beyond energy, decarbonization efforts extend to industries such as manufacturing, agriculture, and construction, where practices like recycling, sustainable materials, and circular economies reduce the carbon footprint. The transition also requires systemic changes, such as upgrading infrastructure, supporting innovation, and ensuring equitable transitions for workers in carbon-intensive industries.

Decarbonization can offer significant benefits to society. It mitigates climate change, improves public health by reducing air pollution, creates new economic opportunities in green industries, and enhances energy security by reducing reliance on imported fossil fuels. As a cornerstone of sustainability, decarbonization is not just about reducing emissions but also about reimagining economies and lifestyles to achieve long-term resilience and environmental balance.

There is a lot of crossover between our concept of sustainable investing and decarbonization efforts. The key principles of decarbonization include the following:

- Reduction in fossil fuel use
- Energy efficiency
- Clean energy adoption
- Electrification
- Circular economy

So, when you see the term decarbonization or have requests from clients about it, know that sustainable investing can provide many of the solutions necessary for decarbonizing the economy.

WHERE DOES BANKING FIT IN?

One area that we, as financial advisors, tend to overlook is our clients' banking relationships – unless, of course, we're an advisor in the bank channel. Where a client conducts their banking is just as important as how they invest.

For convenience, many people do their banking at large, national banks. The ability to walk into a Bank of America, Citibank, or Chase branch in just about any city is appealing to many. But with the advent of online banking, the ease of automated clearing house (ACH) transfers, and the availability of local credit unions and values-based banks, there really is no excuse for anyone to continue using the big banks anymore.

The Net-Zero Banking Alliance was started in 2021 as an initiative of the United Nations Environment Programme Finance Initiative. The objective of the Alliance was to align banks' lending, investment portfolios, and capital markets activities with the goals of the Paris Accord – specifically to limit global temperature increases to 1.5 degrees Celsius. The Alliance started out very successfully with 43 founding banks in 23 countries and over $28.5 trillion in assets.[7]

Unfortunately, just as we've seen with many diversity, equity, and inclusion initiatives, many of these banks have been pressured by political interests to leave the Alliance. In late 2024 and early 2025, six of the largest US banks – JPMorgan Chase, Citigroup, Bank of America, Morgan Stanley, Wells Fargo, and Goldman Sachs – all pulled out of the Alliance. These departures will have a negative effect. According to Todd Cort, co-director of the Yale Center for Business and the Environment, "From an economy-wide perspective, this exodus will only increase the risk of climate impacts on the banks and the rest of society. It sends a signal from large lenders that they care less. Smaller banks may be less inclined to navigate the climate risk waters, and borrowers may be less pressured to focus on their own emissions and climate resilience."[8]

Not surprisingly, those same banks had done little since forming the Alliance in 2021 to limit their fossil fuel financing. I'll discuss more about greenwashing in Chapter 5, and the roles that banks play, but for now, consider these numbers:

Since the Alliance was formed, according to the 2024 Banking on "Climate Chaos Fossil Fuel Finance Report," those six banks financed a total of $181.5 billion in 2022, and $173 billion in fossil fuels 2023. In fact, JPMorgan, Goldman Sachs, and Morgan Stanley each financed more in 2023 than they did in 2022.[9]

---

[7] United Nations Environment Programme Finance Initiative, "Net-Zero Banking Alliance," https://www.unepfi.org/net-zero-banking/.
[8] Yale School of the Environment, "Net-Zero Banking: Dead or Alive?" https://environment.yale.edu/news/article/net-zero-banking-dead.
[9] Rainforest Action Network et al., "Banking on Climate Chaos 2024: Fossil Fuel Finance Report," July 2024, https://www.bankingonclimatechaos.org/wp-content/uploads/2024/07/BOCC_2024_vF3.pdf.

If we're educating our clients on sustainable investing, we also need to educate them on their banking relationships. As I said, with easy access to online banking, ACH functionality, and credit unions and values-based banks, there is no reason why anyone would want to use the big banks anymore. The Global Alliance for Banking on Values is an international organization dedicated to promoting values-based banking. The organization was founded on six core principles that all members agree to live by the following:

- Social and environmental impact at the heart of the business model
- Grounded in communities, serving the real economy and enabling new business models to meet the needs of both
- Long-term relationships with clients and a direct understanding of their economic activities and the risks involved
- Long term, self-sustaining, and resilient to outside disruptions
- Transparent and inclusive governance
- All these principles embedded in the culture of the financial institution[10]

Can you imagine one of the big banks adopting any one of these principles, much less all six? Of course not. Because their purpose, ultimately, isn't to serve their customers but to make as much money as possible from them. Which is why it's up to you to ask about clients' banking relationships. Yes, I realize that with a bunch of ACH connections, checks, debit cards, and other "sticky" services that the big banks promote, it will be a pain to move the banking relationship. However, when you're working with clients who want to be sustainable and responsible, the work is worth the impact.

---

[10] Global Alliance for Banking on Values, "Banking on Values," https://www.gabv.org/banking-on-values/.

It still baffles me that one of the biggest banks in the country, Wells Fargo, is still in business. Aside from being a major fossil fuel funder, the bank was embroiled in a massive scandal that started in 2016. Among other things, the company opened approximately 3.5 million fake accounts for clients, added unnecessary or unwanted products such as auto and life insurance, wrongfully foreclosed on homeowners, intimidated employees as well as discriminated against them, and overcharged asset management clients.[11]

Two institutions that I have used, both professionally and personally are Self-Help Credit Union in North Carolina and Climate First Bank in Florida (full transparency – I am personally an equity investor in Climate First). Both have great origin stories. From Self-Help:

> Initially we helped employees in rural NC form worker-owned cooperatives and gain ownership of local mills that were being shut down. Over and over, we saw workers stopped in their tracks because they couldn't get conventional financing. In response, we started Self-Help Credit Union and a nonprofit loan fund. Our first capital was $77 raised through a bake sale organized by a baker that Self-Help assisted. Early investors also included Catholic women religious orders.
>
> Self-Help co-founders are Martin Eakes and Bonnie Wright, and Self-Help's first "office" was Martin's VW Bug. After the car caught fire (taking Self-Help's files with it!), Martin tried towing a trailer around to meet with rural customers. Finally, in 1982 we got "real" office space in an unheated, unfurnished office building in downtown Durham, NC. Today, we have over 75 credit union branches and lending offices nationwide.[12]

---

[11] Congressional Research Service, "Introduction to Financial Services: The Securities and Exchange Commission (SEC)," IF11129, https://crsreports.congress.gov/product/pdf/IF/IF11129

[12] Self-Help, "Our Story," https://www.self-help.org/who-we-are/about-us/our-story.

Climate First was founded in June of 2021 by my friend, Ken LaRoe. This is Ken's third bank and second values-based bank after founding First Green Bank back in 2009 and subsequently selling it to Seacoast Bank in 2018. After Ken sold First Green, he had sellers' remorse, and after long discussions with his wife, Cindy, decided to work on the trifecta and Climate First was born.

Since its founding in 2021, Climate First has been one of the fastest growing banks in the United States, reaching $1 billion in assets in early 2025. More important, they have financed millions of dollars in solar installations, nurtured their communities in Florida, and begun to expand their footprint across the United States.

Find a bank that you can refer your clients to that has an authentic mission, a great story, and good people. Your clients will be grateful.

RESILIENCE AND ADAPTATION: THE HIDDEN KEY TO SUSTAINABLE INVESTING AND THE CLEAN ECONOMY

Now that we better understand the concept of sustainable investing, decarbonization, clean economy, values-based banking, and the desire to create not just a sustainable economy, but a thriving one, let's introduce a concept that goes hand in hand: resilience and adaptation. At this point in time, we are now facing a changed climate – we have moved from a future event to a current reality. From the hurricane that devastated Asheville, North Carolina, to the uncontrolled wildfires in Los Angeles, the changed climate is making its presence felt. We are seeing its effects globally: ice sheets in both the Arctic and Antarctic are disappearing, wildfires are now a common threat on just about every continent, hurricanes are getting so intense that meteorologists are considering adding a sixth category to the scale, and the list goes on.

How do we, as a species and a society, deal with the ever-intensifying effects of the climate emergency? How do low-lying cities like New York City and Miami prepare for rising sea levels? And how do we feed the soon-to-be 10 billion humans in an age of climate instability? All these questions are questions of resilience and adaptation and are an important category that should be included in any sustainable portfolio.

According to a report from Standard Chartered, the "Global Risks Report 2023" from the World Economic Forum rates failure of climate change adaptation as the seventh biggest risk faced by businesses and governments over the next two years, but the second biggest risk for the next decade. That report goes on to say that "for every dollar spent on adaptation, an economic benefit of $12 could be generated."[13]

The risks include compromised operations to supply chain disruptions – it's clear that any investment in adaptation and resilience can be viewed as a long-term investment in stability. Marissa Drew, chief sustainability officer at Standard Charter says, "Investors are still asking how many of their dollars invested might be at risk. So, we're saying to them that if you flip that and look at the opportunity, there's an enormous return potential from allocating capital to the space – because there's a need, and necessity breeds an attractive commercial return opportunity."

The report says, "Products and services, including climate-resistant infrastructure and agriculture, early warning systems for extreme weather

---

[13] World Economic Forum, "The Global Risks Report 2023," https://www3.weforum.org/docs/WEF_Global_Risks_Report_2023.pdf.

and parametric insurance tied to climate events, offer a multitude of adaptation spaces ripe for investment. 'You can go to almost any industry and see opportunity everywhere,' says Drew."

A 2024 report for the World Economic Forum entitled "The Cost of Inaction: A CEO Guide to Navigating Climate Risk," discusses the risks and opportunities for companies related to resilience and adaptation. The report says that risks related to climate are already influencing the economy globally, and that the business case for taking collective action is quite clear. In addition, it says that there are considerable physical risks that are becoming quite material for businesses which will put "significant value" at risk.[14]

The report goes on to say, "Corporate inaction also comes at a cost: there is a clear business case for adaptation and a better case for mitigation than most might think. Companies report that their current adaptation and resilience investments could yield between $2 and $19 for every dollar invested. On mitigation, while full decarbonization across sectors comes at a cost, sustainability leaders can still find cost-efficient ways to reduce emissions in the short term. Addressing these risks also informs companies how to navigate the transition and adaptation opportunities and develop innovative offerings fit for a warmer and greener world."

Because we tend to focus only on solutions that make us less impactful on the planet in sustainable investing, resilience solutions are sometimes overlooked. This is a mistake because sustainability and resilience are inextricably linked at this point because of the ever-intensifying effects of climate change.

MSCI produced a report in late 2024 entitled "Sustainability and Climate Trends to Watch 2025." In it, they analyze the impact of Hurricane

---

[14] World Economic Forum, "The Cost of Inaction 2024," https://reports.weforum.org/docs/WEF_The_Cost_of_Inaction_2024.pdf.

Helene on Asheville, North Carolina. They identified 259 corporate assets in the area and ranked all of them as having above-average exposure (the 57th percentile) to extreme levels of precipitation. Of those assets 83 face higher levels of "pluvial flooding" in the 67th percentile, while 11 are in the 100th percentile in terms of flood-related risks.[15]

The report summarizes the risk by saying, "As climate change increases the frequency and severity of extreme-weather events in highly insured regions like Europe and the U.S., corporates and homeowners may face rising insurance premiums or, in the worst-case scenario, find their properties uninsurable. This issue could also extend beyond the insurance industry and specific regions and potentially affect the financing of properties and the entire real-estate market, which could create economy-wide negative impacts."

A 2017 paper from insurance giant, Marsh & McLennan entitled "How Climate Resilient Is Your Company?" defines climate resilience as "the capacity to adapt and succeed in the face of the direct and indirect impacts of climate change. In addition to addressing and managing risks, it encompasses the ability to capitalize on the strategic opportunities presented by the shift to a lower carbon and resource-constrained economy."[16]

We want to capitalize on this combination of both adaptation and opportunity when constructing sustainable portfolios. Resilience is not just about surviving in a changing climate; it's also about identifying and realizing the opportunities to lead in sustainability, innovation, and responsible business practices. As public awareness and regulatory pressures increase, companies that prioritize resilience are likely to fare better in

---

[15] MSCI, "2025 Sustainability & Climate Trends to Watch," https://www.msci.com/research-and-insights/2025-sustainability-climate-trends-to-watch.

[16] Oliver Wyman, "How Climate-Resilient Is Your Company?" November 2017, https://www.oliverwyman.com/our-expertise/insights/2017/nov/how-climate-resilient-is-your-company.html.

terms of reputation, investor confidence, and long-term viability. Some key aspects of corporate resilience include these issues:

- **Risk assessment and management.** Understanding a company's vulnerability to climate-related risks is vital, for example, impacts such as damage to facilities from extreme weather and indirect impacts such as disruptions in supply chains. Businesses can use these types of assessments to develop strategies to manage and mitigate these risks.

- **Adaptive capacity.** Once an assessment has been completed, researching and developing the ability and capacity to adapt to changing conditions is crucial. This likely would involve multiple areas, such as investing in hardened infrastructure capable of withstanding extreme weather, diversifying supply chains to minimize vulnerability to climate disruptions, or adopting new technologies and systems that are more efficient and less dependent on legacy systems, such as the fossil fuel economy.

- **Stakeholder engagement.** Beginning conversations with a wide range of stakeholders goes a long way in incorporating a complete resilience strategy. Engagement that includes feedback from employees, customers, investors, and especially local communities and governments can help corporate leaders understand risks outside of the boardroom.

- **Financial resilience.** The company must ensure that it has adequate financial resources to withstand and recover from climate-related impacts. This includes moves such as setting aside funds for recovery efforts, making sure insurance coverage is adequate, or accessing securities such as green bonds to finance sustainability and resilience-related projects.

An example of a company that is considered both sustainable and resilient is CBRE. CBRE manages almost three billion square feet of real estate in over 40 countries. They are charged with both reducing the impact of their managed buildings and ensuring that they are ready for climate change impacts.

The company has created a guide that they use to judge different cities, based on their resiliency plans. The metrics are broken down into three main categories and several subcategories. It looks like this:

- Transition risk
  - Net zero or carbon neutral targets
  - Building performance standards
- Physical climate risk
  - Physical climate risk
  - Water stress
  - Air pollution
  - Heating degree days
- Mitigation and adaptation measures
  - Renewable energy
  - Green bonds
  - Green buildings[17]

Using these guidelines, CBRE can judge which cities are most prepared for climate impacts and then put into action a plan to deal with the effects in buildings located in less-prepared cities.

CBRE's approach to resilience and adaptation is a model that many companies need to adopt no matter the sector or industry. It's a forward-thinking model that incorporates long-term investment instead of short-term speculation. Unsurprisingly, CBRE also scores well in both MSCI's and Sustainalytics' ESG risk ratings.

---

[17] CBRE, "North American City Sustainability Study 2023," https://www.cbre.com/insights/reports/north-american-city-sustainability-study-2023.

THE UNITED NATIONS SDGs

In 2015, the United Nations released its 2030 Agenda for Sustainable Development. An important part of that agenda was the 17 Sustainable Development Goals (SDGs), intended to "end poverty and other deprivations which go hand in hand with strategies that improve health and education, reduce inequality, and spur economic growth – all while tackling climate change and working to preserve our oceans and forests." And while that's a mouthful, it really describes the strategy and intent of sustainable investing and the clean economy.

A goal of some sustainable investors is to address as many of the 17 SDGs as possible when constructing a portfolio. It certainly is a good idea to incorporate as much data related to the SDGs as possible in the analytical process. It also helps with client reporting, which is a topic that we haven't yet discussed.

The concept of trust but verify certainly applies to sustainable investing. In Chapter 5, we'll address greenwashing and the how companies and investors often say one thing and do another. So, in a world with rampant greenwashing, reporting becomes vital.

United Nations' 17 Sustainable Development Goals include the following:

1. **No poverty:** End poverty in all its forms everywhere.
2. **Zero hunger:** End hunger, achieve food security and improved nutrition, and promote sustainable agriculture.
3. **Good health and well-being:** Ensure healthy lives and promote well-being for all at all ages.
4. **Quality education:** Ensure inclusive and equitable quality education and promote lifelong learning opportunities for all.

5. **Gender equality:** Achieve gender equality and empower all women and girls.

6. **Clean water and sanitation:** Ensure availability and sustainable management of water and sanitation for all.

7. **Affordable and clean energy:** Ensure access to affordable, reliable, sustainable, and modern energy for all.

8. **Decent work and economic growth:** Promote sustained, inclusive, and sustainable economic growth, full and productive employment, and decent work for all.

9. **Industry, innovation, and infrastructure:** Build resilient infrastructure, promote inclusive and sustainable industrialization, and foster innovation.

10. **Reduced inequality:** Reduce inequality within and among countries.

11. **Sustainable cities and communities:** Make cities and human settlements inclusive, safe, resilient, and sustainable.

12. **Responsible consumption and production:** Ensure sustainable consumption and production patterns.

13. **Climate action:** Take urgent action to combat climate change and its impacts.

14. **Life below water:** Conserve and sustainably use the oceans, seas, and marine resources for sustainable development.

15. **Life on land:** Protect, restore, and promote sustainable use of terrestrial ecosystems, sustainably manage forests, combat desertification, and halt and reverse land degradation and halt biodiversity loss.

16. **Peace, justice, and strong institutions:** Promote peaceful and inclusive societies for sustainable development, provide access to justice for all, and build effective, accountable, and inclusive institutions at all levels.

17. **Partnerships for the goals:** Strengthen the means of implementation and revitalize the global partnership for sustainable development.[18]

Several third-party firms provide the resources to report on the sustainability and impact of a portfolio. Using the SDGs as guidelines helps to focus on the positive aspects of sustainable investing.

INDEXING AND SUSTAINABLE INVESTING

Over the years, we've seen a movement away from active management toward a more passive, index-based approach to investment management. Along with this transition has come the concept of tracking error. *Tracking error* is the term used to describe the difference between an investment portfolio and its benchmark index.

You cannot index where the economy is going by looking in the rearview mirror, which is how most traditional indexes are created. The S&P 500 and other major indexes are based on the legacy economy and are slow to integrate the clean economy and solutions-based sustainable companies into their ranks. For example, you should never include a fossil fuel company in a sustainable portfolio, but because the traditionally accepted benchmarks include the sector, and institutions frown on high tracking error, there is pressure to include it. And many institutional investors have investment policies that limit tracking error, thus causing inherent conflict in the adoption of sustainable portfolios.

The clean economy is constantly in flux as new innovations hit the market. And while there are thematic indexes that focus on subsectors of

---

[18] United Nations, "Sustainable Development Goals," https://sdgs.un.org/goals.

the economy like clean energy or water, there isn't a broad index that truly incorporates the sustainable economy. Some providers have attempted to create ESG indexes. These indexes layer ESG risk metrics over traditional indexes to create what I call "less bad" investments. What you end up getting is an ESG index that reduces its exposure to ExxonMobil because of the risk – but it doesn't make the index sustainable, just a less bad version of the original index.

Ultimately, the most important thing to remember is that retail clients want solutions. The risk you run as a financial advisor when you use a less-bad ESG index is that the client looks under the hood and sees companies that you would never consider sustainable and calls you out on it. We'll discuss fund selection and greenwashing in Chapters 10 and 5 but just keep this in mind as we move forward.

SUSTAINABLE INVESTING IS GROWTH INVESTING

Sustainable investing is, by definition, growth investing. It's investing in innovation. It's investing in where the economy is going. Innovation investing is the key that brings together both the sustainable aspect of SRI as well as resilience. The Motley Fool defines growth stocks, in part, saying "Growth stocks can be big or small companies. They can operate in any industry, although many are involved in some form of technology. The characteristics these stocks share are more nuanced than size, age, or market segment. They include competitive advantages, an innovation focus, experienced leaders, and a large addressable market."[19] Helping to save the planet from the climate crisis will require innovation and most definitely is a large addressable market among other things.

---

[19] The Motley Fool, "Growth Stock," https://www.fool.com/terms/g/growth-stock/.

Yes, sustainable investing can be more aggressive. It can be more volatile. But, for clients who are investing for the long term, not speculating on short-term profits, they are likely to benefit tremendously from this responsible investing approach.

ESG INVESTING IS NOT SUSTAINABLE INVESTING

It might seem like I'm talking out of both sides of my mouth when I discuss the use of ESG, and the reality is that I am. ESG is a method to assess external environmental, social, and governance risks *on* a company. However, the system is not standardized, and there are a lot of disparities between how different rating agencies gauge companies, and so this demands criticism. At the same time, integrating ESG metrics during the due diligence process ultimately helps with fiduciary duty and is in the client's best interest. Why? Because the more data you have, the better decisions you can make. The biggest problem I've found, however, is when large asset managers equate ESG with sustainable investing, which can be very misleading.

Picture this:

- An ESG portfolio that has reduced its exposure to ExxonMobil – I call it a less bad portfolio.
- An ESG portfolio that has eliminated ExxonMobil entirely – I call it a better portfolio.
- An ESG portfolio that has replaced ExxonMobil with First Solar – I call a sustainable portfolio.

I use this analogy all the time, from TV interviews to my PowerPoint presentations, and over the years, when using it, I've seen hundreds of lights go off in peoples' heads when they say, "Oh, now I get it." Now, there's obviously a lot of nuances beyond this, but it's a great way to start a conversation with someone who is curious about the difference. Or someone who isn't curious about the difference but assumes they're the same thing. As a financial advisor focusing on sustainable investing, your job, day in and day out, as much as managing portfolios and taking care of clients, is communicating and educating. The more you practice, the better you'll become.

ESG is a set of metrics. What is the environmental risk on a company? What is the social risk on a company? And what is the governance risk on a company? ESG is a vital component of modern securities analysis. It is enhanced due diligence. It is *not* a portfolio.

The large asset managers like to equate ESG with sustainable investing, and they do it with impunity. They understand that most investors don't understand all the terms and acronyms that we, as financial advisors, deal with every day. So, they create their Large Cap ESG mutual fund, market it as sustainable, and sell it to the retail investor who thinks they're getting climate or sustainable solutions. What they're really getting is a watered-down version of the S&P 500 or the Russell 1,000.

Now, there's nothing wrong with creating a basic ESG portfolio to reduce risk. In fact, every fund manager should be doing this. Just don't call it sustainable, because it's not.

MEASURING, REPORTING, AND TRANSPARENCY

If this book were focused on ESG investing, there would likely be an entire chapter dedicated to ESG measurement of portfolios, comparisons versus benchmarks, and justifications for investing in the likes of McDonald's, JPMorgan, or ConocoPhillips. Luckily, because we're not trying to build a less bad portfolio and need to justify our holdings decisions, measurement and relativity are less important.

Because we are focused on investing in solutions providers, we aren't forced to make judgments by investing in *the best of the worst*. Is ExxonMobil better than Chevron or is JPMorgan better than Citigroup isn't a question that we must ask. Instead, you'll see me figuring out if First Solar is a better investment than Canadian Solar, or if Autodesk is better than Adobe. By actively maintaining a universe of companies focused on sustainability, resilience, and innovation, we eliminate most of the companies that many ESG funds and portfolios must justify owning.

Through our Morningstar Direct subscription, we have access to Sustainalytics data. Their data effectively enables me to make like for like comparisons when building a portfolio, as well as judging the entire portfolio once it's completed. For example, using Sustainalytics' Sustainability Score tool, I can see that our Green Sage Sustainability Portfolio has a 20% better score than the MSCI All Cap World Index.

Sustainability Score

Benchmark: MSCI ACWI

I can also see the carbon metrics of the portfolio, and that Green Sage's carbon risk score is 41% less than its benchmark, the MSCI All Cap World Index. It lists fossil fuel involvement, which is zero, and gives the portfolio a "Low Carbon" designation. If I was investing to the index, which means minimizing tracking error by including the energy sector, and other polluting industries, both the sustainability score and the carbon metrics would be much higher.

Carbon Metrics

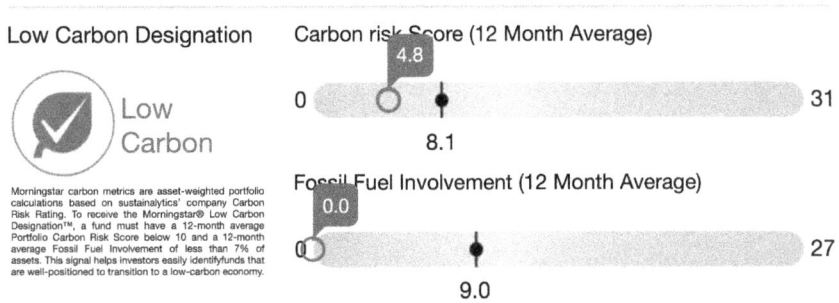

We also use software called YourStake. YourStake performs some similar functions to what we get with Morningstar Direct, but analysis of individual ESG areas is much more granular. I use YourStake for two functions: analyzing portfolios as I build them and comparing prospective clients' current portfolios to Earth Equity's models to show how much more sustainable ours are.

In this section, we'll focus on analyzing our portfolios instead of prospect comparisons. Like I said, we can get very granular on a portfolio basis. Because it is so powerful, I'm including several pages of the report which covers five different metrics:

- Health
- Environment
- Human Rights
- Equal Opportunity
- Accountability

Asset Class -- Corporate

Aggregate Impact

Style Comparison

Methodology

Impact data about corporations is collected from over 100 publicly available sources and grouped together into five main categories -- Environment, Human Rights, Equal Opportunity, Health, and Accountability. Overall aggregations by issue area are a coverage-weighted average of each metric's comparison between the portfolio and MSCI ACWI. For portfolios that include funds, managers' shareholder engagement activities are included in the overall comparisons for each of the 5 major issue areas if at least three companies have improved, or committed to improve disclosure or performance in that issue area following shareholder engagement by the fund managers in your portfolio over the last two years.

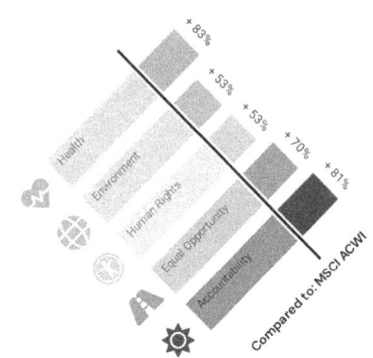

Benchmark Comparison

The particular issue areas for your report are filtered based on your impact objectives. The displayed comparisons are based on a dollar-weighted average based on the portfolio constituents with data coverage for each metric. For example, 30% less animal exploitation (-30%) means that, as a dollar-weighted average, 30% fewer constituents in the selected portfolio have ties to animal testing and animal food products, compared to their respective benchmarks. Funds are assigned a value for each metric based on a dollar-weighted average of the companies held by that fund with data coverage for that metric.

	Green Sage Sustainability Portfolio	MSCI ACWI

 Health

Weapon Industry Exposure
Companies involved in the manufacture or sale of weapons.

59% Less

Tobacco Producer Exposure
Companies that produce cigarettes or tobacco products.

100% Less

Health and Safety Violations (US + UK)
Penalties paid to the US government or UK government for public and workplace health and safety failures.

96% Less

Toxic Air Hazard
Harm done by toxic air pollution released in the U.S. by the company, using EPA data.

64% Less

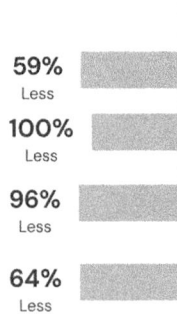

Toxic Water Pollution
Amount (weighted by toxicity) of toxic water pollution from
facilities in the U.S. and European Union.

98%
Less

Agricultural Chemicals Manufacturers
Companies that manufacture agricultural chemicals.

100%
Less

Gun & Ammunition Exposure
Companies that produce or sell guns and ammunition.

100%
Less

Military Weapons Exposure
Companies involved in the manufacture or sale of military weapons
and major military contractors.

49%
Less

Unconventional Weapons Exposure
Companies involved in the manufacture or sale of nonconventional
weapons.

68%
Less

Civilian Firearms Manufacturers Exposure
Companies that manufacture civilian firearms.

100%
Less

SIN Chemicals
How many hazardous chemicals does a company produce based
on the EU REACH criteria.

91%
Less

Environment

Clean Energy Companies
Companies with the highest clean economy revenues, and pure-play
clean energy companies.

26%
More

Deforestation Producers Exposure
Agricultural commodity producers and traders linked to
deforestation

100%
Less

Fossil Fuel Industry Exposure
Companies operating in the fossil fuel industry, and utilities
powered by fossil fuels

84%
Less

Go to page 1

Strong Climate Commitments
Companies with substantial climate pledges that include third-party
accountability measures

1%
More

Total GHG Emissions
Company scope 1 + 2 + 3 GHG emissions.

43%
Less

Scope 1 + 2 + 3 GHG Emissions
Total greenhouse gas emission reported by the company across all
scopes.

23%
Less

Environmental Violations (US + UK)
Penalties paid to the US government or UK government for harming the environment.

95% Less

Water Withdrawal
Company water withdrawal.

4% Less

Total GHG Emissions Intensity
Company scope 1 + 2 + 3 GHG emissions.

7% Less

Industrial GHG Emissions
Amount of greenhouse gas emissions from facilities in North America and European Union.

86% Less

Fossil Fuel Extraction Exposure
Companies operating or servicing fossil fuel extration.

100% Less

Single Use Plastics Companies
Companies that produce plastic.

100% Less

Loans to Fossil Fuel Companies
Fossil fuel finance dollars from banks since 2016.

77% Less

Human Rights

Animal Exploitation
Is a company involved in animal testing, and/or food + clothing containing animal products.

34% Less

Wage and Hour Violations (US + UK)
Penalties paid to the US government or UK government for exploiting wage laborers.

80% Less

Labor Relations Violations (US + UK)
Penalties paid to the US government or UK government for violating labor laws.

93% Less

Meat Producer Exposure
Companies involved in meat and poultry production and processing.

100% Less

Data Privacy Violations (US + UK)
Penalties paid to the US government or UK government for abusing data privacy.

21% Less

Sub-minimum Wage Compensation
Companies that pay their employees below a minimum wage.

100% Less

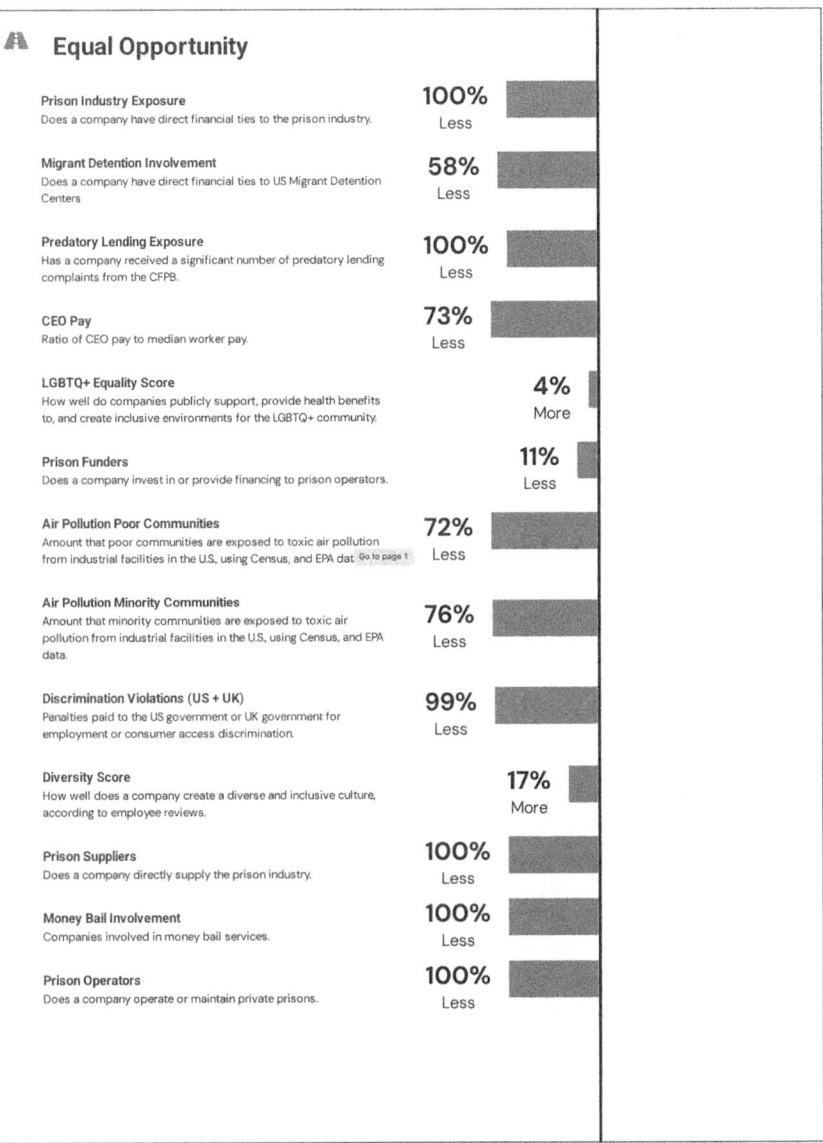

🛣 Equal Opportunity

Prison Industry Exposure
Does a company have direct financial ties to the prison industry.

100%
Less

Migrant Detention Involvement
Does a company have direct financial ties to US Migrant Detention Centers

58%
Less

Predatory Lending Exposure
Has a company received a significant number of predatory lending complaints from the CFPB.

100%
Less

CEO Pay
Ratio of CEO pay to median worker pay.

73%
Less

LGBTQ+ Equality Score
How well do companies publicly support, provide health benefits to, and create inclusive environments for the LGBTQ+ community.

4%
More

Prison Funders
Does a company invest in or provide financing to prison operators.

11%
Less

Air Pollution Poor Communities
Amount that poor communities are exposed to toxic air pollution from industrial facilities in the U.S, using Census, and EPA dat _{Go to page 1}

72%
Less

Air Pollution Minority Communities
Amount that minority communities are exposed to toxic air pollution from industrial facilities in the U.S, using Census, and EPA data.

76%
Less

Discrimination Violations (US + UK)
Penalties paid to the US government or UK government for employment or consumer access discrimination.

99%
Less

Diversity Score
How well does a company create a diverse and inclusive culture, according to employee reviews.

17%
More

Prison Suppliers
Does a company directly supply the prison industry.

100%
Less

Money Bail Involvement
Companies involved in money bail services.

100%
Less

Prison Operators
Does a company operate or maintain private prisons.

100%
Less

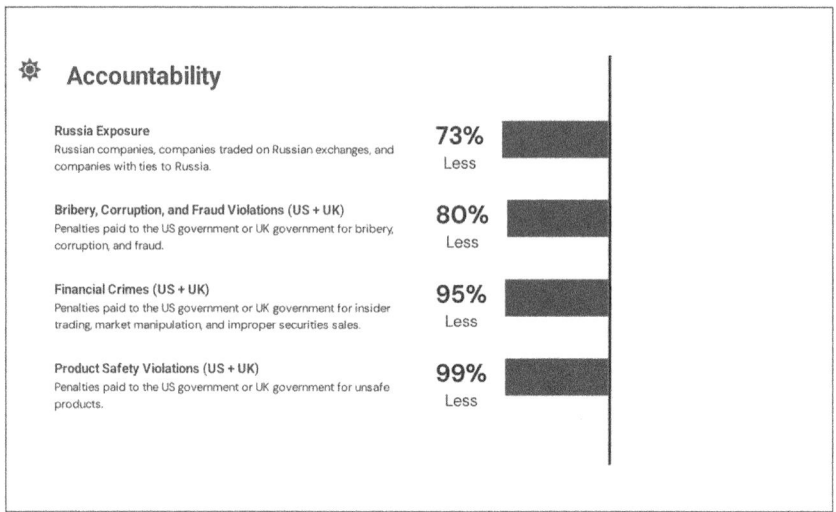

In addition, the report creates real-world metaphor-based metrics that are easy for clients to visualize. These reports are for illustrative purposes only.

Your Impact Metaphor Metrics

Methodology

Each metaphor represents how the dollar weighted impacts of your fund holdings compare to your chosen benchmark.

The relevant metrics are calculated for the portfolio and the benchmark on the basis of ownership percentage of each company. For example, a portfolio that owns 1% of a company that slaughters 1,000,000 chickens is proportionally responsible for 10,000 chickens slaughtered.

In order to make output more readable, for portfolios with under $10 million in assets covered by YourStake.org, the portfolio value is scaled up to $10 million to calculate annual metrics, and displayed as $1 million over 10 years, keeping holdings and company activities constant. For example, a portfolio with $300 in Company A and $200 in Company B is scaled up to a portfolio with $6 million in Company A and $4 million in Company B, and associated metaphors reflect the annual metrics associated with this scaled up portfolio.

If you invest $1M in your portfolio over 10 years, you may be responsible for the equivalent of approximately:

Fewer Cars Driven For A Year	Fewer cigarettes produced	Fewer victims of data breach
39	**285,916**	**357**
Direct GHG Emissions	Cigarettes Produced	Data Breach Victims
Amount of greenhouse gas emissions released directly by the company or through producing electricity for the company.	The number of equivalent cigarettes produced by a company.	The number of people impacted by data breaches.

Fewer garbage bags of waste	Fewer hours of incarceration	More meetings led by women
594	**3**	**34**
Waste Produced	Individuals Incarcerated	Women in Management Positions
The amount of waste to landfill.	The number of individuals detained.	Number of women in management positions.

Fewer pieces of plastic in the ocean	More solar panels	Fewer toilet flushes of water
1,371,579	**9,124**	**71,987**
Plastics in the ocean	Clean Energy	Water Footprint
Annual production of plastics that reach the ocean.	Amount of equivalent clean energy (MWH) produced by a company based on revenue supporting a clean energy economy.	The amount of water used.

Using the YourStake tools, I can test holdings as I'm building the portfolio, and then once the portfolio has been built, compare it versus benchmarks and other portfolios. Using a combination of Morningstar Direct and YourStake tools, I can effectively communicate with prospects and clients how sustainable and responsible their portfolio is rather quickly and at scale.

CONCLUSION

Sustainable, resilient, and innovation investing, or SRI, is about solutions to our biggest challenges. While I believe that, long term, there will be lower systemic risk on the portfolio, lowering risk is not the main driver of a SRI portfolio, unlike an ESG portfolio. Using tools such as Morningstar Direct and YourStake, we can efficiently communicate both value and values to our prospects and clients. The main driver of SRI is creating a portfolio for the economy of tomorrow.

CHAPTER FIVE

GREENWASHING

OVERVIEW

Greenwashing is defined as "the act or practice of making a product, policy, activity, etc. appear to be more environmentally friendly or less environmentally damaging than it really is."[1] Greenwashing is rampant in the investment management industry, and, at least in the United States, there is very little chance that the offenders will be disciplined.

According to the US SIF "2022/2023 Report on US Sustainable Investing Trends," there were 645 different funds incorporating some form of environmental, social, governance (ESG) into their process. The majority of these are mutual funds at 444, followed by 177 exchange-traded funds (ETFs). The rest are variable annuities and closed-end funds.[2]

---

[1] Merriam-Webster, "Greenwashing," https://www.merriam-webster.com/dictionary/greenwashing.
[2] US SIF Foundation, "2022/2023 Report on US Sustainable Investing Trends," December 2022.

That's a lot of funds, and likely a lot of different interpretations of responsible investing, running the gamut of truly sustainable funds to the "less bad" ESG versions peddled by the big investment houses.

GREENWASHING AND YOUR CLIENTS

The danger of greenwashing for financial advisors relates to the interaction you may have with your clients and what their expectations are. As I've said, retail investors are looking to invest in companies that provide solutions to our biggest challenges, such as the changed climate, resource scarcity, and equity. What happens when you buy that client a less bad ESG fund that owns ExxonMobil, McDonald's, and Northrop Grumman? What happens when that client looks at the annual report because they were wondering what the underlying holdings were in the "sustainable" fund you bought for them? Odds are, they're not going to be happy.

This is why due diligence is so important. We'll examine the process of mutual fund and ETF due diligence in Chapter 10, but for now, know that what's under the hood matters.

The problem with so many funds is that they are being managed like they would be for an institutional client, such as managing to an index, reducing tracking error, and using a "best-in-class" strategy, which just doesn't work for sustainable portfolios. These funds include every sector of the market, even when some sectors, such as energy, would never be considered sustainable. They use a best-in-class strategy to determine the best of the worst using ESG metrics. The retail investor doesn't care about institutional metrics or owning the best of the worst in a sector. They just want to own solutions-based companies and to make a competitive return. Period.

CASE STUDY

The best way to understand greenwashing is to review an actual fund. So, we're going to look at the iShares ESG Aware MSCI USA ETF, symbol ESGU.[3] The fund is the second largest in the space, has over $13 billion in assets as of January 2025, and has only been around since 2016. By comparison, the Parnassus Core Equity Fund has about $29 billion, but has been around since 1992. The power of Blackrock's marketing machine has driven much of ESGU's asset growth.

Let's first discuss messaging. The Blackrock website equates sustainable investing with ESG investing.[4] As we have discussed, there is a big difference between solutions-based, sustainable investing and the risk mitigation strategy of ESG investing. Again, there's nothing wrong with ESG investing, but Blackrock should not equate the two. For example, the company's website lists three "sustainable building blocks for your portfolio," which are three, "less bad" ESG funds. This can be misleading and could be construed as greenwashing.

Next, let's look at the fund's allocation to the energy sector. Remember that the energy sector is fossil fuels, not clean energy. Solar usually falls under the technology sector while wind is in the industrial sector. As of January 14, 2025, according to Morningstar Direct, the fund had 3.81% in the energy sector. We'll compare this with a non-ESG index, the S&P 500. As of January 14, 2025, the S&P 500 held 3.35% in energy. The "sustainable" ESGU portfolio holds more fossil fuels than the S&P 500. Retail investors looking for a solutions-based portfolio will have a hard time swallowing the rationale for owning nearly 4% in energy, the sector with the biggest climate liability.

---

[3] iShares, "iShares ESG Aware MSCI USA ETF," https://www.ishares.com/us/products/286007/ishares-esg-aware-msci-usa-etf.
[4] BlackRock, "Sustainable Investing Products," https://www.blackrock.com/us/financial-professionals/investments/products/sustainable.

Finally, we'll scrutinize actual holdings. The top 10 holdings are the exact same as the S&P 500, including Meta Platforms, which decided in early 2025 to discontinue its fact-checking program which will ultimately lead to more disinformation being spread. Certainly not what I would call a responsible company.

It also includes JP Morgan Chase in the top 10. The bank financed nearly $41 billion in fossil fuel projects in 2023 according to the "Banking on Climate Chaos 2024: Fossil Fuel Finance Report" issued by Rainforest Action Network. From 2016 to 2023, its fossil fuel financing topped out at over $430 billion.[5]

The following highlights the fossil fuel financing banks in ESGU from this report:

Bank	2023 Fossil Fuel Financing	2016–2023 Fossil Fuel Financing
JP Morgan	$40.9 billion	$430 billion
Citigroup	$30.2 billion	$396 billion
Bank of America	$33.7 billion	$333 billion
Wells Fargo	$30.3 billion	$296 billion
Goldman Sachs	$18.8 billion	$185 billion
Morgan Stanley	$19.1 billion	$184 billion
PNC Financial Svs	$12.1 billion	$108 billion
Truist Financial	$14.2 billion	$105 billion
US Bancorp	$12.8 billion	$97 billion

These eight US banks financed a total of $202 billion for fossil fuels in 2023 and over $2.1 trillion from 2016 to 2023. These are all holdings in an ETF marketed as being sustainable, and we haven't even started looking at the actual fossil fuel holdings yet, so let's do so.

---

[5] Rainforest Action Network et al., "Banking on Climate Chaos 2024: Fossil Fuel Finance Report."

Energy Sector Companies in ESGU by Portfolio Weighting

Company	Allocation %
ExxonMobil	0.5
ConocoPhillips	0.45
Kinder Morgan	0.42
Chevron	0.36
ONEOK	0.32
Williams Companies	0.28
Hess	0.28
Targa Resources	0.17
Ovintiv	0.16
Baker Hughes	0.13
EQT Corp	0.12
Diamondback Energy	0.10
Schlumberger	0.09
Phillips 66	0.09

I have yet to see adequate justification for any ESG/responsible fund to hold energy stocks. Some say that it's important to have a voice for proxy voting, but this strategy, when it comes to fossil fuel companies, is weak.

Take for example activist hedge fund Engine No. 1's bid to add environmentally conscious members to ExxonMobil's board in 2021. The hedge fund succeeded in adding three of its four candidates to the company's board, supposedly to shift the company's focus from fossil fuels to clean energy. In the ensuing three-plus years, these board members have done little to shift ExxonMobil's business strategy other than some obscure net-zero targets and the purchase of a lithium mine in Arkansas. Instead, according to an article in the *New York Times*, the company actually "doubled down on oil and gas, significantly increasing drilling in the Permian Basin, and expanding offshore drilling in Guyana."[6]

In that same article, experts criticized the lack of progress at ExxonMobil after the board election. Danielle Fugere of As You Sow, a shareholder advocacy organization, said that it "has not made a discernible difference in the way Exxon is addressing climate change." And Mark van Baal of Follow This said that it was "the biggest disappointment in the fight against climate change." Voting your proxy for fossil fuel companies might make you feel good, but the actual results are considerably less concrete.

Another less-discussed fossil fuel related sector is utilities. While electricity generated by clean energy continues to grow at an unprecedented pace, far too many utilities still rely on fossil fuels for electricity generation or are distributing natural gas.

Here's a list of utilities using or distributing fossil fuels in ESGU:

Company	Fossil Fuel (%)	Solar/Wind/Battery (%)	Nuclear (%)
Next Era Energy	46	32	22
Nisource	57	37	n/a
Dominion Energy	50	5	29
CMS Energy	68	23	9
Constellation Energy	11	2	87
Edison International	22	34	6

And of course, there are a lot of other companies in the ESGU portfolio that should never be a part of a truly sustainable portfolio – from defense contractors to fast food to health insurers. Here are some of the

---

[6] Michael J. de la Merced, "Engine No. 1's Battle with Exxon Mobil: Two Years Later," *New York Times,* May 31, 2023, https://www.nytimes.com/2023/05/31/business/dealbook/engine-no-1-exxon-mobil.html.

others that make me scratch my head and may lead to headaches with your SRI clients:

Company	Industry	Allocation %
Newmont	Mining	0.15
Mosaic	Chemical fertilizers	0.10
Meta Platforms	Media	2.43
McDonald's	Fast food	0.41
Flutter Entertainment	Gambling	0.20
Royal Caribbean	Cruise line	0.10
International Paper	Paper	0.10
Coca Cola	Snacks and drinks	0.62
PepsiCo	Snacks and drinks	0.37
Molson Coors Beverage	Alcoholic drinks	0.17
Bunge	Big agriculture	0.16
Hormel foods	Big agriculture	0.11
Kimberly-Clark	Paper	0.11
Conagra Brands	Big agriculture	0.10
Keurig Dr. Pepper	Beverages	0.09
Visa	Credit cards	1.10
Mastercard	Credit cards	1.09
United Healthcare	Health insurance	0.84
Elevance Health	Health insurance	0.36
The Cigna Group	Health insurance	0.23
HCA Healthcare	Private hospitals	0.09
RTX Corp	Defense contractor	0.44
Delta Airlines	Airline	0.19
Axon Enterprises	Defense contractor	0.17
Northrop Grumman	Defense contractor	0.16
Weyerhauser	Timber	0.09

Frankly, I was shocked to see companies such as Flutter Entertainment, which is the parent company of FanDuel, the sports betting operator; Keurig Dr. Pepper, which produces Keurig K-Pod Cups, a very unsustainable way to brew coffee and other beverages; United Healthcare, a health insurer that has been accused of unfairly denying coverage to customers; and three defense contractors, two of which, RTX and Northrop Grumman, develop and supply fighter jets for the military. I would be very surprised if retail clients interested in sustainable investing would be comfortable owning most, if not all, the companies in this list.

Now, to be fair, there are many solutions providers held in ESGU that we include now or have included in our Green Sage Sustainability Portfolio over the years. Here is a list of those companies:

Company	Industry	Allocation %
Linde	Industrial gasses	0.31
Air Products & Chemicals	Industrial gasses	0.10
Tesla	Electric vehicles (EVs) and clean energy	2.18
LKQ	Recycled auto parts	0.26
Deckers outdoor	Apparel	0.21
Lululemon Athletica	Apparel	0.12
Marsh & McLennan	Insurance	0.30
Intuitive Surgical	Medical devices	0.38
Vertex Pharmaceuticals	Biotechnology	0.30
Amgen	Biotechnology	0.26
Regeneron	Biotechnology	0.15
Moderna	Biotechnology	0.10
Trane Technologies	heating, ventilation, and air conditioning	0.41
Conagra Brands	Big agriculture	0.10
Veralto	Water technologies	0.25
Xylem	Water technologies	0.24
Johnson Controls	Building controls	0.16

Company	Industry	Allocation %
Hubbell	Lighting	0.10
Owens Corning	Insulation	0.09
American Tower	Real estate investment trust (REIT)	0.35
Digital Realty	REIT	0.21
CBRE	Real estate management	0.15
Prologis	REIT	0.13
Iron Mountain	REIT	0.11
NVIDIA	Semiconductors	6.61
Microsoft	Software	5.83
Broadcom	Semiconductors	1.90
Salesforce	Software	0.68
IBM	Software	0.52
Applied Materials	Semiconductors	0.46
Accenture	Consulting	0.45
Adobe	Software	0.45
Autodesk	Software	0.34
Lam Research	Semiconductors	0.31
Arista Networks	Software	0.24
Palo Alto Networks	Software	0.24
Cadence Design Systems	Semiconductors	0.21
First Solar	Solar panels	0.11

You'll notice the last holding listed, First Solar, is one of only two companies, along with Tesla, held in ESGU that manufactures solar panels or builds EVs. That's only 2.29% of a "sustainable" portfolio, considerably less than any sustainability-minded client would like to see in their portfolio.

CONCLUSION

When you are deciding which funds to use with your SRI clients, you cannot spend enough time in the due diligence process. Outside of the traditional investment style, domicile, market cap, and performance considerations, check the sector allocations. If you see a large allocation to the energy sector, it should raise red flags for you. But ultimately, you'll want to lift the hood and carefully examine the underlying holdings – this is vital. You don't want to get that call from your client asking why you bought a greenwashed ESG fund for them when they were expecting to see solutions providers.

CHAPTER SIX

SHAREHOLDER ADVOCACY

OVERVIEW

Back when I started in the business and SRI was called *socially responsible investing*, I used to break down the style of investing as a three-legged stool:

- **Positive and negative screening.** Deciding which sectors and industries you wanted to own and which ones you didn't (i.e., no to fossil fuels, guns, or tobacco; yes to solar, organic food, and green real estate)
- **Shareholder advocacy and corporate engagement.** Using your proxy vote or direct engagement, as a shareholder, to push companies to be better corporate citizens
- **Community investing.** Allocating a percentage of the portfolio that went to investments such as low-income housing, affordable health care, and so on

The first leg of the stool is easy to understand, and we will cover it in much more detail in Chapter 10. The third leg is a topic that I'll address in Chapter 6. That leaves the second leg, shareholder advocacy and corporate engagement.

When you own a stock, you have the right to input via proxy and shareholder resolutions with management. Usually when you're reading a proxy, you'll see issues such as voting on board members, approving executive pay and the auditor, or stock grants for employees. Management puts forth these topics, and they must receive shareholder approval.

Shareholder approval is also required when a company decides to merge with another regardless of whether the board has voted in favor of the merger. Ultimately, the shareholders make the decision, and it's up to management and the board to make the case to the owners (or shareholders).

Occasionally, you will see an item on the proxy that was not put forth by management but by a shareholder instead. This is called a *shareholder resolution*. According to US SIF, The Sustainable Investment Forum, "Shareholders in a publicly traded company are entitled to introduce shareholder resolutions, or proposals, to the company management to be voted on in the next annual meeting. These resolutions may pertain to company policies and procedures, corporate governance, or social or environmental concerns. Shareholder resolutions are a meaningful way for shareholders to encourage corporate responsibility and discourage company practices that are unsustainable or unethical."

When you read through the proxy, there will be a notation with each item, listing how management recommends the shareholder to vote. Of course, for all the management-listed topics, they recommend voting "for." Usually, because most shareholder resolutions are critical of management, they recommend voting "against" those resolutions, even when they are calling for more transparency and other issues that would be in shareholders favor.

THE RULES

One thing to keep in mind is that shareholder resolutions are nonbinding. For example, a resolution could receive 80% for votes and still the management team would not have to do a thing. There would likely be repercussions for ignoring the will of the shareholders, however, from the greater stakeholder community, as well as the media. It's this pressure that can be a powerful tool for change.

According to the Securities and Exchange Commission (SEC), there are several requirements to submit a shareholder resolution, but the most important is the amount of shares the client owns, and for how long continuously. These are:

- At least $2,000 in market value of the company's securities entitled to vote on the proposal for at least three years, or
- At least $15,000 in market value of the company's securities entitled to vote on the proposal for at least two years, or
- At least $25,000 in market value of the company's securities entitled to vote on the proposal for at least one year[1]

These rules are in place to discourage abuse of the system by very small shareholders, but also because corporations don't like dealing with shareholder resolutions – they are bad for publicity.

TEAMWORK IS KEY

As a lone investor, initiating a shareholder advocacy campaign is very difficult. It is the stereotypical David and Goliath analogy, as the corporation

---

[1] US Securities and Exchange Commission, "Rule 14a-8: Shareholder Proposals," https://www.sec.gov/divisions/corpfin/rule-14a-8.pdf.

has millions to spend on legal fees and communication strategies, whereas the client is oftentimes a basic retail investor. This is where teaming up with other organizations and investment managers can make a huge difference.

Within the SRI industry, there are known organizations that specialize in shareholder advocacy, both on the investment management side and on the nonprofit side. Three investment management firms that I have worked with over the years that are experts on filing shareholder proposals are Green Century, Calvert Investments, and Impax Asset Management (formerly known as Pax World Funds). These firms run mutual funds and exchange-traded funds that own the shares and are then able to vote proxies for clients. They often work together to create scale.

They will also team up with a group of nonprofits focused on advocacy. Some of the nonprofits that have had an impact in shareholder advocacy include As You Sow, Ceres, and The Interfaith Center for Corporate Responsibility. These organizations do not typically own the shares but form coalitions of asset owners, including fund companies and individual investors, and sometimes even large institutional investors.

Other organizations address specific issues, such as Climate Action 100+ work on advocating companies to address greenhouse gas emissions and other climate-related disclosures. The Thirty Percent Coalition was created to "increase diversity in boardrooms and senior leadership at both public and private companies through investor engagement and collaborative action."

Remember that most companies' majority ownership is funds and institutions, so having their support is critical. Working as a group of investors provides the most significant opportunity for the proposal to win large enough support for the company to take action.

THE ISSUES

Shareholder advocates typically file proposals on several recurring issues, and over the years, these priorities and issues shift depending on a number of factors including regulation, corporate behavior, and even politics. For example, after the Citizens United Supreme Court decision in January 2010 giving corporations the ability to donate unlimited amounts to political campaigns, investors became interested in corporate transparency related to political activity and lobbying. In fact, many of the resolutions filed have to do with transparency and improving operations on several ESG topics.

In US SIF's "US Sustainable Investing Trends 2024/2025 Report," climate change was the leading shareholder proposal at 124. Those proposals were dominated by issues such as energy transition planning, as well as emissions and target setting. About half of those proposals were withdrawn because an agreement with the company was reached. The following shows the different shareholder proposals from 2020 through 2024:[2]

Here are some more trends from the US SIF report:

- Average support for 308 pro-ESG proposals came in at 21.8%.
- Three proposals garnered more than 50% of the vote in 2024 – two on climate change and one about political spending. Twelve earned between 40% and 49% and 47 between 30% and 39%. Six proposals addressing climate change and four related to corporate political influence were among the highest scorers.

---

[2] US SIF Foundation, "US Sustainable Investing Trends 2024/2025 Report," December 18, 2024.

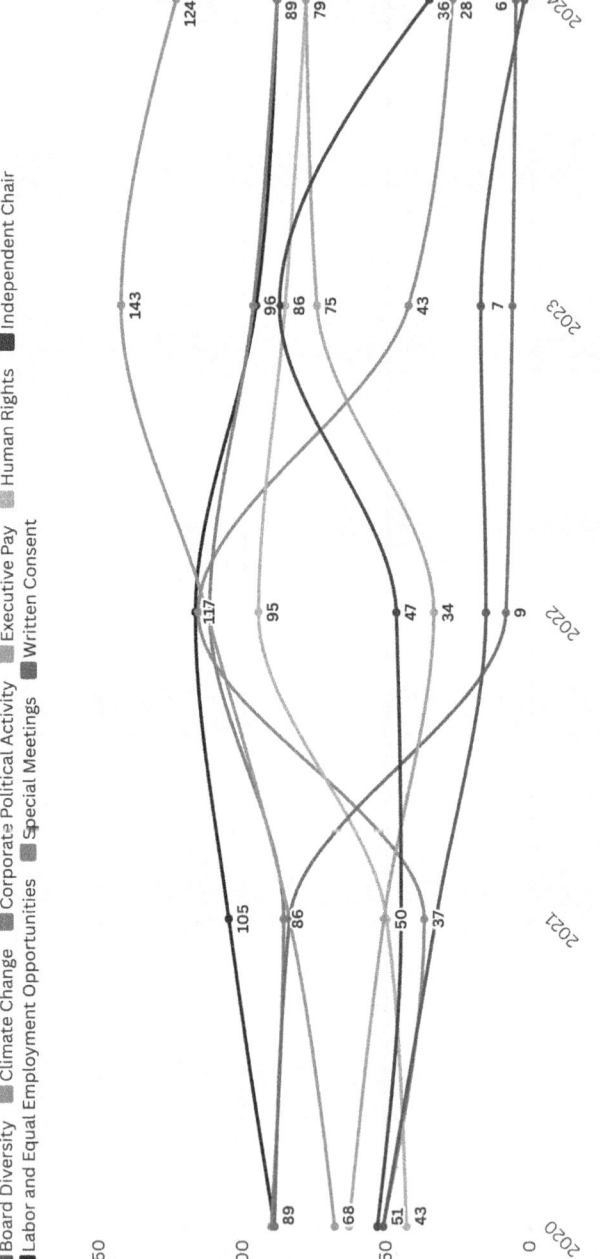

Numbers of proposals filled for 2020 meetings through July 15

Board Diversity ■ Climate Change ■ Corporate Political Activity ■ Executive Pay ■ Human Rights ■ Independent Chair
Labor and Equal Employment Opportunities ■ Special Meetings ■ Written Consent

Source: ISS, Sustainable Investments Institute, Sullivan & Cromwell. *Note:* Data for 2020 show numbers of proposals filled for 2020 meetings through July 15

EXAMPLES OF SHAREHOLDER ADVOCACY VICTORIES

Green Century Funds is a great organization. The firm is the only mutual fund company in the United States owned by environmental and public health nonprofits, and all the profits go to support those organizations. This is in addition to the work that Green Century does to invest in responsible companies and advocate for better environmental practices.

In June of 2023, Kraft Heinz announced that it was adopting a no-deforestation policy to protect tropical forests. The policy set a 2025 deadline for eliminating deforestation related to its global commodity supply chains and is an expansion of its 2018 commitment to source 100% of its palm oil sustainably.

These actions came about because of shareholder proposals filed by Green Century. Ultimately, the proposals never made it to a shareholder vote because Kraft Heinz agreed to the stipulations. It is not unusual for resolutions to be withdrawn after they are filed, and engagement begins.[3]

In its "2023 Shareholder Impact Review," As You Sow described their impact for the year. "In total, the As You Sow team led 210 engagements with 169 companies across 11 issue areas. In proxy year 2023, a total of 111 of these engagements were escalated, and shareholder resolutions were filed on behalf of 73 shareholders. We successfully withdrew 51 resolutions in instances where companies agreed to take requested actions; 48 resolutions went to a vote and received an average support of 23%. A total of

---

[3] Green Century, "Kraft Heinz Sets Global Policy to Eliminate Deforestation in Response to Green Century Shareholder Proposal," https://www.greencentury.com/kraft-heinz-sets-global-policy-to-eliminate-deforestation-in-response-to-green-century-shareholder-proposal/.

almost $2 trillion of share value was voted in support of our resolutions." It goes on to say, "Our 210 engagements addressed a range of issues: climate change (81); diversity, equity, and inclusion (43); racial justice (28); governance (13); ocean plastics, single use plastics, and recyclability (11); retirement plan climate risk (10); sexual and reproductive health (7); petrochemicals (6); water use (5); environmental health, including antibiotics in factory farming, pesticides, and PFAs(4); and political spending (2)"[4]

One of the highlights from this report was AT&T's commitment to political spending transparency. As You Sow had filed a shareholder resolution asking the company to publish a report "analyzing the congruence of the Company's political and electioneering expenditures during the preceding year against publicly stated company values and policies, listing and explaining any instances of incongruent expenditures, and stating whether the Company has made, or plans to make, changes in contributions or communications to candidates as a result of identified incongruencies." Once again, this resolution did not make it to a shareholder vote as AT&T agreed to publish such a report. It was one of nearly 300 resolutions filed asking companies for greater transparency on political spending from 2020 to 2023.

ENGAGEMENT

You'll notice that, in these two examples, the resolutions were withdrawn before they went to a shareholder vote. According to As You Sow, in 2023, about half of the resolutions they were involved with were withdrawn, and an agreement was made with the company. These withdrawals are the direct result of engagement with the company. From the As You Sow report,

---

[4] As You Sow, "2023 Shareholder Impact Review," https://www.asyousow.org/2023-shareholder-impact-review.

"It is our practice to work collaboratively with companies. We nearly always engage in dialogue prior to filing a resolution, and, unless there are extenuating circumstances, we will have multiple conversations with companies to resolve issues through discussion and agreement. Where we are not able to reach an agreement, we frequently file a shareholder resolution to be voted on at the company's annual general meeting (AGM). Filing a resolution elevates the issue to a shareholder vote at the meeting. Discussions with companies often continue after filing a resolution and after the AGM."

Impax Asset Management publicly publishes its engagement policy online. The firm's engagement process and strategy enable them to do the following:

- "Manage risks by proactively identifying and mitigating issues
- Enhance company analysis; how companies respond to engagement is informative of their character
- Strengthen investee companies over time, improving quality, processes, transparency, and resilience"[5]

Many corporations look at investor-sponsored proposals negatively and prefer to have them removed from a proxy if possible. Some attempt to do so via the SEC and others, such as ExxonMobil, via the courts. In January 2024, ExxonMobil filed a lawsuit against two shareholders who had filed a proposal requesting that the company do more to reduce its greenhouse gas emissions. This lawsuit sent a shockwave through the investment industry resulting in considerable negative press for ExxonMobil.

Tim Smith, an SRI pioneer who has been working in the field for 50 years, wrote in an article in the *Harvard Law School Forum* about corporate governance:

---

[5] Impax Asset Management, *Engagement Policy 2022*, May 2022, https://impaxam.com/wp-content/uploads/2022/05/Impax_Engagement_Policy_2022.pdf?pwm=4427.

The response to the lawsuit was global in scope and included several sizeable institutional investors. These investors viewed the unprecedented invocation of the courts to block a shareholder proposal as unnecessarily punitive and akin to a "SLAPP" suit meant to silence shareholder dissent on climate risk and ward off future shareholder filings. Most concerning to investors was the company's flagrant "end run" around the Securities and Exchange Commission (SEC), the federal regulator charged with protecting investor interests and adjudicating proxy disputes. The lawsuit quickly became a lightning rod for the attack on shareholder rights, raising the specter of future lawsuits against shareholder proponents seeking more information and improved corporate policies to better manage climate risk.[6]

The lawsuit was eventually dismissed in court, but not before sending the message that some corporations do not like shareholder interference and will do anything within their means to muzzle dissent. But what it also did was to galvanize the investment community and their right, as shareholders, to have a voice in corporate decision-making. As Smith said in summarizing his article, "It was both important and gratifying to see such a broad spectrum of global investors standing in solidarity to protect shareholder rights."

CONCLUSION

As the changed climate continues to affect more and more people, we will likely see more shareholders attempting to hold corporations accountable for their contribution to the crisis. The right of shareholders to file proposals and to subsequently vote on them is a cornerstone of our financial system. Does it work perfectly? Absolutely not. Does it have an impact? Absolutely.

---

[6] Harvard Law School Forum on Corporate Governance, "ExxonMobil's Lawsuit Against Its Shareholders: A Cautionary Tale," June 12, 2024, https://corpgov.law.harvard.edu/2024/06/12/exxonmobils-lawsuit-against-its-shareholders-a-cautionary-tale/.

CHAPTER SEVEN

COMMUNITY, IMPACT, AND PRIVATE INVESTING

OVERVIEW

In Chapter 6, I introduced the three-legged stool of socially responsible investing: positive and negative screening, shareholder advocacy, and community investing. Community investing from an SRI perspective includes investing in financial institutions and other organizations that support underserved communities. This might include using local banks or credit unions, community development financial institutions (CDFIs), or venture or microfinance funds. The goal of allocating funds to community investing organizations is to ensure that capital flows to places where it historically has not.

Remember that this is still an investment and not charity. By investing in these institutions, you are typically making a yield on a fixed-income instrument, and the institution is then loaning that money out to the community. The return is usually a below-market-rate yield, but then again, the typical allocation to community investments is 1–5%, so its impact on the investor is small, but the community impact is big.

According to the "US Sustainable Investing Trends 2024/2025 Report," "In 2014, US SIF identified 800 Community Investment Institutions that collectively managed $64.3 billion in assets. By 2022, this figure had surged to $458 billion, representing a 615% increase. The number of institutions has also surged. In 2000, the Community Development Financial Institution (CDFI) Fund reported 430 CDFI institutions. In 2023, that number had grown to almost 1,500."[1] This growth has fueled investments in projects such as affordable housing, microenterprises, and community services.

COMMUNITY AND IMPACT INVESTING

Calvert Impact Capital (not to be confused with Calvert Investments) has been focused on community investing since 1995. The organization, in many ways, serves as a facilitator for individuals and institutions that want to make an impact on underserved communities, both domestically and internationally. Instead of choosing which on-the-ground organization to support, investors rely on Calvert Impact Capital to conduct the due diligence, make the investment, monitor progress, and report back. We have

---

[1] US SIF Foundation, "US Sustainable Investing Trends 2024/2025 Report."

used Calvert Impact Notes for years as a part of our community investing allocation, and couldn't be happier with the organization, their communications, and reporting.

A page out of their latest "2023 Impact Report" looks like this:[2]

In 2022, our Community Investment Note® portfolio partners served nearly 150 million individuals by supporting small businesses, building or preserving affordable homes, creating or retaining jobs, and improving energy access in communities around the world. Separately, the Small Business Programs we have arranged through our syndications and structuring service supported small businesses across 19 states and DC.

Impact on Communities

149.9 mil
individual clients served

41.8 mil
people with improved access to energy

3.3 mil
small businesses financed

22,134
affordable homes created or preserved

905,015
jobs created or retained

Impact on the Climate

621 mil
kWh energy conserved

4.2 mil
MWh of clean energy generated by solar, wind, and other renewables

8.5 mil
solar products financed

25 mil
metric tons CO_2 reduced

648,097
acres managed sustainably

Gender and Racial Equity

91,847
entrepreneurs of color

62%
end clients of color

139,223
women-owned businesses

66%
women clients

Small Business Programs

48%
entrepreneurs of color

5,805
small businesses financed across 5 funds

40%
women-owned businesses

---

[2] Calvert Impact, "2023 Impact Report," https://calvertimpact.org/resources/2023-impact-report.

This is the type of reporting that sustainable investing clients like to see. They are looking for solutions to our biggest challenges, and being able to show them how many women or people of color had their businesses financed, or how many megawatt hours of clean energy they helped produce, brings it home to them.

One of the institutions that Calvert Impact invested in is the Clearinghouse CDFI. Its mission since the new millennium has been to "bridge the gap between conventional lending standards and the needs of low-income and distressed communities and communities of color." Some of the funds that Calvert Impact invested in Clearinghouse were used to provide "construction and permanent financing of the Paul Quinn College (PQC), one of 107 historically black colleges and universities in the US. As a working college, PQC offers paid jobs for every student, as well as reduced student tuition and fees." This is a story to tell your clients.

A theme throughout this book is that sustainable investing clients want their portfolios to be solutions-based, and using community investments most fulfills that desire. But buying individual notes from Calvert Impact is not exactly a scalable solution, so how else can you help implement community investments?

As of now, there are a few mutual funds and exchange-traded funds that invest in community impact and Community Reinvestment Act (CRA) bonds. If you're running a sustainable fund portfolio, they make it easy to integrate community investments into your model.

One company that we have used for years is Community Capital Management (CCM). The origin of the firm was to help banks meet their CRA requirement mandated by the Federal Reserve and other banking regulators. The goal of the legislation was to "encourage financial institutions to help meet the credit needs of the communities in which they do business, including low- and moderate-income neighborhoods."[3]

---

[3] Board of Governors of the Federal Reserve System, "About the Community Reinvestment Act (CRA)," https://www.federalreserve.gov/consumerscommunities/cra_about.htm.

CCM focuses on several impact themes in its funds. You can see the variety of themes in this chart from their Community Impact Bond Fund Fact Sheet Q4 2024:[4]

Impact by Theme

The chart shows current CIB Fund holdings and their alignment with our impact themes as of 12/31/24. One investment can align with multiple impact themes. Impact by theme is calculated using the current face value of individual securities (original par value minus any principal paydowns, if applicable). Each security's contribution is counted in the impact themes it supports. Percentages are based on total portfolio exposure, including cash holdings.

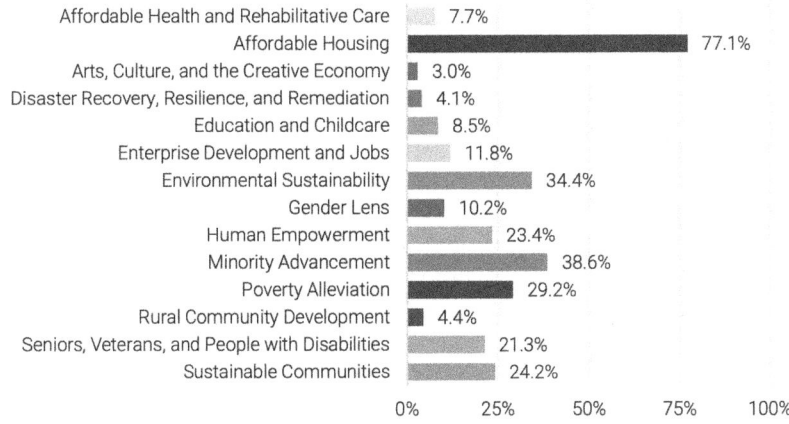

Again, communicating a client's impact based on the investments you choose for them helps to solidify the relationship and could lead to referrals and other opportunities in the future. Always be thinking of ways to make that connection.

Another example of the direct impact of using community investments comes from CCM. The fund made an investment in Hawthorne Eco Village Apartments in Minneapolis, Minnesota. This affordable rental

---

[4] Community Capital Management, "Community Impact Bond Fund Fact Sheet: Q4 2024," January 2025, https://www.ccminvests.com/wp-content/uploads/2025/01/CCM-Community-Impact-Bond-Fund-Fact-Sheet-4Q24.pdf.

development sits in an area that used to be home to vacant lots, drug crime, foreclosures, and crumbling houses.

According to CCM, the impact on the community is substantial:

Project for Pride in Living (PPL) built and manages the property. The 75 units at Hawthorne Eco Village are part of over 1,300 units of safe, quality, affordable housing built and managed by PPL throughout the Twin Cities available to households making less than 60% of the area median income. In addition to affordable housing, PPL also provides no cost employment readiness services for residents and the greater community. Other property and features and amenities include a green roof, playground for children, fitness room, and community garden. Up to four of the apartments will be set aside for those experiencing long-term homelessness and earning at or below 30% of the area median income.[5]

Several impact themes are addressed with the Hawthorne Eco Village project:

- Affordable housing
- Education and childcare
- Enterprise development and jobs
- Environmental sustainability
- Healthy communities
- Human empowerment
- Minority advancement
- Neighborhood revitalization
- Poverty alleviation
- Transit-oriented development

All of this is accomplished within a publicly traded mutual fund that isn't charity, but capitalism focused on stakeholder returns.

---

[5] Community Capital Management, "Stories of Impact," https://www.ccminvests.com/impact/stories-of-impact/.

PRIVATE INVESTMENTS

Although Earth Equity rarely uses venture capital or private equity investments in client accounts, I felt it important to at least mention the opportunity in the sustainable investing space. For the high and ultra-high net worth investor, complementing a public equity and bond portfolio with private investments is usually the prudent thing to do. Of course, there is usually added due diligence responsibilities that go along with private investments as they are not as regulated as public investments.

Because I'm not an expert in the space, I consulted ChatGPT to come up with a list of themes that private investors are currently targeting:

- Renewable energy transition
  - Solar, wind, hydro, and geothermal energy projects.
  - Energy storage technologies (batteries, grid-scale solutions)
  - Investments in clean hydrogen and fuel cell technology
  - Distributed energy resources and microgrids
- Energy efficiency
  - Smart building technologies (e.g., IoT for energy management)
  - Retrofitting infrastructure for energy conservation
  - High-efficiency heating, ventilation, and air conditioning systems and lighting (e.g., LED solutions)
- Electric mobility and transportation
  - Electric vehicle (EV) manufacturers and component suppliers
  - EV charging infrastructure and networks
  - Shared mobility and sustainable logistics solutions
- Circular economy and waste reduction
  - Recycling and upcycling technologies
  - Waste-to-energy projects
  - Sustainable packaging solutions (e.g., biodegradable and compostable materials)

- Sustainable agriculture and food systems
  - AgTech innovations (e.g., precision farming, vertical agriculture)
  - Plant-based proteins and alternative food products
  - Sustainable aquaculture and regenerative farming practices
- Water and resource management
  - Water treatment and desalination technologies
  - Smart water management systems (e.g., leak detection, efficient irrigation)
  - Investments in clean and accessible drinking water
- Carbon reduction and capture
  - Carbon capture, utilization, and storage technologies
  - Reforestation and afforestation projects
  - Carbon credit marketplaces and trading platforms
- Green real estate and infrastructure
  - Development of green-certified buildings
  - Renewable energy integration in real estate projects
  - Sustainable urban development and "smart cities" initiatives
- ESG and data analytics
  - Platforms that provide ESG data and compliance solutions
  - Tools for supply chain transparency and sustainability
  - AI and machine learning applications for tracking and improving ESG metrics
- Sustainable supply chains
  - Technologies for reducing emissions and waste in logistics
  - Innovations in material science for greener supply chains
  - Blockchain for supply chain transparency and traceability
- Biodiversity and ecosystem restoration
  - Nature-based solutions (e.g., conservation projects)
  - Investments in ecosystem restoration (e.g., wetlands, coral reefs)
  - Sustainable forestry and land management

- Health and Well-being
  - Technologies addressing environmental health risks (e.g., air and water quality)
  - Mental health and wellness platforms focused on holistic care
  - Development of sustainable health care facilities
- Green finance and climate tech
  - Startups developing solutions to decarbonize industries
  - Platforms for green bonds, sustainability-linked loans, and ESG investments
  - Fintech enabling better tracking of individual or corporate carbon footprints
- Sustainable consumer goods
  - Eco-friendly fashion and textiles (e.g., recycled fabrics)
  - Sustainable personal care and household products
  - Ethical and traceable supply chains in consumer goods

I do have experience working with two firms: Alante Capital and Greenbacker Capital. Both are sustainable private investments, but with very different foci. Alante is in the consumer products space while Greenbacker invests in sustainable infrastructure.

One of the themes that Alante invests in is the circular economy. I mentioned back in the Introduction how green architect William McDonough was one of my influences when I founded the firm back in 2004. He is the author of *Cradle to Cradle*, which is a breakthrough work on the importance of the circular economy. The basic philosophy behind a circular economy is one of waste elimination. In a traditional linear economy, a product has three stages: creation, use, and waste. What a circular economy model does is eliminate the waste component and transition what would have been waste back into a new product without degradation.

This diagram from Alante's impact report lays out what a circular economy looks like:[6]

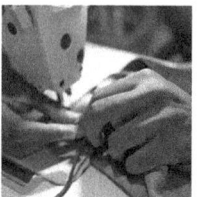

PRODUCTION
*raw materials, sourcing,
manufacturing, supply
chain management*

**DESIGN &
DEVELOPMENT**
*design, product
development, sampling,
assortment & demand
planning*

FROM LINEAR
TO CIRCULAR

**DISTRIBUTION
& SALES**
*inventory, logistics,
ecommerce, retail,
omnichannel, packaging,
returns*

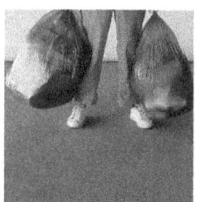

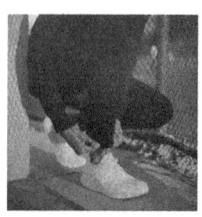

WASTE RECOVERY
*collection, deadstock,
sorting, recycling*

USE
*resale, rental, wardrobe
optimization, aftercare,
repair, refurbish*

One of Alante's portfolio companies, Circ, is a leading textile recycler, a key component of the circular economy. In a world of fast fashion, the amount of textile waste continues to pile up. According to the Ellen McArthur foundation, in the current fast fashion trend, garments are worn

---

[6] Alante Capital, "The Alante Approach," https://www.alantecapital.com/alanteapproach.

only 7 to 10 times before being discarded.[7] An estimated 92 million tons of textile waste is created annually.[8] And, about 30% of clothing that is manufactured is never sold, and those unsold clothes are often burned or sent to landfills without anyone ever having worn them.[9]

The answer is recycling and circularity. Circ's groundbreaking technology can separate polyester from cotton, leaving both fibers fully reusable as if they were new. Growing technology companies like Circ need funding to innovate and grow. That money, more often than not, comes from private investors.

Greenbacker is another private investment company that focuses on funding renewable energy projects. Many of Greenbacker's projects are focused on solar, wind, and battery installations. They sell the renewable energy to utilities, municipalities, and other entities that can provide reliable income for more conservative investors.

In addition, one of the firm's investment funds called the Greenbacker Development Opportunities Fund invests in a range of industries, not just clean energy, and, like many in the space produces an insightful impact report.[10]

These are just two examples of private sustainable investment opportunities. For high and ultra-high net worth clients, complementing their public markets investments with private investments can give them the opportunity to increase their impact with potentially cutting-edge companies as well as income.

---

[7] Circ, "The Cost of Clothing," https://circ.earth/the-cost-of-clothing/.
[8] World Economic Forum, "Textile Recycling Can Create Jobs and Reduce Pollution," August 2023, https://www.weforum.org/stories/2023/08/textile-recycling-create-jobs-reduce-pollution/.
[9] FashionUnited, "Infographic: The Extent of Overproduction in the Fashion Industry," December 12, 2018, https://fashionunited.uk/news/fashion/infographic-the-extent-of-overproduction-in-the-fashion-industry/2018121240500.
[10] Greenbacker Capital, "Impact Report 2023," April 2024, https://greenbackercapital.com/wp-content/uploads/2024/04/GDEV_Impact-Report_2023.pdf.

OUR PORTFOLIO AT A GLANCE[1]

In 2023, our portfolio partners made steady progress toward their goals for environmental and social impact. We're proud to support their work and to work alongside them toward our shared vision for the future of the industry.

Environmental offsets[2]

240 MW+
Generation capacity per annum

391 GWh+
Clean energy generated in 2023

333 GWh
Grid flexibility per annum

441,818 MT+
Carbon abated in 2023

16 Portfolio companies[3]

- Solar
- Storage
- Hydro
- Fleet Electrification
- Energy Efficiency
- Waste to Value

Combined pipeline includes:

$27 Billion
In CapEx

16+ GW
Of power generation

23+ GWh
Of storage capacity

2,740
Projects in pipeline

Total Reported Portfolio Emissions (metric tons CO_2e[1])

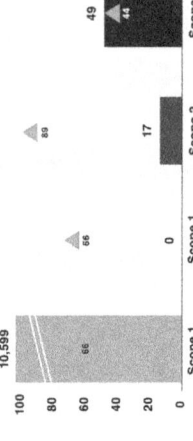

684
235
1
22,118
21,198

- Scope 1 (Net Neutral/Negative)
- Scope 1 (Rest of Portfolio)
- Scope 2
- Scope 3

Two portfolio companies reported Scope 1 emissions stemming from their operations of combined heat and power and biomass plants. These plants are designed to be carbon negative to neutral when compared to the status quo.

Reported Average Portfolio Emissions (metric tons CO_2e)

■ Portfolio average ▲ Benchmark

10,599		
66	66	89
	0	17
Scope 1 (Net Neutral/Negative)	Scope 1 (Rest of Portfolio)	Scope 2

44 / 49 — Scope 3

[1] Data based on self-reporting per respective portfolio company as of 12/31/2023.
[2] Carbon abatement is calculated using the EPA Greenhouse Gas Equivalencies Calculator which uses the Avoided Emissions and generation Tool (AVERT) US national weighted average CO_2 marginal emission rate to convert reductions of kilowatt-hours into avoided tons of carbon dioxide emission
[3] Represents all portfolio companies, including both exited and currently in portfolio, as of 12/31/2023. 14 portfolio companies remain in portfolio.
We use industry-level benchmarks based on company stage (e.g. Series A–C) and type of industry estimated from Metric ESG to benchmark DCO2 emissions from our portfolio companies.

13

CONCLUSION

Be intentional about how you round out your client's portfolio matters. Using vehicles like Calvert Impact Notes accomplishes three things: it provides stable income, has on-the-ground impact, and provides a good story that clients love to hear. And when it's appropriate with higher net worth clients, using thematic private investments extends that impact, and you can tailor the theme depending on the client's interests.

SECTION II

INVESTING

CHAPTER EIGHT

THE INSTITUTIONAL VERSUS RETAIL INVESTOR DILEMMA

OVERVIEW

This book is written for the financial advisor who generally works with retail clients. For over 25 years, I have worked mostly with retail clients: individuals, couples, families, and small values-based nonprofit organizations. I've learned a lot about their preferences, how they feel about sustainable investing and other values-based services, and how they can be best serviced.

Much of what I'll talk about in this chapter is very subjective – your experiences may be very different than mine, but I would bet they aren't. When I generalize, they are just that: generalizations. But they're based on over 25 years in the financial services industry, plus an additional five years in consumer retail sales and management.

THE INSTITUTIONAL INVESTOR

I will contrast my retail experience with another animal: the institutional investor. The institutional investor wants a certain level of client service, but what's most important to them is hitting their benchmarks, doing it with minimal risk, and doing so with as little cost as possible. Does an institutional investor care about climate change? Typically, not as an entity. Do they care about environmental, social, and governance (ESG) issues? Only if ESG has been added to the list of priorities by the governing board or body. We rarely work with institutional investors because we are a relatively small investment manager, and we are not the cheapest index-based investment solution. Plus, institutional demand is for vanilla ESG portfolios and not solutions-based sustainable portfolios.

Institutional investors care about the metrics: benchmarking to an arbitrary index, reducing tracking error, and their quarterly reports. They have a fiduciary duty just like you do, but they typically look at it differently. Working with institutional investors is a business transaction – the goal is to remove all emotion from the relationship and just focus on the facts and metrics.

In discussing institutional investors with financial advisor colleagues, we all tend to have the same impression: avoid them if you can. There is very little room for nuance. They are purely results and performance driven and will probably drive you a little crazy. During the times that we have presented to institutions that were open and interested in sustainable investing (usually smaller environmental nonprofits), we often run into one board member who insists on using a Vanguard S&P 500 index exchange-traded fund (ETF)[1] because it's cheaper and easier. I'm not telling you to avoid institutional opportunities; I'm just saying that you should go into the process with high intentions but low attachment.

The problem with institutional investors is that they are also the mutual fund and ETF managers, so when they manage a fund, they manage it like they think an institutional manager would want it managed. Since most mutual funds and ETFs are geared toward retail investors, this creates a disconnect. Sustainable retail investors don't care about arbitrary indexes, and they don't care about tracking error. So much of the investment industry is centered on indexing, but, as I mention several times throughout this book, you can't index the next economy by looking in the rearview mirror. Indexing the next economy is the same as active management: technology and innovation, as well as resilience in the face of the changed climate, are changing the playing field every day. Trying to create a static index to track it is a fool's errand.

With all of that being said, I don't want you to get the wrong impression about *all* institutional investors. There are many that are serious about investing responsibly. In a conversation with Tim Smith from the Interfaith Center for Corporate Responsibility, he said, "I have worked with many foundations, pension funds, unions and NGY investors for many decades. And while many are totally focused on returns, there are institutional investors with trillions of dollars that are very active in the fights on climate, diversity, etc. CalPers is a perfect example of an institutional investor that has set up a climate solutions fund." So, there are opportunities in the space if you're willing to put the time and effort in.

---

[1] Vanguard. "Vanguard S&P 500 ETF (VOO)," https://investor.vanguard.com/investment-products/etfs/profile/voo.

THE RETAIL INVESTOR

Unlike an institutional investor, working with a retail investor almost always has an emotional element to the relationship. When you're working with a retail investor, you're typically working with what I call a board of one or two. Unlike the 10-plus person board you are faced with in an institutional setting, you only have a couple of people to engage with, and if they're coming to you because they're interested in sustainable investing, they're already friendly. They might need financial planning, help with retirement, or education of their kids or grandkids. They know that they don't want to own ExxonMobil because they're concerned about the planet. You are uniquely equipped to work with these folks.

Retail investors are unlikely to have heard of tracking error and don't really care how the portfolio you create for them aligns with the S&P 500, Russell 2000, or Europe, Australasia, and Far East markets. They care about hitting their goals, not some arbitrary index. They want to enjoy a comfortable retirement or send little Susie to college. Benchmark their progress based on the plan you've laid out for them, not how they align with the index. If you're doing your job well, many of your interactions with your clients will be 20% business and 80% social.

WHAT DOES THE RETAIL INVESTOR WANT?

In my experience, the retail sustainable, responsible, and impact investor is interested in solutions. They want to own the companies that are innovators: the companies that see the unique challenges that we are facing globally and turn them into opportunities to benefit everyone. They feel a sense of connection when you begin to tell them the names of some of the companies in their portfolio, and with that comes a sense of pride: "I'm part of the solution, are you?"

I started publishing an electronic fact sheet a few years back that listed all the holdings in our Green Sage Sustainability Portfolio. The piece not only lists the companies but also has a link to the sustainability/ESG/corporate responsibility page on each company website. This enables the client to better understand sustainable investing and how their investment fits into the solution. I've received feedback, such as, "I never thought about including that kind of company into a sustainable solution, but after visiting their website, now it makes sense to me," and "I really appreciate the work that you do to put together this group of companies that are making a difference." Clients often brag about their portfolio holdings at parties or events, "I own First Solar in my portfolio," or "I'm thinking about buying a Rivian because I own their stock. Have you checked those pickup trucks out yet?"

By contrast, how would a client react if I were to buy the iShares ESG Aware MSCI USA ETF for them, and they received their annual or semiannual report that lists all their holdings? They would come to me scratching their heads and wondering why they hired me to invest sustainably for them. They would ask why ExxonMobil or McDonald's was in their portfolio. Retail clients don't want to own a less bad portfolio; they want to own the companies innovating in the face of our greatest challenges.

CONCLUSION

Retail clients come to Earth Equity Advisors for a very specific reason: we offer what they're searching for. I make it known that our investment philosophy isn't about being less bad, it's about being positive. It's about more than just what's sustainable; it's about thriving. What can we do to give that client peace of mind to know that not only are they going to be able to send their kids to college, or retire in comfort, but do so by investing in a way that enables them to sleep at night? That's what retail investors want.

CHAPTER NINE

FIDUCIARY DUTY AND PERFORMANCE

OVERVIEW

Fiduciary duty. It's the core principle governing what we do as advisors and how we interact with our clients. It is putting the client's interests first and always doing what is in their best interest.

The Consumer Financial Protection Bureau (CFPB) details the responsibilities of a fiduciary, which includes four basic duties:

- **Act only in their best interest.** Because you are dealing with someone else's money and property, your duty is to make decisions that are best for them, not you.
- **Manage their money and property carefully.** You will have important financial responsibilities and must carry them out with care.

You might pay bills, oversee bank accounts, and pay for things they need. You might also make investments, pay taxes, collect rent or unpaid debts, and get insurance for them, if needed.

- **Keep their money and property separate.** Never mix their money or property with your own or someone else's. Confused records can get you in trouble with government agencies, like adult protective services and the police.
- **Keep good records.** You must keep true and complete records of their money and property, or you could face legal consequences.[1]

Traditionally, when it comes to investments and financial services, one aspect of fiduciary duty relates to conducting due diligence on any investments you recommend and buy for a client. For example, buying Enron, Tyco International, WorldCom, or Adelphia Communications for a client back in the early 2000s might have been problematic as all of them had accounting scandals and lost money for clients. Churning a client's account to generate commissions with little to no benefit for the client might be a breach of fiduciary duty. And failing to reveal a conflict of interest with a friend, family member, or business associate might be a breach of fiduciary duty. Fortunately, most financial advisors take their fiduciary duty seriously, and unfortunately, it's a small minority who make the rest of us look bad.

Fiduciary duty is, in a sense, about reducing risk. It is about setting guardrails for advisors to help maintain their objectivity while working to reduce as much risk for the client as possible. The CFPB list? It's about reducing risk. The examples I provided? They're about reducing risk as well.

---

[1] Consumer Financial Protection Bureau, "What Is a Fiduciary?" https://www.consumerfinance.gov/ask-cfpb/what-is-a-fiduciary-en-1769/.

ESG AS FIDUCIARY DUTY?

An investment manager who recommends a security or fund without first conducting appropriate due diligence might be in breach of fiduciary duty. Is the investment manager licensed, and if so, what is their experience and track record? Does a company file its required regulatory documents on time? Is the asset manager your brother-in-law? All of these, and many more, are generally accepted as reasons to question whether a financial advisor is abiding by their fiduciary duty. But what about environmental, social, and governance (ESG)? Does ESG belong as a fiduciary duty metric? And if so, which metrics do you use, and how material are they? I would argue that in many cases, yes, incorporating ESG data into security analysis is part of your fiduciary duty, and I believe that if you don't include ESG in your security analysis, you might be in breach of fiduciary duty. Let's explore this further.

When I am working on rebalancing and reallocating our Green Sage Sustainability Portfolio, I'm looking at several company metrics, from price-to-earnings (P/E) ratios to debt ratios to profitability. These are fundamental metrics that are generally accepted as necessary to evaluate a company effectively. Traditional investment managers will tell you that all you need are fundamental measurements to gauge a company. I believe that fundamentals only tell half of the story; the other half – the ESG risks – gives you a much broader picture of the company and helps you perform your job more effectively.

The United Nations Principles for Responsible Investing produced in 2020 "Fiduciary Duty in the 21st Century: Final Report," which states that incorporating ESG issues into investment analyses and decision-making processes is in alignment with fiduciary duty. It says, "Empirical and academic evidence demonstrates that incorporating ESG issues is a source of investment value. ESG analysis assists investors to identify value-relevant issues. Neglecting ESG analysis may cause the mispricing of risk and poor asset allocation decisions and is therefore a failure of fiduciary duty."[2]

It goes on to support this by saying, "Systemic issues, like climate change, may significantly alter the investment rationale for particular sectors, industries and geographies and may have generalized negative impacts on economic output. Ultimately, the consideration of ESG issues has become one of the core characteristics of a prudent investment process."

Let's talk about materiality with an easy to understand hypothetical. You're considering investing in a manufacturer of widgets. The company is very profitable, with a low P/E ratio, little debt, and high growth (widgets are in demand). The company is run well by a CEO with years of experience, and a very capable management team. They invest heavily in research and development, so they always have cutting edge widgets. Sounds good, right?

The information that you won't find in the company's financials is that they have widget manufacturing facilities across the country. Many of these are located in Florida, Arizona, and California. If you ignore ESG metrics, you might never find out that the facility in Florida is on the coast in an area where king tides are now regularly flooding the roads in and out of the plant. In addition, the plant is also in the path of hurricanes on a regular basis.

It takes water to manufacture widgets, and that plant in Arizona is beginning to run into difficulties with its water supply. As Colorado River water gets squeezed more and more, less and less is ending up farther south. And as residents in the Arizona location are asked to conserve water, they're asking why the widget plant doesn't have to. Not only is there a risk of not having enough water to produce widgets but there is also the public relations risk in the local community.

---

[2] Principles for Responsible Investment, "Fiduciary Duty in the 21st Century: Final Report," https://www.unpri.org/fiduciary-duty/fiduciary-duty-in-the-21st-century-final-report/4998.article.

Finally, the facility in California is in a drought-prone area, just like Arizona. The only difference here is that the vegetation surrounding the plant is a major risk for wildfires. As we've seen with the Los Angeles wildfires in early 2025, the changed climate is causing unpredictable weather patterns leading to destruction and tragedy.

If this hypothetical widget company teaches us anything, it's that ESG risk is most definitely material, and performing this level of due diligence is most definitely a part of your fiduciary duty. How much of a hit does the company take when they can't ship widgets out of the Florida factory during high winds and king tides? What about the public relations fallout when the community in Arizona complains about water use? And what about the loss of the plant when a wildfire sweeps through the California facility?

SRI OR SUSTAINABLE, RESILIENT, AND INNOVATIVE INVESTING AND FIDUCIARY DUTY

Because there is enough difference between ESG and SRI investing, I thought it prudent to address it as well in a fiduciary context. As I've said, investing sustainably can very well be defined as growth investing. The idea behind it is to invest in companies set to be market leaders in the next economy: one that is cleaner, more resource efficient, more resilient, and more equitable. It is an investment style, and although I would argue that it is not thematic, I can see where some might call it thematic investing. Either way, for clients who want to invest with their values, it is indeed in alignment with your fiduciary duty.

As I put together our portfolios, my job is to assess where the economy is going and what are the technologies and innovations that will be moving it forward. This is the very definition of growth investing. For example, I believe that a healthier society is a more sustainable society. Biotechnology is a component in our portfolios because of this concept. What is the next step in biotech research? Artificial intelligence (AI).

We may own stocks that are researching cutting-edge biotechnology using AI-based learning models. The average time it takes to bring a new drug to market is 10 years and the average cost is about $1 billion. Using data from previous drug trials, AI can learn and predict possible uses for current drugs outside of their intended disease, which expands treatment opportunities.

What the AI also does, however, is through in-silico trials, make formulation and compounding changes to create new drugs based on the learning models and previous trials. The potential to address cancer, diabetes, psoriasis, and other widespread diseases is exponential. In addition, the time to market could potentially be halved as well as the cost to market. This is innovation investing. This is sustainable investing, and it is within your fiduciary duty.

PERFORMANCE

So how does ESG/sustainable/responsible investing perform? Well, just like any investment style, it depends on the portfolio, how it's constructed, and over what time period you're measuring. If you're looking at short-term returns, any investment can beat or underperform its benchmark. So, I prefer to look at the long term.

Unfortunately, since we work in a "what have you done for me lately" culture, oftentimes media headlines focus on short-term returns, without adding context. For example, sustainable investing, because of its nature, tends to fall into the growth investing style (as opposed to value investing.) So, when the markets shifted to a value bias in 2021 and 2022, most sustainable portfolios underperformed, even though they had solid longer-term returns. I did not see a single story highlighting this shift in investment style and linking it to sustainable investing's short-term underperformance.

A headline from Morningstar in early 2024 said, "ESG Fund Returns Recover, but Still Trail Conventional Peers by a Small Margin." What you would miss if you only read the headline, though, was the quote, "Sustainable Equity Funds Lagged in 2023 but Performed Well Over the Trailing Five Years."[3] This is obviously frustrating, but ultimately, it's our job to see past the noise, and tell clients and prospects the real story.

Now, I'm not one to read academic papers, but when it comes to investment performance and reporting on it, I think it's best to leave it up to the academics to do the research, not Wall Street, and certainly not the media. In a paper entitled "Does Sustainability Generate Better Financial Performance," the authors found that returns with traditional investments was comparable. In the abstract, they said, "We surveyed 1,141 primary peer-reviewed papers and 27 meta-reviews (based on ~1,400 underlying studies) published between 2015 and 2020. Aggregate conclusions from a sample suggest that the financial performance of ESG investing has on average been indistinguishable from conventional investing (with one in three studies indicating superior performance)." The authors went on to say, "We developed three propositions: first, ESG integration as a strategy seems to perform better than screening or divestment; second, ESG investing provides asymmetric benefits, especially during a social or economic crisis;

---

[3] Morningstar, "ESG Fund Returns Recover in 2023: Most Sustainable Funds Trail Conventional Peers by a Small Margin," https://www.morningstar.com/sustainable-investing/esg-fund-returns-recover-2023-most-sustainable-funds-trail-conventional-peers-by-small-margin.

and third, decarbonization strategies can potentially capture a climate risk premium."[4]

This particular meta-analysis was reviewed in a separate article published by a team at New York University Stern Center for Sustainable Business. They came up with six clear conclusions:

- "Improved financial performance due to ESG becomes more marked over longer time horizons.
- ESG integration, broadly speaking as an investment strategy, seems to perform better than negative screening approaches.
- ESG investing appears to provide downside protection, especially during a social or economic crisis.
- Sustainability initiatives at corporations appear to drive better financial performance due to mediating factors such as improved risk management and more innovation.
- Studies indicate that managing for a low carbon future improves financial performance.
- ESG disclosure on its own does not drive financial performance."[5]

Morgan Stanley issued a report on sustainable fund performance in mid-2024, saying that "sustainable equity funds had a median return of 5.2% in the period, in line with traditional funds at 5.1%." But the report goes on to specifically point out the advantage of long-term investing. It said, "In the past five years, sustainable funds have delivered superior median returns in eight of 10 of the past half-year intervals. A hypothetical

---

[4] Ulrich Atz, Tracy Van Holt, Zongyuan Zoe Liu, and Christopher C. Bruno, "Does Sustainability Generate Better Financial Performance? Review, Meta-Analysis, and Propositions," *Journal of Sustainable Finance & Investment* 13, no. 1 (2023): 802–825, https://www.tandfonline.com/doi/full/10.1080/20430795.2022.2106934.

[5] Tensie Whelan, Ulrich Atz, Tracy Van Holt, and Casey Clark, "ESG and Financial Performance: Uncovering the Relationship by Aggregating Evidence from 1,000 Plus Studies Published Between 2015 – 2020," NYU Stern Center for Sustainable Business and Rockefeller Asset Management, 2021, https://www.stern.nyu.edu/sites/default/files/assets/documents/NYU-RAM_ESG-Paper_2021%20Rev_0.pdf.

$100 investment in December 2018 would have risen to $135 by June 2024 if a sustainable fund achieved the median return in each period. That return is 4.7% higher than the median performance of traditional funds."[6]

I think, ultimately, when discussing the performance of ESG, responsible, or sustainable portfolios, the best route is to just say that they are competitive with traditional investments. And remember, you're typically not managing a client's portfolio relative to an arbitrary benchmark but to their particular risk and return needs. It's how you structure their portfolio that makes the difference. Sustainable fund performance shouldn't be a consideration if you're performing adequate due diligence, which we'll discuss in Chapter 10.

CONCLUSION

Some out there question whether responsible investing falls within an advisor's fiduciary duty because they say it's based on preferences and not material. I would counter that argument by saying that ESG risk metrics are absolutely material, especially considering the examples I've provided. In addition, sustainable, resilient, and innovative investing is growth investing, focused on the clean economy of tomorrow. I believe the exact opposite is true of the skeptic's belief: not using ESG risk metrics and incorporating SRI is in violation of fiduciary duty because you're not taking all the available information into account when investing for a client.

And when it comes to performance, the studies show that investing with your values provides competitive returns, so don't let the media headlines stop you from doing what you know is right. Invest responsibly.

---

[6] Morgan Stanley, "Sustainable Funds Performance: First Half 2024," https://www.morganstanley.com/ideas/sustainable-funds-performance-first-half-2024.

CHAPTER TEN

BRINGING IT ALL TOGETHER

CONSTRUCTING YOUR FIRST SRI PORTFOLIO

OVERVIEW

Most of the assets I manage are in mutual funds and exchange-traded funds (ETFs). Using funds enables me to create multiple portfolios at scale for a range of different risk profiles and give clients adequate diversification. Are these portfolios perfect? No, they're not. Would I put them up against any other sustainable portfolios? Absolutely!

The key to creating a portfolio that incorporates competitive performance with sustainable holdings while avoiding greenwashing as much as possible is due diligence. I use Morningstar Direct as my portfolio creation and research tool, and with it, I'm able to look not only at performance but also take a deep dive on fund holdings.

THE HOLDINGS MAKE THE DIFFERENCE

In Morningstar, I maintain a list of environmental, sustainable, governance (ESG)/responsible funds that I can access anytime. Luckily, I have a core set of funds that I've been using for several years, so my quarterly rebalances are made easier because of this, but I still review holdings regularly to make sure that managers haven't added companies that I don't consider to be sustainable.

Morningstar Direct enables me to sort the list by any number of metrics, from manager tenure to performance to portfolio makeup, and I take advantage of this functionality regularly. I manage our portfolios using modern portfolio theory, so I want to see investment style, domesticity and market cap. I try to find funds without a lot of crossover between these. I will typically sort by fund category, and then by performance, and begin the process there.

One thing to remember is that when you're putting together a fund portfolio is that you can't be as picky as you can if you're creating an individual stock portfolio – we'll cover our individual stock portfolio in Chapter 11. So, in many cases, you will have to work with several "less bad" portfolios which makes your job even more difficult, judging what you should or shouldn't own.

I have used the Brown Advisory Sustainable Growth Fund for many years, so when it comes to domestic large cap, a fund is going to have to really stand out in terms of both performance and sustainable holdings to unseat Brown. It's a decent size fund with nearly $7 billion in assets. I know what I'm getting with Brown – no fossil fuels, a decent allocation to technology, and nothing egregious.

Here are some of the fund's top holdings as of the end of February 2025:

Holding	Allocation %	Holding	Allocation %	Holding	Allocation %
Amazon	7.8	Arthur J Gallagher	3.82	Uber	2.43
NVIDIA	7.14	Marvell Technology	3.70	Dynatrace	2.41
Microsoft	6.71	ServiceNow	3.53	West Pharma Svs	2.37
Visa	4.88	Alphabet Class A	3.23	Workday	2.31
Progressive	4.69	Ares Management	2.56	Monolithic Power	2.18
Intuit	4.50	Airbnb	2.52	KLA	2.16
KKR	4.18	Danaher	2.51	Veralto	2.16

Again, nothing screams sustainability, but nothing is egregious either. In fact, of the 21 stocks listed, we have owned one-third of them in our Green Sage Sustainability Portfolio over the years, and 10 are in our Green Sage stock universe. One thing I appreciate about this portfolio is that it is not a quasi-index like so many ESG funds are.

Speaking of quasi-indexes, let's look at one and compare. The Vanguard ESG US Stock ETF, ESGV, is more of a blend fund, but it has accumulated over $10 billion in assets, and I would have a hard time distinguishing it from the S&P 500. Let's check out the top 15 holdings as of February 28, 2025:

Vanguard ESG US Stock ETF	Allocation %	S&P 500	Allocation %
Apple	7.29	Apple	6.97
Microsoft	6.22	Microsoft	6.02
NVIDIA	6.16	NVIDIA	5.66
Amazon	4.20	Amazon	3.94
Meta Platforms	3.08	Meta Platforms	2.73
Alphabet Class A	2.04	Berkshire Hathaway Cl B	2.03
Broadcom	1.91	Alphabet Class A	1.96
Alphabet Class C	1.83	Broadcom	1.67
Tesla	1.71	Alphabet Class C	1.61
JPMorgan Chase	1.57	Tesla	1.58
Eli Lilly	1.55	JPMorgan Chase	1.44
Visa	1.20	Eli Lilly	1.34
Mastercard	0.99	Visa	1.25
Costco Wholesale	0.98	Exxon Mobil	1.06
UnitedHealth Group	0.92	UnitedHealth Group	0.98

Not a whole lot of difference between the two portfolio holdings which is one of the reasons why we won't own it. If I wanted to own the S&P 500 minus energy, I would buy the ProShares S&P 500 ex-Energy ETF, SPXE.[1]

When you're buying the basics – large, mid-, or small cap domestic; international or emerging markets – you're likely not going to find a super-sustainable portfolio. But, because modern portfolio theory dictates a mix of these asset classes, you work to find the best of the bunch, which is why conducting your due diligence, looking under the hood, and putting in the time is critical.

I avoid indexes because I believe, as my colleagues at Green Alpha Investments say, that indexing is just slow-motion active management.

---

[1] ProShares. "S&P 500 Ex-Energy ETF (SPXE)." ProShares. https://www.proshares.com/our-etfs/strategic/spxe.

And in a rapidly advancing arena such as sustainability, indexes just move too slow to be able to take advantage of new technologies.

To make my job a little easier, I can add a column that shows net fossil fuel exposure in Morningstar and then sort by that metric. Often, this is the start of my process, because I know that I want to avoid fossil fuels, and I also know that excluding the sector has little effect on overall long-term performance.

DIVESTING FROM FOSSIL FUELS ISN'T JUST ABOUT RISK, IT'S ABOUT PERFORMANCE, TOO

Fossil fuels add risk to the portfolio, from stranded asset risk to regulatory risk, to the risk that fossil fuels companies' main product is the driver of our existential crisis in climate change. Many traditional investment managers claim that you cannot exclude a sector and still generate competitive returns. That's simply not the case.

An important point to remember is that the energy sector includes only fossil fuels; it does not include wind, solar, geothermal, or batteries. Those industries are represented by industrials, technology, and basic materials. Jeremy Grantham, a legendary hedge fund manager, commissioned a report from the Grantham Research Institute on Climate Change and the Environment in 2018. The Institute looked at the performance of the S&P 500 and NASDAQ if you removed any one sector from the calculations.

What they found is that over the period 1989–2017 there was only a 50 basis points difference between the best-performing portfolio

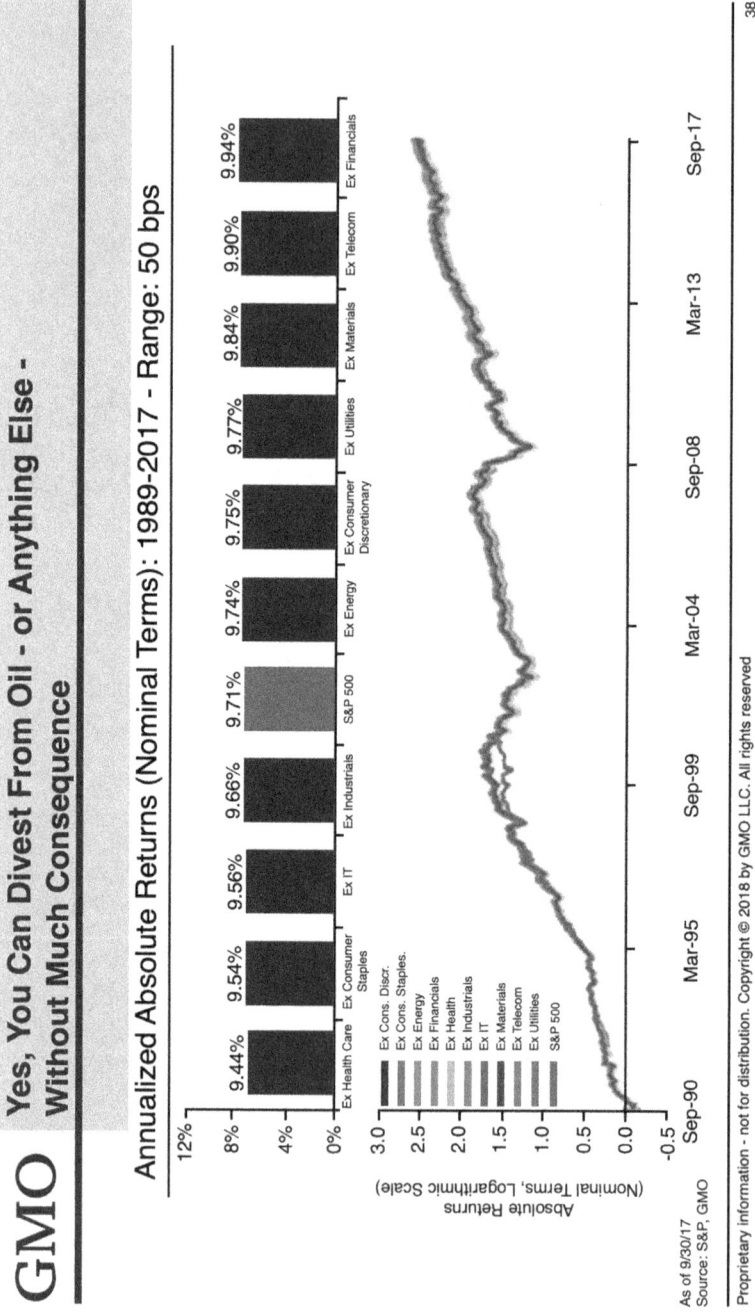

GMO

Yes, You Can Divest From Oil - or Anything Else - Without Much Consequence

Annualized Absolute Returns (Nominal Terms): 1989-2017 - Range: 50 bps

As of 9/30/17
Source: S&P, GMO

38

(9.94% for Ex Financials) and the worst performer (9.44% for Ex Healthcare). The full S&P actually performed worse than six iterations without a sector and better than four. The Ex Energy portfolio returned 9.74% over that period, which was 0.03% better than the full S&P 500 which returned 9.71%. Over this period, it was better not to own fossil fuels.[2]

But over the last 10 years, that disparity has grown even more. From August 2014 through August 2024, SPY, the SPDR S&P 500 ETF Trust[3] had a total return of 236% according to Morningstar Direct. Over that same period, XLE,[4] The Energy Select Sector SPDR ETF returned 40% for a difference of nearly 200%. You don't have to own fossil fuels to generate alpha, or for any other reason.

MODERN PORTFOLIO THEORY STILL APPLIES

Creating a portfolio with a broad mix of securities is just as important in a sustainable portfolio as in a traditional portfolio. When I'm creating a portfolio, I break it down as such:

Equities

- Domicile
  - Domestic
  - International – Developed markets
  - International – Emerging markets

---

[2] London School of Economics and Political Science, "The Mythical Peril of Divesting from Fossil Fuels," Grantham Research Institute on Climate Change and the Environment, https://www.lse.ac.uk/granthaminstitute/news/the-mythical-peril-of-divesting-from-fossil-fuels/.
[3] State Street Global Advisors. "SPDR® S&P 500® ETF Trust (SPY)." State Street Global Advisors, https://www.ssga.com/us/en/intermediary/etfs/spdr-sp-500-etf-trust-spy.
[4] State Street Global Advisors. "The Energy Select Sector SPDR® Fund (XLE)." State Street Global Advisors, https://www.ssga.com/us/en/intermediary/etfs/the-energy-select-sector-spdr-fund-xle.

- Size
  - Giant/large cap
  - Mid cap
  - Small cap
- Focus/thematic
  - Clean energy/energy transition
  - Biotech
  - Water
  - Real estate
  - Infrastructure

Bonds

- Quality
  - High quality
  - High yield
- Duration
  - Short term
  - Intermediate term
- Yield
- Domicile
  - Domestic
  - International
- Focus
  - Green bonds
  - Climate bonds
  - Sustainability focused

Alternatives

- Long/short strategies
- Commodities
- Currencies

- Put/call option strategies
- Futures
- Arbitrage

I use most of these security styles to construct our portfolios, using individual funds for each style. Most are as described previously in this chapter: the best of a particular style based on performance and holdings, as well as manager tenure.

TARGETING SPECIFIC OPPORTUNITIES: THEMATICS

I like to call the market cap and domesticity-based funds the core part of the portfolio. Yes, they're ESG screened, and sometimes include some positive, solutions-based companies, but mostly they're role is to provide market exposure without being egregious. It's very important to find the best of the best in this "less bad" category. However, by complementing these funds with thematic funds, you can make a much bigger difference and fulfill your goal of creating a truly sustainable portfolio.

Some might argue that it's cheating to use these funds, but as a fiduciary, you need to do what is in the client's best interest. Creating a solid portfolio of core funds does just that. But again, it's how you complement these funds with core sustainable solutions that makes the difference.

Let's look at a truly sustainable ETF run by Green Alpha Investments, the AXS Green Alpha ETF, NXTE. In Chapter 4, I discussed Green Alpha's *next economy* philosophy. To remind you, from Green Alpha: "The Next Economy is the emerging, de-risked, solutions-driven way goods and services are produced and consumed. As systemic risks—the climate crisis, resource degradation, disease burdens, and eroding social cohesion—continue to manifest, demand for solutions is accelerating. As a result, innovative companies addressing systemic risks are leading long-term economic growth. Investing in them is our best opportunity to preserve and create wealth. By directing capital to the most competitive solutions creators, investors can both catalyze and benefit from the highly efficient, sustainable Next Economy."[5]

Green Alpha manages their portfolio in much the same way that I manage our Green Sage Sustainability Portfolio. We both focus on finding solutions to our greatest challenges and the opportunities that they will provide long-term. Here are the top 20 holdings as of February 27, 2025:

Holding	Allocation %	Holding	Allocation %
Taiwan Semiconductor	7.23	Vestas Wind Systems	2.93
International Business Machines	6.47	Infineon Technologies	2.89
Sprouts Farmers Markets	4.75	Digital Realty Trust	2.78
Applied Materials	4.13	HA Sustainable Infrastructure	2.50
ASML Holding	4.01	Brookfield Renewable	2.46
Lam Research	3.87	SL Green Realty	2.45
Qualcomm	3.84	ABB	2.42
Natural Grocers by Vitamin Cottage	3.77	Equinix	2.26
CRISPR Therapeutics	3.06	Jinko Solar	1.87
Contemporary Amperex	3.04	Vornado Realty Trust	1.87

You can immediately see the difference between this fund and others we have reviewed. Yes, there is a lot of technology, but there is also

---

[5] Green Alpha Advisors, "Investing in the Next Economy: A New Definition of Portfolio Risk" (white paper).

organic food, solar, and wind. There are batteries, semiconductors, and real estate. Each company is contributing to sustainability in a unique way.

I use this fund to complement the vanilla standard market-cap-based funds that modern portfolio theory dictates. This fund is a go-anywhere global fund searching for solutions wherever they might be.

And it's not the only thematic fund I use. I'm a huge fan of biotechnology because I believe that a healthier society is a more sustainable society. I'll get into my biotech philosophy a bit more when I discuss our Green Sage Sustainability Portfolio in Chapter 11 but know that adding it to our fund portfolios is a priority. Sustainable investing is about investing in the future, it's about investing in growth opportunities, and I would argue that there are few investments with the growth potential of biotechnology.

I use the AlphaCentric LifeSci Healthcare Fund for this theme. I regularly talk with the fund manager, Dr. Mark Charest, who holds eight drug patents himself from his days as a researcher. So, it's not surprising that I have learned much from him about biotech investing. Mark says that only 18% of rare diseases, the kind that affect fewer than 200,000 people, have an FDA-approved therapy. Those are the types of companies and solutions that this fund invests in. And they are the type of companies that I want to include in our sustainable portfolios.

The built environment is responsible for about one-third of our carbon emissions, as well as their use of huge amounts of both energy and water. Many real estate investment trusts (REITs) understand this and are making the transition to greener and healthier building technologies. This is another sector that we want to highlight and overweight.

Sam and Sarah Adams run the Vert Global Sustainable Real Estate ETF, VGSR. They take a very intentional approach to managing this real estate portfolio, which makes it easy to talk about with clients. Look at their ESG Criteria maps:[6]

---

[6] Vert Asset Management, "VGSR ESG Tear Sheet 2023," September 2024, https://vertfunds.com/wp-content/uploads/2024/09/VGSR-ESG-Tear-Sheet-2023.pdf.

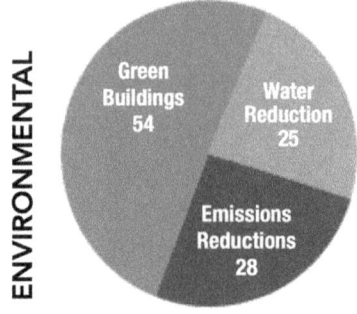

ENVIRONMENTAL

Green Buildings 54
Water Reduction 25
Emissions Reductions 28

Green Buildings	Share of buildings with a qualified green certification.
Water Reduction	Average reduction in water use and consumption.
Emissions Reductions	GHG emissions reduction that meet or exceed a decarbonization pathway by 2050.

SOCIAL

Affordable Housing 12
Urbanism 19
Diversity 25

Affordable Housing	Provision of below median market rate housing.
Urbanism	Share of portfolio near public transit options.
Diversity	Evidence of diversity in employee, management and executive teams.

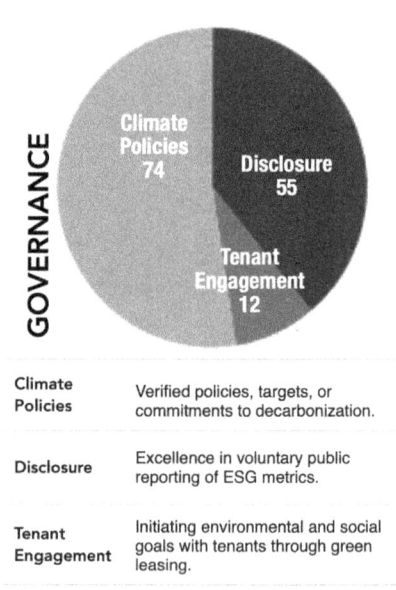

GOVERNANCE

Climate Policies 74
Disclosure 55
Tenant Engagement 12

Climate Policies	Verified policies, targets, or commitments to decarbonization.
Disclosure	Excellence in voluntary public reporting of ESG metrics.
Tenant Engagement	Initiating environmental and social goals with tenants through green leasing.

I pulled this graphic from the firm's annual ESG report. In addition to being very transparent on the ESG criteria they use they also discuss things like engagement, and compare the portfolio versus the benchmark as seen here:

As an aside, when a fund prepares and shares an impact report or ESG report, it shows that they are going the extra mile and documenting their commitment. This level of transparency is so important to sustainability clients, especially clients who may have been burned by other advisors who have provided lip service and used greenwashed funds in the past.

I include a thematic investment focused on water. In Chapter 1, I described the problems in Utah with the Great Salt Lake drying up. It is no different with fresh water globally. According to the World Resources Institute, "more than a billion people currently live in water-scarce regions, and as many as 3.5 billion could experience water scarcity by 2025. Water-related risks are linked to conflict, instability, migration, and food insecurity, making water crises an urgent challenge that demands immediate action."[7]

The ability to provide people with access to affordable and safe water is one of the biggest challenges facing humanity in the 21st century. When combined with climate change, we certainly have our work cut out for us because they exacerbate each other.

Our challenge when investing in water is how do we find and invest in companies that are not involved in privatizing this necessary component for human life. The danger in privatizing water is equity, and how do we make it accessible to everybody, no matter the location, social status, or wealth. We want to invest in companies that are focused on equitable distribution, filtration, and efficiency whenever possible.

---

[7] World Resources Institute, "Water Security." World Resources Institute, https://www.wri.org/freshwater/water-security.

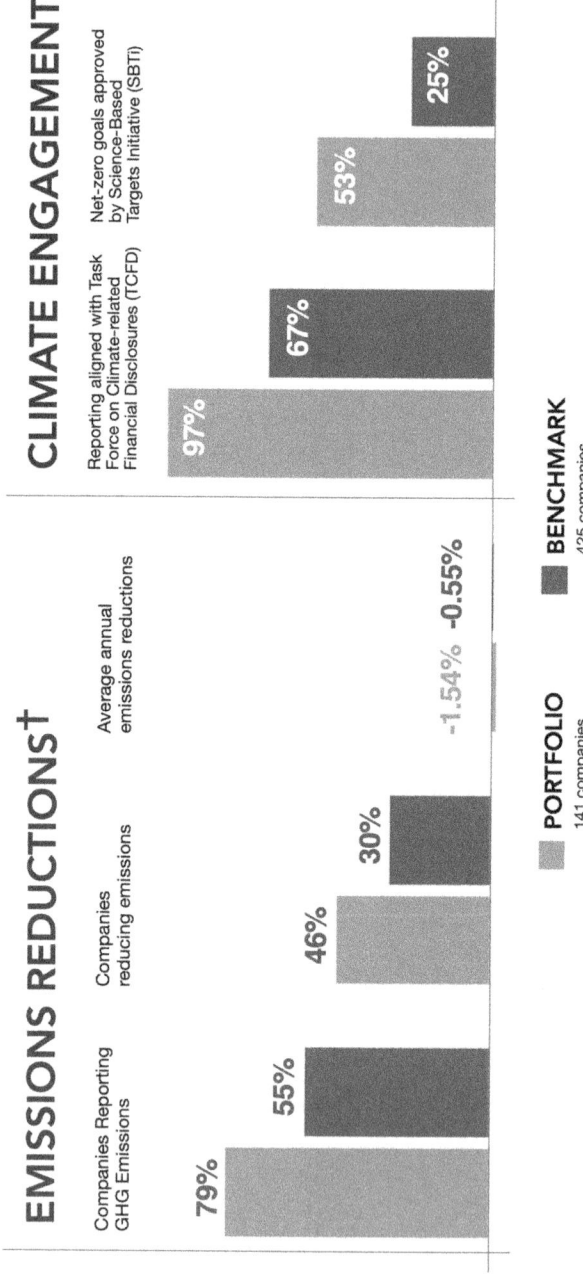

EMISSIONS REDUCTIONS†

Companies Reporting GHG Emissions	Companies reducing emissions	Average annual emissions reductions
79% / 55%	46% / 30%	-1.54% / -0.55%

CLIMATE ENGAGEMENT

Reporting aligned with Task Force on Climate-related Financial Disclosures (TCFD)	Net-zero goals approved by Science-Based Targets Initiative (SBTi)
97% / 67%	53% / 25%

PORTFOLIO 141 companies

BENCHMARK 425 companies

† Portfolio emissions reductions represent 79% of the holdings that publicly report. Emissions reductions are calculated as the total change in company reported like-for-like Scope 1 (direct) + Scope 2 (indirect) greenhouse gas emissions in carbon dioxide equivalents (CO2e) between the 2023 and 2022 reporting years. This methodology is subject to change with data developments or other findings.

We have recently added a thematic fund focused on infrastructure to the portfolios. In the aftermath of the Hurricane Helene disaster, I realized the massive need and opportunity in strengthening and hardening our infrastructure and systems against the effects of the changed climate. Using resiliency and adaptation as the basis for this theme, I was able to find an infrastructure fund that was diversified into several areas of infrastructure, without owning fossil fuels, called the Global X US Infrastructure Development ETF. Because pipelines are often a core of infrastructure funds, it took some work to find the right one.

Finally, we include a clean energy or energy transition fund. Since I believe this theme is at the core of a sustainable portfolio, its inclusion is mandatory. The fund includes solar and wind, smart metering, batteries, and several other complementary industries. This is likely one of the more volatile themes, so make sure to pick the right fund and allocate prudently depending on the risk level of the portfolio.

Complementing the basic core portfolio holdings with specific themes shows your value as an sustainable, resilient, and innovative (SRI) expert. Are the five themes we use the only ones? Absolutely not. Bring your expertise to the table and include themes that you believe and have researched to be sustainable. Or there might be new ones that haven't been launched yet. Keep your eyes open for new opportunities in new technologies that are providing solutions to our greatest challenges.

AVOID THE CROSSOVER TRAP

Have you ever had a prospective client share their current investment statement with you, and it consists of 10+ large cap domestic funds? Or a bunch of funds from the same fund company? While this is not an issue specific to SRI, it's important enough when you're building a diversified, cohesive portfolio for me to address it. When you're creating a portfolio, make sure to run a report on fund crossover. What I mean by crossover is buying multiple funds that have the same holdings.

Here is an example of a report I run in Morningstar Direct called "Stock Intersection" (for illustrative purposes only). This is using an actual prospective client's portfolio. All 50 of the top holdings were held in at least 6 of the 10 funds. This gives the client a false sense of diversification, and I would argue, is not in alignment with our fiduciary duty as investment advisors. We brought this prospect on as a client because we conducted our due diligence, communicated and educated the investor, and helped them rebalance their portfolio.

Stock Details			
Stock	Ticker/ISIN	Market Value $	% of Investments
Microsoft Corp (USD)	MSFT	37,819	3.47
Source of Stock			
T. Rowe Price Blue Chip Growth (USD)	TRBCX	13,557	1.24
Vanguard Total Stock Mkt Idx Adm (USD)	VTSAX	8,186	0.75
Vanguard 500 Index Admiral (USD)	VFIAX	8,117	0.75
T. Rowe Price Spectrum Diversified Eq (USD)	PRSGX	4,322	0.40
Vanguard LifeStrategy Mod Gr Inv Shrs (USD)	VSMGX	2,755	0.25
Vanguard LifeStrategy Income Inv (USD)	VASIX	883	0.08
Apple Inc (USD)	AAPL	36,468	3.35
Source of Stock			
T. Rowe Price Blue Chip Growth (USD)	TRBCX	10,944	1.00
Vanguard Total Stock Mkt Idx Adm (USD)	VTSAX	8,893	0.82
Vanguard 500 Index Admiral (USD)	VFIAX	8,818	0.81
T. Rowe Price Spectrum Diversified Eq (USD)	PRSGX	3,861	0.35
Vanguard LifeStrategy Mod Gr Inv Shrs (USD)	VSMGX	2,993	0.27
Vanguard LifeStrategy Income Inv (USD)	VASIX	960	0.09
NVIDIA Corp (USD)	NVDA	33,213	3.05
Source of Stock			
T. Rowe Price Blue Chip Growth (USD)	TRBCX	12,527	1.15
Vanguard 500 Index Admiral (USD)	VFIAX	7,369	0.68
Vanguard Total Stock Mkt Idx Adm (USD)	VTSAX	7,034	0.65
T. Rowe Price Spectrum Diversified Eq (USD)	PRSGX	3,158	0.29
Vanguard LifeStrategy Mod Gr Inv Shrs (USD)	VSMGX	2,367	0.22
Vanguard LifeStrategy Income Inv (USD)	VASIX	759	0.07

Stock Details			
Stock	Ticker/ISIN	Market Value $	% of Investments
Amazon.com Inc (USD)	AMZN	24,457	2.25
Source of Stock			
T. Rowe Price Blue Chip Growth (USD)	TRBCX	9,849	0.90
Vanguard Total Stock Mkt Idx Adm (USD)	VTSAX	4,900	0.45
Vanguard 500 Index Admiral (USD)	VFIAX	4,805	0.44
T. Rowe Price Spectrum Diversified Eq (USD)	PRSGX	2,725	0.25
Vanguard LifeStrategy Mod Gr Inv Shrs (USD)	VSMGX	1,649	0.15
Vanguard LifeStrategy Income Inv (USD)	VASIX	529	0.05
Meta Platforms Inc Class A (USD)	META	15,249	1.40
Source of Stock			
T. Rowe Price Blue Chip Growth (USD)	TRBCX	5,728	0.53
Vanguard Total Stock Mkt Idx Adm (USD)	VTSAX	3,349	0.31
Vanguard 500 Index Admiral (USD)	VFIAX	3,321	0.30
T. Rowe Price Spectrum Diversified Eq (USD)	PRSGX	1,362	0.13
Vanguard LifeStrategy Mod Gr Inv Shrs (USD)	VSMGX	1,127	0.10
Vanguard LifeStrategy Income Inv (USD)	VASIX	361	0.03

WHAT ABOUT BONDS?

Modern portfolio theory dictates a blend of securities are required to create a diversified, risk-balanced portfolio. We've talked a lot about stock funds up until this point, but what about bonds? Most of the time, bonds, with their steady interest rate and relatively stable value, act as a buffer to the volatility that oftentimes is associated with stock investments. Of course, there are exceptions to this rule, such as in 2022 when both stocks and bonds were down double digits. In general, however, stocks and bonds move in different cycles. They're not completely uncorrelated like some alternative investments that we'll discuss soon, but they have less correlation with each other. I mentioned previously the different types of bonds we allocate to, but let's take a closer look. I typically break my bond portfolios down by quality, duration, and theme.

I want to emphasize the same thing I discussed with market-cap-focused, core equity portfolios: it's very difficult to find a purely sustainable bond portfolio. You must take the time to look under the hood and check out holdings. This is especially hard with high-yield bonds as they often will have fossil fuels as part of the investment mix.

When it comes to bonds, I want to see a majority of the portfolio in investment-grade securities. Since our equity allocation tends to be focused more on aggressive growth, having a more stable complement will help to reduce volatility in our portfolios. Like stock funds, you don't have to buy a bunch of them, just the best you can find for each specific style. There will be adequate diversification built into most bond funds.

As happens sometimes with SRI funds, when I wrote this chapter, we used the Climate Focused Bond Fund from Lord Abbett as our core bond holding and had been using it since 2020. Between writing and editing, Lord Abbett decided to liquidate the fund, so I needed to replace it in our diversified fund portfolios. I replaced it with the Pimco Climate Bond Fund, which had very similar characteristics to the fund from Lord Abbett. The main unique feature about these funds is that they are global instead of just US-focused. The reason I chose these particular funds is that much of the corporate and municipal climate action is happening overseas. Climate action in the United States has been held up by the politicization of the subject. So, why not add more international investments in our stock mix? Purely based on performance, international stocks simply haven't performed as well as domestic. Bonds don't have the same performance characteristics, which gives us more freedom to invest.

Here is the bond current breakdown of Pimco's Climate Bond Fund as of January 31, 2025:[8]

---

[8] Pimco, "Climate Bond Fund (Class I)," https://www.pimco.com/us/en/investments/mutual-fund/pimco-climate-bond-fund/inst-usd.

Maturity %		Sector Allocation Market Value %	
0-1 yrs	0.00	US Government Related	21.87
1-3 yrs	0.00	Securitized	11.16
3-5 yrs	47.30	Invest. Grade Credit	21.70
5-10 yrs	49.60	High Yield Credit	1.40
10-20 yrs	3.92	Non-USD Developed	44.72
20+ yrs	-0.83	Emerging Markets	0.39
Effective Maturity (yrs)	6.25	Other	2.73
		Net Other Short Duration Instruments	-3.96

Many companies in the world of sustainability are smaller and don't have the track record or credit history of huge multinationals. So, if we want bond exposure to these companies, we are forced to use high-yield bonds. Outside of the sustainability theme, high-yield bonds have different performance cycles than investment-grade bonds, so our allocation to the style changes as interest rates and other economic factors change.

I have used other fixed-income instruments over the years as well. During times of higher inflation, inflation-protected bonds have performed well, and convertibles have outperformed during periods of growth. So long as I have my core taken care of, as I do with the Lord Abbett fund, I have the flexibility to move the rest of the portfolio around based on other economic factors.

For example, when interest rates were rising because of inflation, I reduced our overall bond allocation and transitioned that money over to alternatives, which I'll discuss next. But, when all indications were pointing to a peak in interest rates, I directed more money to bonds to take advantage of both the higher yields available and the opportunity for capital gains in a decreasing rate environment. Being able to allocate based on current economic conditions will benefit your clients.

ALTERNATIVES

I am a strong believer in creating well-diversified portfolios and that diversification includes truly noncorrelated investments. Historically, alternatives (alts) were available only in private investment form, but over the last several years, more liquid alts have hit the market in mutual fund and ETF form. Having access to these securities gives us more options to create truly risk-adjusted portfolios for our clients.

I use the JPMorgan Guide to the Markets as a source for high-quality charts and illustrations, which is produced quarterly by their asset management business. These graphics enable me to explain complex principles in a way that our clients can better understand. I recommend you use this free resource when communicating with your clients.

One of the better graphics that they have produced over the past few years shows the effect that adding a diversified alts component to a portfolio has in terms of both volatility and performance. Simply adding a 30% alts allocation to any portfolio, conservative to aggressive, has a positive impact according to their calculations. Check out the illustration that covers 1989 through the first quarter of 2023 here:[9]

---

[9] J.P. Morgan Asset Management, "Guide to the Markets," https://am.jpmorgan.com/us/en/asset-management/protected/adv/insights/market-insights/guide-to-the-markets/.

Alternatives and portfolio risk/return
Annuzlized volatility and returns, 1989 – 1Q23

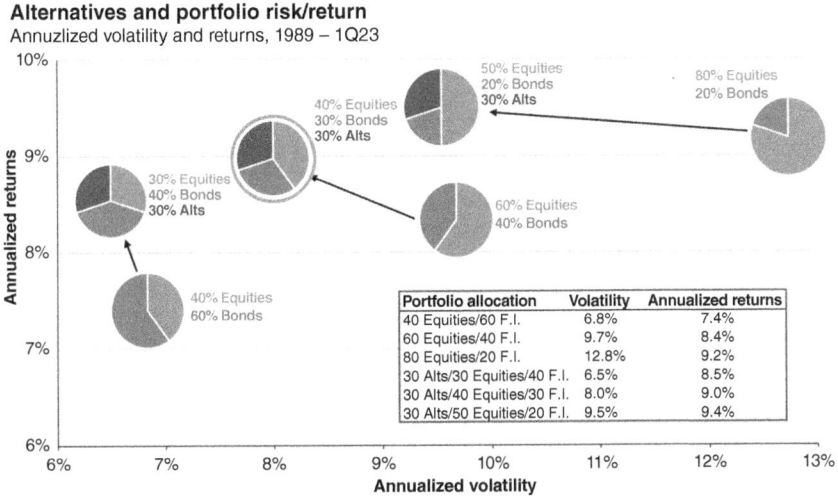

Portfolio allocation	Volatility	Annualized returns
40 Equities/60 F.I.	6.8%	7.4%
60 Equities/40 F.I.	9.7%	8.4%
80 Equities/20 F.I.	12.8%	9.2%
30 Alts/30 Equities/40 F.I.	6.5%	8.5%
30 Alts/40 Equities/30 F.I.	8.0%	9.0%
30 Alts/50 Equities/20 F.I.	9.5%	9.4%

The challenge for sustainable investors is finding liquid alternatives that are acceptable in an SRI portfolio. As of this writing, there are no liquid alternative investment funds that have a sustainable mandate. Knowing this and the importance of including them in a diversified portfolio means that you have extra due diligence to perform. Remember, though, that no portfolio is perfect, but that is no reason to completely exclude an asset class that will help you fulfill your fiduciary duty to the client. You should still conduct your due diligence and find the best possible funds that are as responsible as possible with the best return possible.

Here are the types of alternative investment funds and strategies that I've used over the years:

- Long/short
- Global macro
- Commodities
- Currencies

- Put/call option strategies
- Futures
- Arbitrage
- Flexible bond funds

You can use any one or several different strategies, depending on your preferences, economic conditions, and ability to find managers with whom you are comfortable. Here are a couple of examples of strategies that I'm currently using.

Campbell Systematic Macro Fund. I've been using Campbell since I was at Merrill Lynch a very long time ago. Back then, it was a private investment and was only available by direct subscription. Now, you can buy it as a mutual fund. It's as diversified of a fund as you'll ever see, with the ability to invest in fixed income, equity indices, commodities, and foreign exchanges. It can trade each asset either long or short and is allocated to over 100 different markets globally. If I were going to pick just one alternative to include in my portfolios, it would be one that is this diversified.[10]

One of the main reasons why you purchase an alternative investment is because they are not correlated with the movement of the traditional stock or bond markets. This noncorrelated nature helps to buffer volatility, and, based on the JPMorgan chart previously shown, can also potentially add to returns. Following you can see an illustration from Morningstar Direct showing Campbell fund's negative correlation with both our main equity fund, the Brown Advisory Sustainable Growth Fund, and the Pimco Climate Bond Fund.

---

[10] EBSIX, "Systematic Macro Presentation," https://www.ebsix.com/wp-content/uploads/fund_materials/SystematicMacro_Presentation.pdf?20250125223654.

Where Does Systematic Macro Invest?

CAMPBELL

Global Diversification in a Single Investment

Portfolio spans more than 100 markets across North America, Asia, and Europe

Buy ("Go Long") — *Potential to profit in rising markets*

Sell ("Go Short") — *Potential to profit in declining markets*

FIXED INCOME | 21	EQUITY INDICES | 25	COMMODITIES | 33	FOREIGN EXCHANGE[1] | 24+
3-Month SOFR Futures	CAC 40 Index (France)	Aluminum	Australian Dollar[2]
Australian 10-Year Bond	DAX Index (Germany)	Canola	Brazilian Real
Australian 3-Year Bond	DJ Euro Stoxx 50 Index	Carbon Emission Allowances	British Pound[2]
Australian 90-Day Bill	Dow Jones Index (USA)	Cocoa	Canadian Dollar[2]
Bobl (Germany)	FTSE China A50 Index (China)	Coffee	Chilean Peso
Bund (Germany)	FTSE Index (UK)	Copper	Chinese Yuan
Buxl (Germany)	FTSE JSE Top 40 Index (South Africa)	Corn	Colombian Peso
Canadian 10-Year Bond	FTSE Taiwan Index Futures	Cotton	Czech Koruna
Canadian 3-Month CORRA Futures	FTSE/MIB Index (Italy)	Feeder Cattle	Euro[2]
Euribor (Europe)	Hang Seng China Enterprises Index (Hong Kong)	German Base Month Power Future	Hungarian Forint
Euro Schatz (Germany)	Hang Seng Index (Hong Kong)	Gold	Indian Rupee
Japanese 10-Yr Bond	IBEX35 Stock Index (Spain)	Heating Oil	Indonesian Rupiah
Long Gilt (UK)	IFSC Nifty 50 (India)	High Grade Copper	Japanese Yen[2]
OAT 10-Year Bond (France)	MSCI EAFE Index	Iron Ore	Mexican Peso
Short-Term BTP (Italy)	MSCI Emerging Markets Index	KC HRW Wheat	New Zealand Dollar
Treasury Bond/30-Year (USA)	MSCI Singapore Index	Lead	Norwegian Krone
Treasury Note/10-Year (USA)	NASDAQ 100 Index (USA)	Lean Hogs	Philippine Peso
Treasury Note/5-Year (USA)	Nikkei 225 Index (Japan)	Live Cattle	Polish Zloty
Treasury Notes/2-Year (USA)	OMX Stock Index (Stockholm)	London Brent Crude	Singapore Dollar
Treasury Ultra Long Bond (USA)	Russell 2000 Index (USA)	London Gas Oil	South African Rand
United Kingdom 3-Month SONIA	S&P 400 Index (USA)	Natural Gas	South Korean Won
	S&P 500 Index (USA)	Nickel	Swedish Krona
	S&P Canada 60 Index	Palladium	Swiss Franc[2]
	SPI 200 Index (Australia)	Platinum	Taiwan Dollar
	Tokyo Price Index (Japan)	RBOB Gasoline	
		Silver	
		Soybean Meal	
		Soybean Oil	
		Soybeans	
		Sugar #11 (World)	
		Wheat	
		WTI Crude	
		Zinc	

[1]Traded as forward contracts, not futures. [2]Also may be traded as cross rates. Campbell's portfolios trade different markets and instruments, depending on the strategy and investment objective. The markets traded by a particular portfolio may change at any time, without prior notice to investors.

PAST PERFORMANCE IS NOT INDICATIVE OF FUTURE RESULTS. FUTURES AND FORWARD CONTRACT TRADING IS SPECULATIVE, INVOLVES SUBSTANTIAL RISK, AND IS NOT SUITABLE FOR ALL INVESTORS.

8

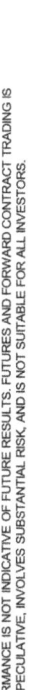

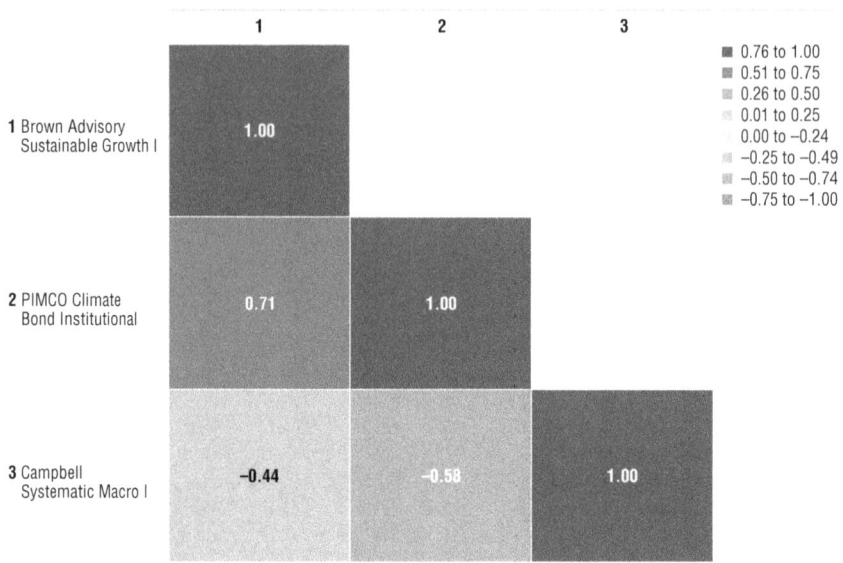

I also think it's important to have a bond alternative as well – especially in environments where interest rates are actively rising. A bond alt can cushion some of the volatility that comes from that inverse relationship between interest rates and bond prices.

Spectrum Low Volatility Fund. Like the Campbell fund, I've used the Spectrum Low Volatility Fund for several years. The fund uses strategies including selective leverage and global allocations to reduce both risk and volatility. For example, in 2022, the Bloomberg US Aggregate Bond Total Return Index[11] had a −13.01% return, while the Spectrum fund was down −4.35%, according to Bloomberg Finance. While not eliminating the loss, it served as a buffer by nearly 9%.

There are many more liquid alternative funds available, so conduct your due diligence and find the one(s) that are right for you and your clients.

---

[11] Bloomberg. "Bloomberg US Aggregate Index." Bloomberg Fixed Income Indices, June 12, 2024, https://assets.bbhub.io/professional/sites/27/US-Aggregate-Index.pdf.

Hopefully, we will see fund companies try to create sustainable versions of their alt portfolios soon.

ASSET ALLOCATION

Asset allocation is the foundation of modern portfolio theory. Obviously, a good mix of stocks, bonds and alternatives within each category is vital. How you put it all together will help determine your risk and your overall performance. I manage four different fund-based portfolios: conservative, balance, aggressive, and global equity. Each model is geared toward a specific risk target, which varies based on the current market and economic conditions.

When I'm constructing these portfolios, I use two pieces of software as my analytical tools: Morningstar Direct and Riskalyze by Nitrogen. Morningstar Direct helps me to create hypotheticals, as well as see my mix of security styles, sectors, countries, and any crossover that there may be between my fund selections. I can look at past performance and compare against the appropriate benchmark. What Morningstar doesn't calculate for me is risk, and that's where Nitrogen (formerly Riskalyze) comes into play.

We've been using Nitrogen for several years now. It's a multifunction software, but its core is determining the risk level of a portfolio based on its components using a 0–100 scale. Clients and prospects can complete a questionnaire to determine their score, and we can then more precisely allocate the assets. But before we even get to that point, I use the software to help me with asset allocation.

Each security has a score from 0 to 100 based on several factors, including volatility, performance, asset class, and the specific holdings of the fund. As I enter each security weighting, it calculates the model's risk in real time. So, if I enter in a portfolio that's supposed to be conservative, and I get a 65 or 70 score, I've probably made it too aggressive. Conversely, a 40 score for an aggressive portfolio would not be appropriate.

Here are some of the real-time indicators that are shown in Nitrogen (for illustrative purposes only):

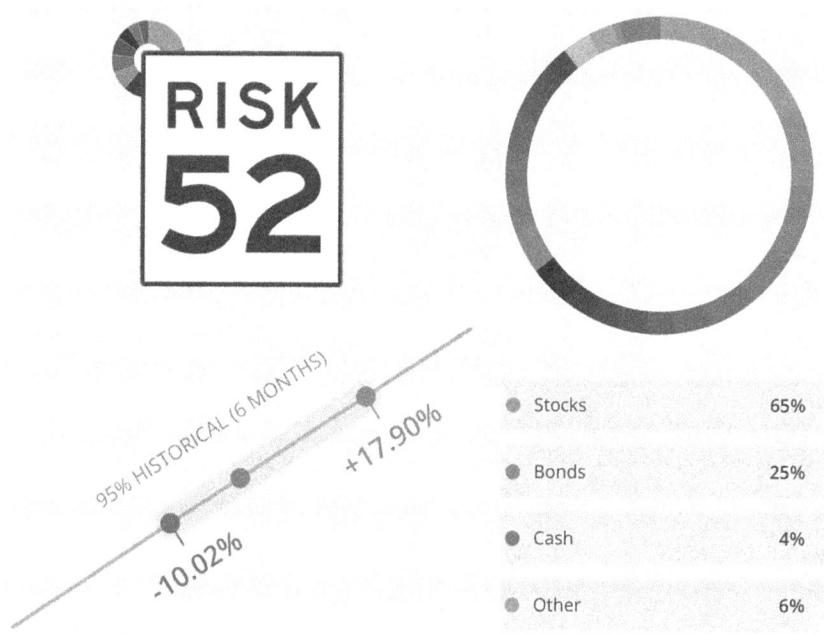

Stocks	65%
Bonds	25%
Cash	4%
Other	6%

The Asset Allocation Heatmap expresses the weighted potential upside and downside that each allocation contributes to the overall portfolio, along with the portion of each allocation's potential downside that has been diversified away due to correlation.

The percentages shown represent a given allocation's potential performance, contextualized to its weight within the overall portfolio. The green percentage represents an allocation's portfolio-weighted potential upside, while the red percentage represents its total portfolio-weighted potential downside. The gold percentage represents the portion of that total portfolio-weighted potential downside that has been diversified away due to correlation.

HDIVX	0.4%	2.4%	4.0%	$1,900	19%
QNZNX	0.3%	0.8%	1.6%	$800	8%
BAFWX	0.3%	1.4%	2.3%	$800	8%
PRBLX	0.2%	1.1%	1.9%	$800	8%
EGRIX	0.1%	0.3%	0.6%	$600	6%
EBSIX	0.5%	0.8%	1.1%	$600	6%
CEFIX	0.2%	0.9%	1.3%	$600	6%
WASMX	0.2%	1.0%	1.3%	$500	5%
NEXTX	0.2%	1.1%	1.5%	$400	4%
CUBIX	0.0%	0.1%	0.3%	$400	4%
GRID	0.1%	0.7%	1.0%	$300	3%
VGSRX	0.1%	0.5%	0.8%	$300	3%
PHO	0.1%	0.6%	0.9%	$300	3%
FHHIX	0.0%	0.3%	0.4%	$300	3%
LYFIX	0.2%	0.6%	0.9%	$300	3%
PAVE	0.1%	0.7%	1.0%	$300	3%
PCEBX	0.1%	0.2%	0.2%	$300	3%
PCMM	0.0%	0.0%	0.3%	$300	3%
ACCSX	0.0%	0.1%	0.1%	$200	2%
Cash / Money Ma..	0.0%	0.0%	0.0%	-$0	-0%
Total				$10,000	

So, I'll adjust each portfolio until I hit the risk number that I'm shooting for. I'll go back to Morningstar and enter those changes to make sure that the portfolio hasn't been negatively affected from a holdings-metrics perspective (market cap, domesticity, etc.) and will repeat this process until I'm comfortable with the model. Now, I don't change funds very often, only when it is necessary, and typically for two reasons. The first reason is simply performance relative to other portfolios of the same style. I'll give a manager one or two quarters, depending on underperformance, to improve make improvements. At that point, I'll replace the fund with an appropriate better performer. The second reason is when I see style drift. For example, if a large cap domestic fund starts to incorporate international companies or starts adding mid- and small cap stocks. I buy a fund because I want them to manage in a particular way. One of the typical situations when this happens is when we see a shift from growth to value or vice versa. If you're a growth fund, invest that way. Back during the dot-com bubble, value funds were vastly underperforming and losing assets. So, instead of sticking to their guns and continuing to invest in value stocks, many started to integrate tech and other growth sectors. And when the bottom fell out of growth stocks, it also fell out of many value stocks, too. In fact, I remember seeing that dot-com darling, pets.com, in a very traditional value fund during that time. Style drift is bad, so make sure you're paying attention.

Occasionally, as happened when I was writing this chapter, a fund will change its investment strategy. In this case, the fund went from being a "low carbon" alternative long/short fund to a tactical trend fund. Oftentimes, this happens with no notification to the investment manager, so make sure you're reviewing all your funds on a regular basis.

I shoot for some pretty standard asset allocations for each of the fund portfolios that I manage:

Portfolio	Equities (%)	Fixed Income (%)	Alternatives (%)
Global Equity	80–90	0–10	10–20
Aggressive	65–80	10–20	10–20
Balanced	50–65	20–30	20–30
Conservative	40–50	30–40	20–30

I also manage what I call a fixed/alt model that can complement any of our other portfolios to really tune in a risk level. This portfolio works well with our individual equity Green Sage Sustainability Portfolio when a client wants to use it as a core holding. I keep this portfolio basic with 50% bonds and 50% alternatives, and I use the same funds in the asset allocation funds just shown. The best part is that it doesn't take a whole lot of extra research to run this portfolio but gives you added flexibility to help clients.

Again, using Morningstar Direct and Riskalyze, you can be sure that your portfolios meet the characteristics that you would like to see in them. Once you're comfortable with what you created, it's time flip the switch and invest.

STRATEGIC VERSUS TACTICAL MANAGEMENT

I do manage our fund portfolios strategically, rebalancing them every quarter. Usually the changes are minor 1% or 2% up or down for each fund. But, at times of economic uncertainty, I have the flexibility to be tactical as well. There are two specific times when tactical management paid off.

The first was back in 2008 when markets were dropping precipitously. In November 2008, I was concerned that there was more pain to come in addition to what we had already endured. I decided at that point to sell off half of our stock holdings (I probably should have sold them all, but that's 20/20 hindsight). I moved the proceeds into cash and bonds and waited. When the S&P hit a low point in March 2009, I felt it was the right time to start buying back. I used a dollar-cost averaging strategy over six months to buy back in (again, I should have bought everything back at that point, but being prudent was more important). This simple yet bold move had a strongly positive impact on all my client's performance at the time.[12]

The second time I used tactical management was during the pandemic. As I've said, my wife has PhDs in microbiology and molecular genetics, so she really understood what was going on in the world. Using her guidance based on what she was seeing and reading about in scientific journals, it looked like the economy was going to grind to a halt because of the need to quarantine and avoid social contact. It was a no-brainer to reduce equity exposure and shift money into bonds and alternatives until there was better visibility. As I often say, the markets hate uncertainty, and I can think of very few times in my lifetime as uncertain as 2020.

We continued to monitor the situation and made several moves to make our portfolios more conservative. But as visibility improved, vaccines became a reality, and businesses were starting to reopen, I began to slowly shift back toward our original equity allocations. The overall process took about a year. But again, not being afraid to make bold moves when the situation called for it, benefitted clients.

At the same time, there have been several times over the years that we've seen corrections, recessions, and other ordinary market and economic events. I rarely make a shift during these times because they are simply a part of the market and economic cycle. Overall, I do believe in the adage about time in the market versus timing the market. Knowing when to stay the course and when to make tactical changes may be one of the hardest things in this job. Ultimately, staying the course is the safer choice, because markets always come back. But if you can, over the course of a decade, make one or two moves that help provide your clients with just a bit of alpha, don't be afraid to be bold.

---

[12] Past performance is not indicative of future results.

BEING AN INVESTMENT MANAGER

I'm not a Chartered Financial Analyst. I wasn't a business, finance, or accounting major in college – I majored in communication. I don't have the typical cred that investment managers on Wall Street do, yet I've succeeded. And I'm also very proud of the portfolios I create and manage, and the returns that we've achieved for our clients. I'm proud that for over 20 years, my firm has been a thought leader in the sustainable, responsible, and impact investing business. And I was smart enough to position even smarter people around me as support and inspiration.

Whether you want to be an investment manager or not, it's very important that you understand the process. It's important that you can communicate your investment philosophy and the rationale for the decisions you make. Investment management is very difficult, especially in a world where so many people are cost-conscious and satisfied with owning the plain vanilla S&P 500 index. But that's not what you do. You are a specialist who brings something extra to the table. You help clients invest responsibly, and with that comes a sense of accomplishment and pride.

I love what I do and am doing so without the fancy letters after my name. Is it stressful? Of course, it is – I'm managing millions of dollars for hundreds of families who are relying on me to both create competitive performance and invest in the clean economy. But it is also incredibly rewarding and fulfilling.

CHAPTER ELEVEN

AN INDIVIDUAL STOCK PORTFOLIO

HOW I RUN THE GREEN SAGE SUSTAINABILITY PORTFOLIO

OVERVIEW

One of the hardest things to do as a financial advisor (any financial advisor, not just sustainable) is to manage an individual stock portfolio. It can also be one of the most rewarding! I've been managing the Green Sage Sustainability Portfolio since the end of 2012, and it is one of my favorite parts of my job.

Determining the scope of your individual stock portfolio is your first task. Will it be domestic, large cap, international, or . . . ? Will it be actively managed on a regular basis or less frequently like we do with Green Sage's semiannual reallocation and rebalance? Where will you pull your data from, and which data will you use? Every portfolio is different, and that's what makes this opportunity so exciting.

The other thing that I love about having managed this portfolio for well over 10 years is how I can look back and view its evolution – an evolution that came because of experience, trial and error, and a growing sustainability movement as opposed to a planned refinement of the process. Over those 10 years, investment management technology improved, ESG and fundamental data and delivery improved, and demand greatly increased. There are now so many more publicly traded opportunities to invest sustainably than I had back in 2012, which makes the job both easier and harder at the same time.

Whether you choose to run an individual stock portfolio is up to you because it's not necessary; there are a lot of good SMAs available (including Green Sage), so maybe you don't want to reinvent the wheel. However, you should know how one is managed and the process by which it becomes sustainable.

IT'S ALL IN THE UNIVERSE

Curating a universe of investible stocks takes time. Our current universe includes over 700 companies that we consider sustainable, either in their products, services, or how they do business. Some are what I'd consider core members of the universe, while others are outliers, but all of them are reviewed and have an opportunity to be a part of the portfolio every six months.

I use Morningstar Direct as my tool for maintaining the list of stocks. What I like about Morningstar is that I'm also able to track my portfolios as well as produce monthly fact sheets using their Presentation Studio tool. It's not perfect, but it works well for my uses.

So, how do I decide what goes into the universe? Well, that's a factor of the industries, sectors, and technologies that, based on continuous research, I've decided are a part of the new economy – the ones that are leading us into a cleaner, more resource-efficient, and more equitable economy. I've discussed this in other chapters, but it's worth reinforcing: we use the philosophy that Wayne Gretzky made famous: we "skate to where the puck is going, not where it's been." It's why I believe that you can't invest the clean economy by looking in the rearview mirror at traditional indexes.

This ever-evolving list is by no means exhaustive but it serves as the core for the construction of Green Sage. It needs to be flexible and evolving because of the speed at which sustainable companies and technologies are arising. Here is the current list:

- **Clean energy.** This is a bedrock for any sustainable portfolio, from solar to wind to geothermal. This is one of the fastest-growing segments of the economy. According to the US Energy Information Administration, 60% of new US grid capacity in 2024 was solar, 23% battery storage, and 10% wind, with only 4% going to natural gas and 2% to nuclear development.[1] Effectively and efficiently distributing this clean energy to areas of demand and adding utility-scale battery systems will only benefit the industry and contribute to greater growth.

- **Battery technology.** When I created Green Sage back in 2012, there was not a single battery-focused individual stock available to purchase. Since then, the battery industry has mushroomed into a global juggernaut, and with the Inflation Reduction Act of 2022, much of that development has happened in the United States. According to S&P Global Market Intelligence, the demand for batteries will continue to increase by over 22% annually through 2030,[2] creating ample opportunities for investors in the new economy. And this technology is quickly moving forward with innovations in charging speed, capacity, less impactful components, and usable life cycle.

- **Energy efficiency.** I like to say that the best kilowatt is the one that is never used. Improving energy efficiency is the focus of several companies and industries, and we have multiple investment opportunities to take advantage of in the category. From technologies that reduce energy consumption to simply insulating our houses better, energy efficiency has been a cornerstone of our society for a long time. In February 1977, President Jimmy Carter gave a televised address in which he called on the American public to be more efficient with their use of energy. He donned his cardigan and asked us to turn down our thermostats. This was in response to winter fuel shortages, which happened for several reasons,

---

[1] Julian Spector, "Chart: 96 Percent of New US Power Capacity Was Carbon-Free in 2024," Canary Media, 2025.
[2] S&P Global Market Intelligence, "Lithium-Ion Battery Capacity to Grow Steadily to 2030," https://www.spglobal.com/market-intelligence/en/news-insights/research/lithium-ion-battery-capacity-to-grow-steadily-to-2030.

including instability in the Middle East. Not a lot has changed over that time from an energy perspective, but we are most definitely more efficient. According to data from the Environmental Protection Agency, from 1975 to 2022, vehicle fuel efficiency increased 101.5% from 13.1 to 26.4 miles per gallon.[3] We still have tremendous opportunities to reduce our energy consumption, many of which are good investments.

- **Water distribution, filtration, and efficiency.** Climate change affects several environmental metrics. One of the greatest impacts is on water and how water is cycled in the atmosphere. Some areas will get more rain, and some will get less. Some regions will have much more intense droughts, and some will experience devastating flooding. All of this will have an impact on how we provide safe and clean drinking water and efficiently irrigate crops to feed a rapidly expanding population. There are two major problems in this category: the aging and precarious water infrastructure in the United States and a lack of water to meet demand in rapidly growing areas like Phoenix and Southern California.

- **Green transportation.** How do we get from point A to point B as efficiently as possible? Obviously walking and bicycling is most efficient, but the United States isn't built for these modes of transportation like many cities in Europe. Rail lines and subways are much more efficient than cars, but again, they are not always practical, and many Americans resist public transportation. So, the pragmatist must focus on cars and electrifying as much of the individual vehicle fleet as possible. Virtually all the major auto manufacturers are in the process of transitioning their fleets to electric vehicles (EVs), but political resistance, along with a slow rollout of charging

---

[3] LendingTree, "Fuel Efficiency Study," https://www.lendingtree.com/auto/fuel-efficiency-study/.

stations (the Inflation Reduction Act is addressing this) has slowed progress. Consumers concerns about range anxiety isn't helping. But the reality is that the future is electric transportation, and as sustainable investors, we're investing for the future. Better battery technology as described will certainly have a positive impact, as will more widely available charging networks.

- **Infrastructure – resilience and adaptation.** As I've said multiple times throughout the book, the changed climate is already affecting us in devastating ways. The hottest year on record was 2024, sending a powerful hurricane 500 miles inland to the mountains of Western North Carolina and 2025 brought us the wildfires in Los Angeles. More intense storms, droughts, wildfires, sea level rise, and other effects are now regular news stories. How do we prepare our communities for these impacts? If you live in a coastal city, what infrastructure is being both added and bolstered to withstand category 5 and potentially new category 6 hurricanes? Miami now deals with flooding during king tides, which happen on a regular basis because of sea level rise. I believe that investing in companies that specialize in infrastructure development is one of the biggest opportunities in a changed climate world. Infrastructure companies are a necessary component of a sustainable portfolio: from sea walls to wind farms to wind-resistant and high-performance buildings.

- **Natural and organic products and services.** I love my Allbirds. They are the best shoes I've ever owned. They're comfortable, durable, and, best of all, they're about as sustainable as you can get. Each shoe has its carbon footprint (pun intended) clearly labeled. Materials are all natural, including the parts of the shoe that are traditionally made from fossil fuels like the sole. Allbirds is a great example of a company that truly walks the walk (again, pun intended) and has been intentional from day one to make a quality product with as little impact as possible. There is a lot of greenwashing in this space, so due diligence is vital when you're putting your individual stock portfolio together.

- **Regenerative and organic agriculture.** The transition to a more plant-based diet is vital for climate impact. One of the most impactful industries when it comes to climate and sustainability is agriculture. From water use to pesticides and chemical fertilizers, to the nonlocal nature of corporate agriculture, we want to invest in companies that buck the growth-at-all-costs model of big agriculture, grocery stores that understand the importance of local distribution, and companies that use fair trade practices with their network of independent farmers.

- **Sustainable real estate.** The built environment accounts for about one-third of all carbon emissions. Most REITs and real estate management companies understand the importance of both building efficient buildings and retrofitting existing buildings to be more efficient. Investments they make in building efficiency almost immediately affect their bottom lines. While a big part of this is energy efficiency, water efficiency is also prioritized, as is healthy spaces, using nontoxic building materials, including community spaces, and building near easily accessible public transit routes.

- **Information technology, big data, artificial intelligence (AI), and the internet of things (IoT).** Let's talk about efficiencies again, because that is what information technology brings to the table. Let's say you own a manufacturing company making widgets. Integrating technology into your manufacturing process will likely do a couple of things: increase your per hour output of widgets, reduce the amount of energy needed to produce those widgets, and maybe even make it safer for your employees to perform their jobs. All these benefits are about efficiency – making more product in less time, spending less on energy, and less on time off for injured employees. It's a win-win-win situation. That's not even getting into the insights that big data and AI can now provide, as well as the monitoring and automation that IoT brings to the table.

- **Green finance, insurance, and community investments.** This is one of my favorite topics to discuss when it comes to sustainable investing because when I talk about finance, most people wonder how I can tie it in. Green finance is important because we need to make sure that up-and-coming sustainable technology is capitalized, and that consumers can get their solar panels and batteries installed. But what I like to discuss is insurance. Exciting right? Hear me out. What is the one industry that has the greatest potential to have an impact on climate policy? Insurance. Why? Because they are the arbiters of risk. The insurance industry prices climate risk, so if you have a manufacturing facility in Florida that has been affected by hurricanes, it's more than likely that your premiums are going to go up or that you might lose your insurance altogether. We want to invest in insurers who are actively integrating climate risk into their models and actively working with their clients to develop resilience and adaptation strategies. Unfortunately, US insurers are way behind European insurers and reinsurers, so that's where we invest right now in insurers: in Europe.

- **Recycling and circular economy.** I mentioned Bill McDonough and his book *Cradle to Cradle* in Chapter 7. Circular economy is the concept of eliminating waste from the product cycle. Let's use your iPhone as an example. When it becomes obsolete, a circular economy version would have a system where it is completely deconstructed, and its components reintegrated into the next product cycle. No need to dig up more rare earth minerals; we're just going to reuse them. We look for companies that either do the work of the recycling as a third party or those that have integrated it into their product life cycle plan.

- **Green building technology.** Closely tied with sustainable real estate, green building technology is investing in the companies that produce products and services to make buildings more efficient. This might include smart metering and smart home systems to give you more information and automate your lifestyle. It might also include a company like Owens Corning. Remember the Pink Panther commercials? It's old school, but insulating buildings is a basic principle when it comes to reducing the impact of the built environment, as is low-emissivity (low-e) windows, heating, ventilation, and air conditioning systems, and nontoxic building materials.

- **Cutting-edge biotechnology.** I believe that a healthier society is a more sustainable society. With biotechnological advances, including CRISPR Cas 9 gene editing, mRNA vaccines, and immuno-medicines (among many others), I have never been more excited about the future of humanity. This is compounded by the opportunity that AI technology presents us by using in-silico research, which should greatly reduce the time and cost of drug discovery, as I mentioned previously.

- **Minerals and materials.** For a long time, I avoided including mining companies in the portfolio. They have a horrible track record of both environmental degradation and employee abuse. However, I've become more open to including this industry for the simple fact that to produce the electric-based economy that we need to build, materials such as nickel, copper, and lithium are necessary. It takes more work to perform due diligence on these companies, but they are an integral part of the sustainable economy going forward, and excluding them would be a mistake.

This is by no means an exhaustive list of areas to include in a sustainable portfolio, but it should be a start for you. Interestingly, as I was writing this, I realized that our marketing materials have never included "regenerative and organic agriculture," even though we have been investing in that industry for years. I had just always included it under "natural and organic products and services," but I thought it deserved its own category. The same will happen to you as you build out your portfolios.

PORTFOLIO ATTRIBUTES

What's interesting is that using the following list as the basis for portfolio construction creates a pretty well-rounded portfolio. For example, our latest sector breakdown looks like this as of April 30, 2025:

Sector	Allocation %
Industrials	20.9
Technology	18.6
Financial services	14.6
Consumer cyclical	12.4
Health care	8.6
Utilities	5.9
Basic materials	5.8
Real estate	5.5
Communication services	4.0
Consumer defensive	3.7

Just like in our fund portfolios, the only sector missing from the portfolio is energy. And recall from Chapter 10, where I described Jeremy Grantham's experiment on the effects of removing any sector from the S&P 500, and its minimal impact on performance.[4] We don't need fossil fuels in our portfolios to be competitive over the long term.

---

[4] London School of Economics and Political Science, "The Mythical Peril of Divesting from Fossil Fuels."

The portfolio is also diversified internationally as well. By investment policy, two-thirds of the portfolio is domestic, and the remaining one-third is international. Country exposure as of April 30, 2025 looks like this:

Country	Allocation %
United States	63
France	4.8
Spain	4.2
Germany	4.2
Canada	3.4
United Kingdom	2.7
China	2.6
Japan	2.6
Italy	2.2
Netherlands	2.2
Austria	1.9
Switzerland	1.8
Australia	1.7
Taiwan	1.6
Brazil	0.8

And investment policy dictates market cap as well, with 50% in large cap, 30% in mid-cap, and 20% in small cap. As of December 31, 2024, the market cap weighting looked like this:

Market Capitalization	Allocation %
Large/giant	55.6
Mid-	27.4
Small/micro	17

Here is the current makeup of the portfolio as of this writing:

Clean Energy	Regenerative and Organic Agriculture	Hercules Capital
Brookfield Renewable	Compass Group	Intesa Sanpaolo
Hannon Armstrong	Givaudan	Marsh & McLennan
First Solar	Ingredion	MunichRE
GE Vernova	Sprouts Farmers Markets	**Recycling and Circular Economy**
Battery Technology	Vital Farms	Brambles
Fluence Energy	**Sustainable Real Estate**	**Green Building**
Energy Efficiency	AvalonBay Communities	Advance Drainage Systems
Badger Meter	CBRE	Carlisle Companies
ICF International	Digital Realty Trust	Hubbell
nVent	Iron Mountain	Installed Building Products
Schneider Electric	**Information Technology**	Meritage Homes
Water	Advantest	Owens-Corning
Mueller Water Products	Applied Materials	Tecnoglass
Veralto	Arista Networks	Trane Technologies
Xylem	Autodesk	**Biotechnology and Science**
Green Transportation	Cadence Design Systems	Amgen
Allison Transmission	Deutsche Telekom	Intuitive Surgical
BYD	ExlService	Thermo Fisher Scientific
Denso	Marvell Technology	United Therapeutics
Infrastructure	NVIDIA	Vertex Pharmaceuticals
MYR Group	Palo Alto Networks	**Minerals and Materials**
Stantec	Pure Storage	Linde
Tetra Tech	Salesforce	Steel Dynamics
Valmont Industries	T-Mobile US	**Utilities**

Clean Energy	Regenerative and Organic Agriculture	Hercules Capital
Natural and Organic Products and Services	Taiwan Semiconductor	Cia Energetica DE Minas Gerais
Accor	Thomson Reuters	Iberdrola
Deckers Outdoor	**Green Finance and Insurance**	
ELF Beauty	ABN AMRO Bank	
Industria de Diseno Textil	Amalgamated Financial	
Gildan Activewear	AXA	
HNI	Erste Group Bank	

Note: Specific investments described herein do not represent all investment decisions made by Peter Krull. The reader should not assume that investment decisions identified and discussed were or will be profitable. Specific investment advice references provided herein are for illustrative purposes only and are not necessarily representative of investments that will be made in the future.

PORTFOLIO HOLDINGS EXAMPLES

Let's pull out a few of the current stocks and take a closer look at why they are considered sustainable, resilient, or innovative. This exercise is intended to give you a sense of how companies from different sectors can contribute and help to diversify a sustainable portfolio.

We'll begin with an easy one: batteries. When most people think about investing in batteries, they usually think of the kind used in EVs. Fluence, however, makes large, utility-scale battery installations. The kind of batteries that are connected to the grid to provide stability and continuity. In addition to energy storage, they also service the installations and develop and provide the AI software to optimize battery use.

In the second quarter of 2024, the United States saw energy storage installations grow by more than 10.5 gigawatt-hours (GWh) – an 86%

increase on a year over year basis according to the American Clean Power Association. John Hensley with the Association said, "Energy storage is becoming a mainstay of the power grid, delivering a more resilient and affordable grid. Additional storage capacity across U.S. markets is helping to provide a cost-effective and reliable solution to serious problems such as rising energy demand, a timely need for more overall capacity, and more volatile and extreme weather events."[5]

A key element to making an investment in Fluence is that the company is a collaboration between Siemens and AES. Siemens is a $160+ billion German conglomerate and AES is an $8 billion US-based utility. The financial backing of these large, well-established companies is different than most battery companies in that, at the R&D stage, most are startups. Fluence has produced and deployed over 225 projects with over 34 GWh of energy storage.

Let's move on to a less obvious selection: Accor. Accor is a $12 billion French hotel chain. Accor is a sustainability leader in the hospitality industry. It created the PLANET 21 program, which sets measurable goals for reducing emissions, conserving resources, and promoting biodiversity. This framework ensures sustainability is woven into daily operations and guest experiences, making it a core part of Accor's identity rather than a corporate afterthought. In a world of greenwashing, having a means to measure goals and report on them is vital.

What sets Accor apart is its integration of sustainability within its brands. Fairmont Hotels champions environmental initiatives like the "Bee Sustainable" program, while Greet Hotels are built on eco-friendly practices and community involvement. These tailored efforts ensure sustainability is authentic and aligned with the distinct character of each brand.

---

[5] Energy Storage News, "US Grid-Scale BESS Deployment Hits Record in Second Quarter of 2024," https://www.energy-storage.news/us-grid-scale-bess-deployment-record-second-quarter-2024/.

Accor's commitment goes beyond the environment to include social impact and innovation. From tracking the carbon footprint of menu items to targeting net-zero emissions by 2050, the company demonstrates leadership in addressing climate change. Transparent reporting and partnerships reinforce its role as a sustainability pioneer, setting a high standard for responsible travel and tourism.

From an investment perspective, the company has been able to consistently grow earnings. Over the past five years, the company has averaged over 42% annual growth rate, which surpasses the hospitality industry's average of 32.5%. When you consider that the global COVID-19 pandemic was during this period, the statistics are even more impressive.

Another less obvious selection is Valmont Industries. Valmont is a nearly $7 billion manufacturer focused on solutions in three main areas: infrastructure, water and resource management, and clean energy. Their infrastructure business manufactures steel and aluminum products, including light poles for safety, as well as communication and transmission towers to move clean energy where the demand is located.

They also manufacture advanced irrigation equipment designed to use less water and digitally monitor fields for moisture. This can be a major contributor to sustainable agriculture. Finally, they design and fabricate wind turbine towers and support structures as well as solar tracking systems. By focusing on resource efficiency and creating solutions for conservation and renewable energy, Valmont aligns with circular economy principles and global sustainability goals.

In addition to manufacturing sustainable products, Valmont is also profitable, and the stock has performed very well. Over the five-year period ending December 31, 2024, the stock averaged over 16% annualized returns, beating the S&P 500 over that time by about 1.5% per year, according to Morningstar Direct.

We often see technology companies in sustainable portfolios, and with good reason. Technology enables us to increase productivity and energy efficiency. One company that has been doing both for quite some time is Salesforce. Salesforce is the leading company that provides database software and services for customer relationship management including sales, customer service, marketing, and analytics.

The company set goals early to attain net-zero carbon emissions across its value chain and accomplished that goal in 2021. Of its operations 100% are powered with clean energy. With its Net Zero Cloud platform, it enables the customers to measure and manage their carbon emissions and hit their environmental and sustainability goals.

Salesforce has been a driving force in workplace equality and inclusivity and reports on its progress to become a more equitable employer. These efforts have led to the company being named number seven on the list of the World's Best Workplaces by Great Place to Work. Businesses with happier employees are typically more successful. It also is a founding partner in 1t.org, which supports the restoration of one trillion trees globally and invests in nature-based solutions.

And, like the other stocks mentioned, the company continues to grow rapidly. It's growth rate over the past five years ending on December 31, 2024, has been greater than 21% annualized. Its stock has returned over 15.5% annualized over the same period, beating the S&P 500 by about 1 %, according to Morningstar Direct.

I love this exercise of describing the varied impacts different companies in the Green Sage Sustainable Portfolio provide. If I had space, I'd write up one for each company, but we need to keep the book flowing, so I'll end here.

These four featured companies, in addition to the other 71 companies identified, were chosen from the 725 that make up the Green Sage universe. I'll get into the process of creating the portfolio shortly, but first let's examine how to create, grow, and maintain a universe.

MORE ABOUT
THE UNIVERSE

The first iteration of the Green Sage Sustainability Portfolio in 2012 owned 30 stocks. This was a factor of a couple of things, but mostly the lack of available publicly traded sustainable investment options. I realized that if I was going to grow the assets in the model and manage it long term, then I needed to create and maintain a list of eligible stocks. So, I took the group that I had used for the first iteration and saved it as a list.

To add to the list, I knew that I didn't necessarily need to reinvent the wheel and that, as a very small firm, I didn't have the ability to hire an analyst. So, I began reviewing other sustainable investment fund holdings and selectively adding to my list. This is where I really became familiar with greenwashing as I continued to find questionable stocks in fund after fund. Most of them were "less bad" versions of traditional indexes, and so I knew that a truly sustainable fund would be in demand and do well in the marketplace.

But I would find some gems amongst the greenwashing, and occasionally, I would find a manager that I would want to use in our fund models, like Green Alpha or Brown Advisory, which have been mainstays for years!

I also began subscribing to useful newsletters that featured sustainable innovation articles, finding writers who were experts on the subject, and reading books. You're not going to be successful in building an individual stock portfolio if you don't put in the time to read as much as you can about a wide variety of topics related to sustainability, resilience, innovation and the like. Some claim that you need 10,000 hours on a subject to become an expert, and I don't know if that's true. But what I do know is that when you live and breathe the topic, it's hard not to be an expert.

In between the six-month reallocation and rebalance schedule in December and June, I regularly add new companies to the mix. But right before I begin the review process, I spend at least a day or two trying to make sure that I haven't missed any companies that should be on the list.

As I've mentioned, I have a huge interest in biotechnology. Having a spouse with PhDs in microbiology and molecular genetics definitely nurtures this interest! As I discussed in Chapter 10, I use a thematic biotech fund in the model and have become acquainted with the manager of the fund. During one conversation, we discussed a company called United Therapeutics, which develops pulmonary therapies, works with transplantable organs, and other solutions. The company was in his portfolio. He talked about how impressed he was with their ownership and leadership team. I took a note and moved on.

Well, right before the last Green Sage reallocation, I saw that note and decided to research the company to see if it was worth adding to the universe. The company was founded by a mother who was looking for a cure for her daughter's life-threatening condition known as pulmonary arterial hypertension. I also found out that in 2021, United Therapeutics became a Public Benefit Corporation, the first of its kind in biotech. This change of corporate designation gives the company license to work, not just for shareholders, but for all stakeholders. Finally, I saw that the company had great financials. I added it to the universe, and ultimately to the portfolio, and it has been one of the better performers since we bought it.

Always keep your eyes open for solutions and possibilities. Read as much as you can from as many sources as you can. Your success in managing a sustainable individual stock portfolio will be a direct result of the time you put into it.

Now that you've created your universe, it's important to remember that it also needs to be maintained. Some companies won't make it and will need to be removed – remember that this is a fast-growing segment, and some promising technologies just won't be able to be scaled to the point of commercialization. I've also added companies to the list that were marginal or what I'd call provisional. I want to keep an eye on them to see if they make strides toward truly being a solution provider. This doesn't always play out as they may have management or strategic changes. This is especially true with the ESG pushback of the last couple of years. Some management teams have given in to the pressure and have scaled back or eliminated sustainable products or services or simply the way a company does business. It's okay to remove a company from the universe if it no longer fits your definition of sustainable.

You can maintain the universe on an ad hoc basis or on a schedule; it just depends on how you want to manage it. I've found reviewing the list to be helpful because it may remind you of a company or sector that you need to review or explore some more.

DATA, DATA, DATA

I'm going to start this section by saying I am not a Certified Financial Advisor, nor do I have any desire to be. I have immense respect for those individuals who dedicate a tremendous amount of time to go through that program to receive this designation. Compared to the elegant analysis these folks do, I consider my process rudimentary, but it works for me and has worked for this portfolio for well over a decade. You'll need to develop your own process, but hopefully, mine can be a start for you.

Twice a year, I export my list of companies to Excel so I can perform the analysis that will lead to the reallocation and rebalance. Along with the list, I also export as much data as I can from Morningstar Direct, usually on the order of 100 or so metrics. I then manually add additional ESG and street opinion data from a variety of sources. Here are some, but not all, of the metrics I use:

Traditional Fundamentals			ESG
Market cap	Relative strength	PEG ratio	Sustainalytics score
Domicile	Enterprise value	P/FCF ratio	MSCI score
Sector	Book value	P/CF ratio	Carbon risk
Industry	Current ratio	ROIC %	Controversy level
Dividend yield %	Quick ratio	ROA %	ESG subindustry Percentile
1-, 3-, 5-, and 10-year returns	P/B ratio	ROE %	Revenue % from fossil fuels
Alpha	P/C ratio	Debt to equity	% female directors
Beta	P/E ratio	Standard deviation	Rev % carbon solutions

Notes: PEG ratio: Price to earnings growth
P/FCF: Price to free cash flow
P/CF: Price to cash flow
ROIC: Return on invested capital
ROA: Return on assets
ROE: Return on equity

For efficiency's sake, I'll start by eliminating companies with low trading prices (usually under $2/share), low volume (usually under 50,000 shares/day), or low market cap (usually under $250 million). When you have a universe of over 700 companies, and you want to reduce that number by about 90%, every little bit helps! Ultimately, this is a process of elimination – comparing companies in similar industries against each other to find the best opportunities for growth in the new economy.

Some data is more relevant than others, and I want some data to play a larger role in analysis. To accomplish this, I create a score for each metric I want to measure. I compare the company's score relative to the median index score and/or to the universe median score. It is a game of relativity.

How does a company stack up against its competitors? How has it performed in terms of profitability, is it overvalued, and what percentage of its revenue comes from carbon solutions? Sometimes, I'll even create my own factors like cash-to-market cap ratio or measure institutional buyers versus institutional sellers and create a score.

What I want to do with all these scores is create four composites: a fundamental composite, an ESG composite, a street consensus composite, and an overall composite. It is these composites that ultimately help guide me to decide which companies stay and which go. I will add up each category (fundamental, ESG, street consensus) at the end columns and create a factor so each composite has equal weighting.

Name	Ticker	Sub-industry	Fundamental Composite	ESG Composite	Consensus Composite	Overall Composite
Mercedes-Benz Group AG ADR	MBGYY	Automobiles	6.58	5.00	8.45	20.03
LiveWire Group Inc	LVWR	Automobiles	1.92	13.00	5.04	19.96
Rivian Automotive Inc Class A	RIVN	Automobiles	1.92	11.00	4.70	17.62
BYD Co Ltd ADR	BYDDY	Automobiles	8.22	1.00	7.80	17.02
Tesla Inc	TSLA	Automobiles	6.85	5.00	4.84	16.69
FREYR Battery	FREY	Batteries	1.92	14.00	4.37	20.29
Fluence Energy Inc	FLNC	Batteries	2.47	13.00	4.54	20.00
EnerSys	ENS	Batteries	3.56	2.00	6.32	11.88

I've put together a set of guidelines for how I want the portfolio to look when all is said and done. I want it to be weighted more heavily toward large cap stocks because of the relative stability they provide versus small and mid-caps. I shoot for 50% large cap, 30% mid-cap, and 20% small cap. These are obviously broad guidelines but keeping them within 5% is a good rule to follow.

I also want the portfolio to be global but still leaning strongly toward US-based stocks. The reality is that many companies based outside of the US have stronger sustainability programs, so it is very important to make an allocation outside of the US. For example, we couldn't allocate to any US-based insurance companies because they have not taken climate risk as serious as the European carriers. The target we use is two-thirds US companies and one-third foreign, with most of the foreign companies coming from developed markets such as Europe and Japan. Like market capitalization, these are guidelines and allow a +/-5% variance at the time of reallocation.

I break companies down by subindustry and will go through each one to make sure I'm comfortable with the categorization. I limit each subindustry to a maximum of four stocks to ensure adequate diversification, but rarely do we have that many. Usually it's one or two.

The process of elimination begins here. I'll sort the spreadsheet by subindustry, from high-composite score to low-composite score, and start removing the low-hanging fruit. I don't simply pick the top scorers, because there is much more nuance than that, but use the scores as a guide. I look at relative composite scores. I know that many foreign stocks don't have a lot of analyst coverage, so their consensus score may be misleading, and I try to complement companies within each subindustry to eliminate as much overlap as possible.

As I get down to the final 200 or so companies, I will take deeper dives into each company's sustainability credentials to make sure that the portfolio is as solutions-based as possible. I'll also sort by domicile to make sure we'll be able to get the appropriate allocation to foreign stocks, as well as sort by market cap to hit that target as well.

I target a total of 70 stocks in the portfolio with a ±5 variance. I have raised this number over the years as we've seen more and more companies added to the universe. I likely won't increase the number from here, as additional companies would only serve to complicate things. Plus, I like the idea that most companies have a 1–2% allocation, which means they can have an impact on the overall performance of the portfolio.

The whole process takes about three weeks to complete, which means that six weeks out of the year I'm working on the portfolio. I decided to use a semiannual reallocation schedule because I wanted to be able to make changes regularly, but I also know that I don't have the bandwidth to be managing the portfolio full-time. This was a good compromise.

CONCLUSION

Whether you choose to manage an individual stock portfolio or not, I believe it's important that you at least have one to use with clients. Running your own takes dedication, a thoughtful plan, and strategy, and the time to do it, but it can be very rewarding. I received feedback from a client a few years ago that they liked having individual stocks because it gave them more of a sense of ownership than funds did. They liked reviewing our holdings sheet, which provides links to each company's sustainability web page, and learning how their investments were making a difference in the world.

CHAPTER TWELVE

FINANCIAL PLANNING

OVERVIEW

I'm not a financial planner, but I truly understand the importance of a well-crafted, comprehensive but concise financial plan. When I was first starting my financial services career at Merrill Lynch many years ago, selling financial plans was a part of how we were evaluated as young advisors. I once sold financial plans to a small trucking company as an employee benefit. It gave me the opportunity to work with several people from different backgrounds and in different financial situations. I learned a lot about how a comprehensive financial plan can help change people's lives.

That was a long time ago, and I focus more now on managing the Earth Equity portfolios and being a thought leader in the sustainable investing space. My Earth Equity team and our financial planning department at Prime Capital Financial handle our clients' financial planning needs.

So, I'm not here to instruct you on how to put together a financial plan for your clients. What I would like to do, however, is give you a couple of topics to think about as you put together your clients' plans.

CLIMATE CHANGE AND FINANCIAL PLANNING

As of this writing, climate change is not a factor when a Certified Financial Planner creates a financial plan. Financial plans typically address issues such as retirement, education, estates, insurance, and taxes. With the changed climate becoming an increasingly prevalent part of our lives, I believe it's important that you add some climate factors into the financial plans you complete for your clients.

The US Department of the Treasury released a report in 2023 entitled "The Impact of Climate Change on American Household Finances." The report says that between 2018 and 2022, the total cost of climate and weather disasters topped $617 billion and that 13% of Americans had experienced economic hardship from those disasters or weather events in the previous year. It goes on to say, "The impacts of climate change are projected to worsen in coming years, putting additional communities and households at risk of financial strain."[1] If you're not including climate change in financial plans, you're missing out on an opportunity to further bring value to your clients, and you'll be doing them a tremendous service when climate impacts hit home.

---

[1] US Department of the Treasury, "The Impact of Climate Change on American Household Finances," https://home.treasury.gov/system/files/136/Climate_Change_Household_Finances.pdf.

LOCATION, LOCATION, LOCATION

For most clients, their largest asset is their real estate holdings. According to the Pew Research Center, in 2021, home equity accounted for about 45% of US homeowner's net worth.[2] Where a client lives will have a bigger impact on how they plan for their long-term financial future. What is the likelihood of a climate-fueled storm hitting your location? Are wildfires a realistic danger? Will the region run out of water? No matter where a client lives, they at least have some climate danger. We never thought we'd see the kinds of flooding in Asheville that we saw in September 2024. And while there is no such thing as a climate haven, there are locations that are more likely to be affected than others.

CoreLogic estimated that one in 10 residential properties in the United States were affected by natural disasters in 2021. According to the report, "Natural disasters are increasing in frequency and severity, impacting regions underprepared to handle an economic disruption, job displacement and the destruction of real estate assets. Community members are often unable to pay their mortgages or afford reconstruction costs. The report analyzes an area like Houma, Louisiana, which was hit head-on by Hurricane Ida, a category 4 hurricane, in August 2021. At the time of impact, delinquency rates hovered around 7.4%. The following month, the delinquency rate nearly doubled to 13.3% and hit 13.5% in October."[3]

---

[2] Pew Research Center, "The Assets Households Own and the Debts They Carry," December 4, 2023, https://www.pewresearch.org/2023/12/04/the-assets-households-own-and-the-debts-they-carry/.
[3] CoreLogic, "2021 Climate Change Catastrophe Report," https://www.corelogic.com/intelligence/2021-climate-change-catastrophe-report/.

In 2023, the First Street Foundation released its "9th National Risk Assessment: The Insurance Issue." The report details the rising risks from climate disasters and the impacts on the United States: "in CA, recent disaster data shows that since 2009, there has also been a 270% increase in the cost of wildfires and a 335% increase in the number of structures destroyed by wildfires. Both statistics highlight the consequence of wildfire management practices and the fact that wildfires are happening more often in, and in closer proximity to, places where people live."[4]

A Forbes Home survey asked participants, "If you were to move in the next year, what would motivate it?" Of the respondents 30% answered climate change, and an additional 34% are motivated by better weather.[5]

How will your clients financially handle a natural disaster event, and how are you integrating the risk into your financial plan?

INSURANCE

Of course, closely tied to real estate is insurance. If you live in states such as California, Florida, or Louisiana, property insurance is becoming more difficult and much more expensive to obtain. According to S&P Global, US homeowners insurance increased by over 11% in 2023,[6] and that trend is unlikely to slow down. Insurers that were slow to integrate climate risk into their underwriting are now being forced to make up for recent losses. Reinsurance rates have increased for insurers, and the responsibility is being passed down the line.

---

[4] First Street Foundation, "9th National Risk Assessment: The Insurance Issue," https://report.firststreet .org/9th-National-Risk-Assessment-The-Insurance-Issue.pdf.

[5] Forbes, "Americans Are Moving Because of Climate Change: Here's Where They're Going," https:// www.forbes.com/home-improvement/features/americans-moving-climate-change/.

[6] S&P Global Market Intelligence, "US Homeowners Insurance Rates Jump by Double Digits in 2023," January 2024, https://www.spglobal.com/market-intelligence/en/news-insights/articles/2024/1/ us-homeowners-insurance-rates-jump-by-double-digits-in-2023-80057804.

From the "9th National Risk Assessment: The Insurance Issue":

The damages associated with that (wildfire) risk are further expected to increase significantly by growing from around $14 billion in forecasted damages today to around $24 billion in damages per year by 2053, in today's dollars. In California, properties in the most at-risk portions of the state are finding it almost impossible to find affordable homeowners' insurance. In fact, recent data from the state suggest that between 2015 and 2021 some of the most at-risk zip codes have seen insurance policy non-renewals (insurer-driven) increase by nearly 800%. Underscoring this broader insurance issue, in Florida the "insurer of last resort", Citizens Property Insurance Corporation, has become the largest insurer in the state due to several bankruptcies and calculated business decisions to leave the market from some of the top providers.[7]

SwissRe reports that in the United States, there is a 42% insurance protection gap – the difference between insured and uninsured losses.[8] Some of this gap exists because of homeowners making the choice to self-insure, which could devastate an individual's financial plan if they aren't prepared for inflation and the realistic costs of repairing or rebuilding.

An appropriate financial planning question could be, "How badly do you want to stay in your current location, and is it worth having to self-insure your property?" For many clients, self-insuring is well out of reach, and they'll have to make the difficult decision to go.

Not to belabor the point, but I think it is so important to emphasize the tremendous risk that climate will have on real estate. Again, from the "9th National Risk Assessment: The Insurance Issue":

In total, there are huge numbers of properties at risk of rising insurance rates and non-renewals due to the growing risk of wildfires for nearly 5 million properties concentrated in the Western US, wind

---

[7] First Street Foundation, "9th National Risk Assessment: The Insurance Issue."
[8] Swiss Re, "Natural Catastrophe Protection Gap Infographic," https://www.swissre.com/risk-knowledge/mitigating-climate-risk/natcat-protection-gap-infographic.html#/.

damage for around 27 million properties in high-risk coastal wind zones, and flooding for around 15 million properties across the US not covered by FEMA flood zones. These millions of properties across the US represent a significant subset of the larger real-estate market which has not adequately priced the cost of climate into its valuation. The unrealized climate-corrected valuation gap represents a growing climate bubble which is just starting to be recognized and quantified.

The report found that a Florida homeowner who is dropped by an insurance carrier can expect their property value to decrease by 19–40%. Take this seriously, and your clients will be grateful!

BANKING

I wrote about banking in Chapter 4, but I thought it would be worthwhile to reiterate the importance of transitioning from the big national banks to local credit unions and values-based banks in the financial planning section. So few people realize that when they make a deposit at their bank, that money is then loaned out to businesses for mortgages and other uses. When you choose a credit union or a values-based bank, that money isn't used to finance the destructive fossil fuel industry. Instead, it is used to support local small businesses, install solar panels, and help those neighbors who have historically had few banking choices.

Adding banking to your financial planning discussion shows your client that you're not just concerned with their investment portfolio but also where their non-investment monies sleep at night. It shows that you're concerned with their overall impact and that you can be a resource to help them bank better.

WATER AND DROUGHT

Drought is one of the major effects of climate change. Vast regions of the American southwest has been feeling the impact of drought since the early 2000s. Yet, people continue to flock to the region for its low humidity and continuous sunshine. In 2023, Arizona limited construction activity in the Phoenix area because there was not enough water supply to meet demands of projects that were already approved.

Many cities that rely on the Colorado River for their water supply will be feeling the pinch as we move forward. From Las Vegas to Southern California, and the surrounding regions, advisors should be asking clients if living in the region is in their long-term future. The UN Environment Programme reports that Lake Mead in Nevada and Arizona and Lake Powell in Utah and Arizona experienced their lowest levels ever. The conditions are no longer categorized as a drought, but aridification, a "new, very dry normal." The lakes are at risk of reaching what is called "dead pool status," meaning the water in the lakes is so low that it could no longer provide enough water to run hydroelectric power facilities – another major problem.[9]

INCOME INTERRUPTIONS

According to FEMA, in 2014, the agency managed 108 disasters per year. In 2024, that number is 311, and more than 20 million individuals and families survive a disaster every year.[10] Clients who reside in areas that

---

[9] United Nations Environment Programme, "As Climate Dries, American West Faces Problematic Future, Experts Warn," https://www.unep.org/news-and-stories/story/climate-dries-american-west-faces-problematic-future-experts-warn.
[10] Performance.gov, "Recovering from a Disaster," https://www.performance.gov/cx/life-experiences/recovering-from-a-disaster/.

are likely to be affected by climate-enhanced storms also run the risk of income interruptions. When you can't work for weeks or months because of a disaster, there is a need to increase emergency cash reserves to be able to cover the time away. And while the federal government provides some disaster unemployment assistance, the process can be time-consuming and difficult. Preplanning and overfunding an emergency fund are vital.

Temperature extremes make it harder for people who work outside and results in lost productivity and income. We will see what is known as "wet-bulb" temperatures rise – a wet-bulb temperature is a measurement of heat plus humidity. According to ClimateCheck, "High heat with humidity poses a more significant risk to human health than high heat alone. The human body relies on the evaporation of sweat to cool itself, but in extreme heat and high humidity, sweat doesn't evaporate effectively. This leads to increased body temperature, heat exhaustion, and potentially fatal heatstroke."[11] Know that if your client is an outdoor worker, there may be times when they are unable to work, resulting in diminished income.

You're likely reviewing health and life insurance during the financial planning process. Keep in mind that as global temperatures rise, so does the risk for heat and microbe-related illnesses. Changing climate will spread diseases to different regions, especially tropical diseases such as Zika, West Nile, malaria, and dengue. Warming temperatures will enable ticks to be active during a wider range of months, leading to more cases of Lyme disease, ehrlichiosis, Rocky Mountain spotted fever, and others. These diseases may be debilitating long term or even deadly, so make sure client insurance is adequate.

---

[11] ClimateCheck, "Understanding Wet-Bulb Temperature: The Risks of High Wet-Bulb Temperatures Explained," https://climatecheck.com/blog/understanding-wet-bulb-temperature-the-risks-of-high-wet-bulb-temperatures-explained.

INFLATIONARY PRESSURES

Climate impacts also bring the potential to negatively affect supply chains, which can lead to inflationary pressures, as we saw during the pandemic. Climate also can have severe impacts on global shipping. *Foreign Policy* reported in January 2024 that the Panama Canal was under threat because of drought conditions, and that fewer ships were being allowed to pass through the vital shipping artery. The article says, "This has created a fraught logistical puzzle amid a simultaneous maritime crisis in the world's other main shipping shortcut: the Suez Canal, which is roiled by war in the Middle East." It goes on to say, "As climate extremes become more common, shipping companies, analysts, and governments fear the Panama Canal crisis may not be an aberration but the new reality. Scrambling to deliver their goods on time has led shipping companies to question whether the canal will remain a reliable artery of global trade. . . ."[12]

This is just the tip of the iceberg when it comes to the economic effects of climate. Changes in water patterns and droughts will affect agriculture and, ultimately, the price of food. An article from Columbia University details some of the impacts, saying increased heat and drought will likely reduce crop yields, and a National Academy of Sciences report states that for every degree Celsius the average temperature rises, there will be a 5–15% decrease in overall crop production. The article says, "Many commodity crops such as corn, soybean, wheat, rice, cotton, and oats do not grow well above certain temperature thresholds. In addition, crops will be affected by less availability of water and groundwater, increased pests and weeds, and fire risk. And as farmers struggle to stay afloat by finding ways

---

[12] Robbie Gramer, "Global Shipping Crisis Looms as Climate Change Dries Panama Canal," *Foreign Policy*, January 15, 2024, https://foreignpolicy.com/2024/01/15/panama-suez-canal-global-shipping-crisis-climate-change-drought/.

to adapt to changing conditions, prices will likely increase and be passed along to consumers."[13]

But it's not just about drought, though, as increased localized flooding has drowned both crops and livestock. According to the Columbia University article, "Extreme rainfall events have increased 37% in the Midwest since the 1950s, and this year, the region has experienced above normal amounts of rain and snowmelt that have caused historic flooding." NOAA, the National Oceanic and Atmospheric Administration, expects extreme rain events to continue. Farmers are planting fewer crops because of access to fields, and this lost yield could "cause prices for animal feed and ethanol to rise and potentially disrupt marketplaces at home and abroad. As a result of climate change impacts, the Midwest is projected to lose up to 25% of its current corn and soybean yield by 2050."

$500,000

In April 2024, *Consumer Reports* commissioned a report entitled "Cost of Climate Change to an American Born in 2024." The report estimates that climate change could cost a baby born in 2024 to be about $500,000 but concedes that when "more uncertain" factors are included, that number could reach $1 million.

The report goes on to say, "For many Americans, this financial loss will require difficult decisions about how to pay for food, housing, and other daily expenses, which climate change will increase by approximately 9 percent over their lifetime. At the same time, climate change is expected to decrease an individual's net income by roughly 10% over their lifetime,

---

[13] Renee Cho, "How Climate Change Impacts the Economy," *State of the Planet*, Columbia Climate School, June 20, 2019, https://news.climate.columbia.edu/2019/06/20/climate-change-economy-impacts/.

leaving that person with less disposable income to cover the higher cost of living. Despite the large uncertainties associated with estimating the impacts of future climate change on personal finances, one thing is clear: climate change will have a significant impact on Americans' standard of living."[14] As difficult as it may be, finding a way to integrate the cost of climate change into your financial plans is vital.

CONCLUSION

Despite all the evidence, people continue to move into areas prone to storms, drought, and fire, including Florida, Texas, Nevada, and Arizona, according to the US Census Bureau. Your actions as a financial advisor can help clients make better decisions for their and their family's futures. Taking the time to understand their specific climate risks and how it affects their financial plan brings value to the relationship. Learn about risks in your locality and become the go-to advisor for your region.

---

[14] ICF Incorporated, "Cost of Climate Change to an American Born in 2024: National Risk Assessment."

CHAPTER THIRTEEN

BUSINESS RETIREMENT PLANS

OVERVIEW

The Morgan Stanley "Sustainable Signals Report" details trends in sustainable investing, attitudes about, and interest in the investment style by demographic. The latest report was released in April 2025, and it shows that 84% of individuals in North America are either somewhat or very interested in sustainable investing.[1]

---

[1] Morgan Stanley Institute for Sustainable Investing, "Sustainable Signals: Individual Investors 2025."

Let's break that number down into age demographics:

Generation	"Very" or "Somewhat Interested" (%)
Baby boomers	72
Gen X	86
Millennials	97
Gen Z	99

Between Gen X, millennials, and Gen Z, most of the working-age population has a considerable interest in sustainable investing. Of the surveyed investors, 64% said that their interest in sustainable investing has significantly or somewhat increased from 2023 to 2025. Some of the top drivers for the increased interest include a desire to support real-world outcomes alongside a market-rate financial return, a belief that sustainable investments could offer stronger financial returns than traditional investments, and an intention to align investments with personal values. And well over half of respondents said that they planned to increase their sustainable investing allocation over the ensuing 12 months.

With all this information in mind, you would think that every 401(k) and 403(b) plan in the United States had at least one sustainable investing option for plan participants, wouldn't you? If you said yes, you would be wrong. In a 2024 article published by *Yale Climate Communications* entitled "Your 401(k) Might Be Feeding the Climate Crisis," the author says, "Fewer than 5% of 401(k)-type plans even offer climate-friendly or fossil fuel-free funds, according to Plan Sponsor Council of America."[2] Five percent of retirement plans offer a sustainable investment option, even though between 85% and 96% of plan participants have an interest.

---

[2] "Your 401(k) Might Be Feeding the Climate Crisis," *Yale Climate Connections*, March 2024, https://yaleclimateconnections.org/2024/03/your-401k-might-be-feeding-the-climate-crisis/.

There's a tremendous disconnect between what plan sponsors offer and what plan participants prefer.

The angle that the Yale Climate Communications article takes is to calculate how much money from retirement plans ends up being invested in fossil fuels. According to their calculations, retirement plans in the United States own upwards of $46.5 billion in fossil fuels, which is almost 5% of the nearly $9.9 trillion held in employer sponsored retirement savings plans. That's a lot of money that could be invested in climate solutions instead of climate change causes.

HOT POTATO

There are a lot of regulations related to retirement plan or Employee Retirement Income Security Act of 1974 (ERISA) accounts – considerably more than we typically see on the individual client side. The ability to include environmental, social, and governance (ESG) or sustainable investments has been thrown back and forth like a hot potato over the past few administrations in Washington, as the Department of Labor (which oversees ERISA regulations) has repeatedly issued contradictory rules.

The issue often comes into play when talking about pensions or omnibus plans, where all participants share one investment account. It just takes one participant who believes the misinformation about ESG or simply doesn't want to invest responsibly to cause a problem. While I wholeheartedly agree that investing responsibly is better for investors in the long run, I also don't think people should be forced to invest in what that they are uncomfortable with – especially with omnibus 401(k)s.

But most plans aren't omnibus, and pension plans are the exception rather than the rule. In a world dominated by individual, personal choice, it seems rather disingenuous to restrict a plan participant's desire to invest sustainably. There is no reason why every plan sponsor doesn't include just one or two sustainable investment options. None!

One of the excuses I hear regularly is that there isn't a demand for sustainable investments in retirement plans – that participants aren't asking plan sponsors for access to the funds. There are likely several reasons for this, the first being that plan sponsors aren't asking participants what they want to invest in. In my experience, plan sponsors are more concerned with not being sued, and including only the most innocuous, inexpensive funds they can find. Their attitude is we know better, we're the fiduciary, and we pick the funds. It has nothing to do with demand.

The second reason is that picking funds that are outside of the traditional S&P 500 clones makes plan sponsors uncomfortable. There is a risk of lawsuit. They don't understand that ESG is a risk mitigation strategy and not "woke investing." They don't know which funds to pick. They don't understand the demographics of their plan participants and their desire to invest sustainably. And they don't understand that the nature of that sustainability desire their participants have is about investing in solutions to make the world a better place.

Sam Adams is the CEO and cofounder at Vert Asset Management and is on the investment committee of the Plan Sponsor Council of America. He has worked in the sustainable investing space since founding Vert in 2014. In a conversation I had with Sam, he said, "We're finding that millennials and Gen Z are choosing to not contribute to their company's retirement plans, instead opening taxable accounts because their retirement plan doesn't have a sustainable or responsible option."

There is a big problem with this – first these employees are missing out on the tax deferral that comes with retirement plan investing, potentially costing them tens of thousands of dollars or more over their working life. Second, they miss out on any company matching dollars they would have received from the employer.

Liana Magner, the Head of Retirement at Natixis Investment Advisors, was interviewed in a November 2022 *Investment News* article on ESG and sustainable investments in retirement plans. She said, "According to Natixis Investment Managers survey results, 86% of millennials say they want their investments to reflect their personal values and 66% of millennials would be more likely to contribute for the first time or increase contributions to their workplace retirement savings plan if they knew their investments were doing social good. This is important considering that in a few short years, 75% of the American workforce will be millennials. It is evident that this is no longer a 'do good, feel good' story, but a movement that will affect the retirement savings outcome of a generation of Americans."[3]

Amy O'Brien, Global Head of Responsible Investing at Nuveen, echoed the thoughts of Magner in a *Plan Sponsor* article. She said, "Plan sponsors should consider adding more options for values-based investing to their menus and understand what's important to younger investors, who are coming out of college well-versed in the ideas behind sustainable investing. Plan sponsors need to take a second look. In the past, we've seen them add options, but in some cases if they did not commit to educating employees, they didn't do the education, and then they didn't see the fund flow they had hoped for. This is a way for companies to attract and retain younger workers."[4]

The Schroders 2022 "US Retirement Survey" found that 87% of plan participants want their "investments to be aligned with their values." When it comes to participation rates, the report said, "Of the 31% of 401(k) plan participants who knew their plan offered ESG options, nine out of ten

---

[3] "Strong Millennial Demand Pushing for Increased ESG Options in 401(k)s," *Investment News*, https://www.investmentnews.com/retirement-planning/strong-millennial-demand-pushing-for-increased-esg-options-in-401ks/228982.

[4] Rhea Wessel, "Investors' ESG Demands: Will Plan Sponsors Be Forced to Act?" PlanSponsor, https://www.plansponsor.com/in-depth/investors-esg-demands-will-plan-sponsors-forced-act/.

invested in those options, and almost three-quarters (73%) estimate they allocate 50% or more of their assets to socially responsible choices."[5]

Including a sustainable investing option in retirement plans is not only in demand by younger workers but it also could be used as a recruiting and retention tool as well. It seems awful short-sighted for plan sponsors to continue avoiding adding sustainable funds, and well worth the "risk."

WHAT'S THE BEST WAY TO ADD SUSTAINABLE FUND(S) TO A PLAN?

It's clear that, based on the demands of employees, every plan should have at least one sustainable or ESG fund for participants to use. But how do you make that selection? I would start out with the knowledge that sustainable investors want to own solutions, not just "less bad" versions of the big indexes. With that in mind you can begin your search.

You'll likely only be able to add one, maybe two funds to the plan. It'll obviously need to be competitive from a performance perspective – that's a necessary ERISA mandate. But beyond that, remember the guidelines I used previously when building a fund portfolio. Look under the hood and see what the fund actually owns. Is it a quasi-index or does it buck convention and own solutions providers? Is it built to invest in a cleaner, more resource-efficient, more resilient and equitable economy? If so, then there's a good chance that participants will invest in it.

If I had a choice of two funds, I would stick with the basics if possible: a US large cap growth fund or a global fund with access to more ESG and

---

5 Schroders, "US Retirement Survey," https://www.schroders.com/en-us/us/institutional/clients/defined-contribution/us-retirement-survey/.

sustainable-friendly regions like Europe. The flexibility of a global fund makes it easier to invest in solutions providers.

But remember, if participants don't know it's there, they may not use it. Or they may not understand what the fund is about, so education is just as important as getting the fund on the menu in the first place. Work with the plan sponsor to host webinars or in-person meetings to grow awareness and answer any participant questions.

This is a very difficult market to break in to. There is a lot of resistance from advisors and plan sponsors who don't understand the demographics and preferences of younger participants. The tendency is to default to the set of funds that are known and "safe," but not necessarily the ones that will drive participation rates and meet participants desires to invest responsibly.

At the end of 2024, I took over management of the Comerica FIT Core Series Large Cap Collective Investment Trust (CIT). A CIT is an investment vehicle that works like a mutual fund but is primarily used in retirement plans. At the time of this writing, we are working on a launch and marketing plan for the fund, knowing that there is demand and that it's in a plan sponsor's best interest to include at least one sustainable fund in every plan.

CONCLUSION

At the end of the day, this is a communication issue. Talking with participants, talking with plan sponsors, and bringing the needs of the two together is vital. Educating both parties on what ESG and sustainable investing really means, not the media or politician's opinions, but what you have learned from this book and other reputable sources, will make a difference. The opportunity is there if you're willing to work for it.

SECTION III

FOR THE INVESTMENT ADVISOR

CHAPTER FOURTEEN

THE SRI PRACTICE

HOW YOU CAN BUILD YOUR OWN

OVERVIEW

When I launched Krull & Company in June 2004, I was truly jumping into the void. I had spent about five years at Merrill Lynch where I learned the business, how to invest and allocate, and how to work with clients. When I realized it was time to leave because of problems with personnel management, I did a short stint at BB&T Securities and quickly realized that I was not cut out for the bank channel! The promises of a stream of prospects from the branches never materialized, the overuse of annuities made me uncomfortable, and the odd way that compliance scrutinized every trade turned me off quickly.

I was at a crossroads and started doing my research, talking with my fiancé, and saving money. Do I stay in financial services, or do I go back to consumer retail, where I was a very successful store manager? I couldn't see myself going back to the long hours of retail, however, so I ruled that out.

The questions were, Can I create my own small financial services firm, hang my shingle out, and be successful? I thought that I could, but I also wondered if my current clients would follow me. The answer to both questions was yes!

As I've said before, I had two main influences on my decision to focus on socially responsible investing. The first was my fiancé (now wife), Dr. Melissa Booth. Melissa has PhDs in microbiology and molecular genetics – yes, she's very smart, and I married well above my station! We were hiking and spending a lot of time outdoors. She was teaching me about climate change, sustainability, and environmental issues, and I was soaking it all up.

In our conversations, I recalled several interactions with my Merrill Lynch trainer and mentor who would often say that sustainable, resilient, and innovative (SRI) investing was an opportunity – especially after the Calvert wholesaler had visited the office. He never followed that path because it didn't align with who he was or what his values were, but I took it to heart and began to integrate what I learned from Melissa with this knowledge.

And, and I've mentioned, about that same time, I accompanied a client to meet with acclaimed green architect, designer, and author, William McDonough at his home in Charlottesville, Virginia. The client was installing a rainwater catchment system at Bill's house, and I was curious to see the system but even more curious to meet Bill.

I had watched his documentary, *The Next Industrial Revolution*, and was fascinated by his cradle-to-cradle concept of circular economies.

In the documentary, Bill talks about how bad design can lead to tragedy, even though tragedy wasn't intended. The lack of a plan becomes your de facto plan, as do the unintended consequences. Conversely, he says "design is the first signal of human intention." Could I create an investment firm with intention? Could I move beyond the "lack of a plan" paradigm that the traditional investment industry purveyed and all its unintended consequences? With all of this in mind, I set out to start my own financial services firm that was intentional and that focused on making the world a better place.

That was in 2004. The selection of SRI mutual funds that were available to me at the time was sorely lacking. Often, in the early years, I had to choose core non-SRI funds because the SRI alternatives simply didn't have competitive performance. I chose funds with holdings that weren't egregious, but it wasn't what I wanted to do. As the industry grew, however, so did the quality of investment management, and within a few years, I was using only SRI funds for equities and bonds.

Lucky for you, you don't have to make the same difficult choices I was making back then. You now have more than enough options (probably too many) to create a sustainable portfolio for your clients. Hopefully, my instructions in previous chapters will help you to craft models that meet your requirements and align with your clients' values.

GREEN OR GRAY?

My business partner Neill Yelverton likes to say that Earth Equity doesn't have a green or gray option; all we do is green. This will be one of the first choices that you'll have to make. If you currently are a financial advisor, you likely have several clients already and have been investing their money traditionally. You'll have to decide how to handle those clients. There can be tax implications to making drastic changes to portfolios, so going slow is the key.

Maintain your traditional investment models while you develop your SRI models, and of course, if SRI is going to be an "add-on," then you'll continue to manage both styles going forward. When it makes sense to transition your legacy clients to your new SRI models, do so in as painless and tax-efficient a way as possible. I can't emphasize how important good rebalancing software is to make portfolio transitions easier!

Whichever way you choose to run your investment management business going forward – green, gray, or both – make sure to employ the portfolio building strategies and techniques I've discussed previously in the book. Conduct in-depth due diligence, use appropriate asset and risk management strategies, and truly understand why the portfolio is structured the way that it is.

START WITH WHY

Clients are smart and can see through bullshit. If you're offering a sustainable investing option but don't understand or believe in it, they will know. Conversely, when a client knows that you share their passion for sustainability, social justice, or whatever the issue may be, you have a chance to nurture a client for life.

While I'm a pragmatist and understand that you don't need to be walking around in Birkenstocks and hugging trees (how's that for a stereotype?) to allocate your clients' assets to an SRI model, it is important to be informed and competent, which, ultimately, is the goal of this book. Speak with confidence, knowing that whatever choice you and the client make for their investment allocation, it is in their best interest.

And as a pragmatist, I also know that the statistics show the continued demand for sustainable investing options. If you're an established advisor, you have likely seen a client or two leave because you didn't have an SRI option. As we know, 70–80% of assets move when an inter-generational transfer takes place – oftentimes to a younger generation with a different value set than their parents or grandparents. This is the reality of the current marketplace. So, while that may be your original motivation, I would suggest that you dig a little deeper to find greater motivation.

If you haven't read the book *Start with Why* by Simon Sinek, I would encourage you to do so if you plan on making SRI the focus of your business. In the book, Sinek talks about what inspires people to act – it's not the *what*; it's not the *how*; it's the *why*. Everybody knows *what* you do – you help them plan and invest their money. Even though we like to think so, most clients don't care *how* you do what you do. However, all of them care *why* you do what you do. It's likely that all of us got into this business to help people – that's a great start on the road to why. But to connect with SRI clients, there must be more. Perhaps it is about social justice for you and the unfair burden that the poor shoulder when it comes to environmental degradation. Perhaps you have children, and you are concerned about the impact of climate change on their lives and future generations. Whatever your why, don't be afraid to let it be known.

Sinek uses what he calls the *golden circle*, which is three concentric circles with the words *what*, *how*, and *why* written in them from outside to in. He says that most businesses start with what and work toward the center. Instead, he says you should start at the center of the circle, start with why, and the how and the what will take care of themselves. He says, "People don't buy what you do; they buy why you do it . . . the goal is to do business with people who believe what you believe."

If you follow Sinek's advice and start with why, are intentional as Bill McDonough advocates, and create competitive, sustainable portfolios, you can be successful as an SRI advisor.

COMMUNICATING WITH CLIENTS AND PROSPECTS

So now you know why you're a financial advisor focusing on sustainable investing. How do you communicate your values and your investment offerings? I'm not going to get into a detailed marketing plan to let the world know that you now offer the best SRI investing options out there. What I am going to do is give you some advice on ways, both subtle and overt, to let clients and prospects know what you do.

At the time of this writing, there is one professional designation related to sustainable investing: the Sustainable Investing Certificate from the CFA Institute. The College for Financial Planning had offered the CSRIC or Chartered SRI Counselor designation since 2018, but dropped it in spring 2025. According to Jenny Coombs, the creator of the CSRIC, there will likely be a new designation offered by US SIF. Keep an eye out for it.

If you currently have a book of business, you likely have a sense of which clients might be interested in sustainable investing. Likewise, you also know which clients to avoid the subject with because the topic has been politicized. So, you start with those who might be open to it by simply letting them know that it is an option and asking if they would like to discuss it further.

When I was making the transition after I started my firm, one of the most important lessons I learned was to allow clients to make their own decisions at first. I was not pushy about offering SRI portfolios or the philosophy behind it. Clients either gravitated to it or not. For those who didn't, I simply maintained their traditional portfolios, while I used the newer, more responsible models for those who did. Eventually, I merged the portfolios because there was not a trade-off in performance, and it's much easier to scale when you have fewer models to manage.

You will want your marketing to reflect that you now offer sustainable investing options. Again, if this is only a part of your business, simply add a page to your website describing how you provide SRI investments and your investment philosophy. If you are going all-in on SRI, then you'll likely need to build a whole new website.

One tip that I would add is rooted in a lot of what we have discussed throughout the whole book – don't focus on ESG: it's too much of a political hot potato. Focus on solutions, growth investing, and the opportunities that sustainable investing has to offer.

Add a simple question to your risk questionnaire or intake form: are you interested in sustainable investing? Ask about the client's interests or groups they belong to. What kind of car are they driving? There are a lot of ways that you can learn about someone just by being intentionally observant.

Create a good presentation. Over the years, one of the most effective new client acquisition strategies I've employed is public speaking. A professionally designed, easy-to-understand presentation goes a long way toward bringing new dollars in the door. Use animations and simple charts. Discuss the new clean economy and changing demographics and consumer interests. Make sustainable investing accessible. And finally, practice, practice, practice. Know your material inside and out, and be prepared for intelligent, insightful questions.

I've had good luck giving presentations at churches and synagogues that have a focus on creation care, environmental nonprofits, and other purpose-driven organizations. Most of these groups will have an events chair who organizes activities and speakers for gatherings, and they often are looking for someone to come and speak. Don't be afraid to ask.

Practice your writing. My degree is in communication, so I've been comfortable writing since college. If you need to improve your writing, take a class at your local community college. Share your writing with your friends, family, and coworkers, and take their feedback seriously. When you're comfortable that your writing is sharable, work to build out your blog or reach out to local publications that could use a finance writer. Put yourself out there and help others in doing so.

Closely tied to writing is media relations. I employ a part-time publicist who helps me book media interviews, create awards submissions, and a range of other services that I couldn't do on my own. Her services are invaluable and because of her, our small firm punches well above our weight class when it comes to the media. From the *New York Times* to the *Wall Street Journal* to *Bloomberg*, I am regularly discussing sustainable investing with journalists. This didn't happen overnight, but now I'm considered one of the thought leaders in the sustainable investing space, and instead of reaching out to journalists, they oftentimes are reaching out to me. If your budget doesn't allow for a PR professional, consider using a service such as Source of Sources, which is a free email list that highlights the stories journalists are currently writing.

Finally, get involved in your community. When I first moved to Asheville, North Carolina, I began attending events like Green Drinks and other networking groups. Through that first Green Drinks, I was introduced to the head of the premier environmental nonprofit in the region. In no time, I was on the board and eventually served as the chair. That nonprofit has done a world of good locally and has also been a great source of new prospective clients. Find clubs, groups, and nonprofits that align with your values and get involved.

These are only a few suggestions that you can use to grow your sustainable investment practice. Spend some time with a sheet of paper and complete a mind map, including all the connections you may have in your town and opportunities to network, write, or be a speaker or media source. Sponsor a festival. Go on a Sierra Club hike. Help raise money for Planned Parenthood. The possibilities are endless.

WORKING WITH VALUES-BASED CLIENTS

Values-based clients are just like any other client. They care about their families; they want a comfortable retirement; they want to efficiently leave their wealth to family and charity; they want to send their kids and grandkids to college; they want to support their community and the local economy. There's nothing unusual about any of this, and so your interaction should be no different than with a traditional investment client.

There are some cues that the clients may pick up from you when you interact with them. If you pull up to their house in a gas-powered Hummer, they might question your environmental credentials. That's obvious. But what about when they visit your office, and you offer them bottled water instead of a pitcher and glasses? Is the default delivery method for your statements and performance reports paper or electronic? When you're working with a male/female couple, whom do you spend your time looking at and talking to? All of these and many more are subtle cues that you give off, and you need to intentionally be aware of them.

When it comes to charitable donations, ask your clients which organizations they regularly give to. Whom a client donates to tells you a lot about who they are and what their values are. You might follow their lead and contribute as well or offer to match clients' donations up to a certain amount. If they support a nonprofit, perhaps you attend a meeting or event with them. This might seem like going above and beyond, but if you are going to be an SRI advisor, it is so important to walk the walk.

And speaking of which, are you walking the walk in your personal life? Does your home have solar panels and batteries? Are you driving an electric vehicle (EV)? Clients notice everything and oftentimes are skeptical of advisors who say one thing and do another. Don't be a greenwasher in your personal and professional practices when you're telling them not to buy a Blackrock ESG fund because it owns Chevron and McDonald's!

CRAFTING YOUR PRACTICE

Going back to the beginning of this chapter, remember what Bill McDonough said? "Design is the first signal of human intention." Craft your SRI practice with intentionality. From your office space to the refreshments you serve, to the e-delivery of statements, take control from the beginning.

What is the client experience like, and how can you make it more true to your mission? The previous sections gave you several suggestions. Here are a few more that are both SRI-focused and good practice in general.

When we formed our independent Registered Investment Advisory firm (we had been working under another RIA previously), we pulled the team together to brainstorm several different aspects of the new firm. We created the name Earth Equity, as a team. We wrote out our vision statement together: Sustainable, responsible, and impact investing for all. We created a mission: Our mission is to empower sustainable, responsible, and impact investing across generations and communities to amplify financial impact and nurture positive change. Finally, we identified our core values: integrity, passion, impact, responsibility, and gratitude. These exercises brought us together with a shared vision for what we wanted Earth Equity to be. Take the time to go through this process. You'll be glad you did!

Build a tech stack that you would want to use yourself. Often, we choose a piece of software because of price or convenience, but is it good for clients, and can we use it without headaches? Can they easily log in and get the information they need? Will you be on the phone with tech support regularly, or does it just work? Is it a legacy product that is widely used in the industry, or is it a nimbler startup that might be better appreciated and used by a younger generation who is more interested in SRI? I've used so many different software packages over the years – some with success and others not so much – so that's why I'm including software in the list. Ask current users if they like it and get an extended trial. Make sure you and your clients are comfortable with your choice before you commit because committing to your software is a lot like a marriage!

You'll need to have a form of SRI reporting software, a category that is continually improving and expanding. We currently use two pieces of software. I have created a custom report in Morningstar Direct that will take a prospect's current portfolio and show them how much they own in fossil fuels, weapons, tobacco, and other non-desirable industries. The second report from YourStake enables us to compare the client or prospect's current portfolio versus one of our SRI portfolios in several metrics, including health, environment, human rights, equal opportunity, and accountability. These pieces of software can be invaluable in convincing that prospect that they should hire you. They also can help you as you construct your portfolios.

Gather the right people around you. Team building is very difficult, but also very rewarding when done right. As you grow your practice, look for others who share your values and who want to be a part of the solution. Nurture your team, and if possible, provide them with as many perks and benefits as you can afford. For example, we covered employee cell phone expenses and paid for annual passes to Biltmore in Asheville. We require that employees use all their vacation time, understanding the importance of downtime and rest.

There was one part of the hiring process that I especially enjoyed. Once we narrowed our search down to two or three candidates, we would invite the candidates individually out to lunch with the team. I can think of no better way to get to know a person than by having a meal with them.

We created a client gifting program that was focused on local businesses and artisans. When we send gifts, we include a card that tells the unique story of our relationship with the company or artist. We even had a potter create Earth Equity–themed pieces, including coffee cups, vases, and dishes. They were a big hit!

As much as we'd like to see a transition to greater use of public transportation, the reality is that most people will arrive at your office in a car. We learned when our office was in downtown Asheville that convenient parking was a problem and that older clients didn't want to come into the office because they couldn't find parking, or the walk was too long. When we changed offices after the pandemic, we found a location that had ample free parking on site. It may be a small thing, but many times, it's the small details that count. And sometimes you don't have any control over this, but we've found that many of our clients drive EVs. Having a free car charger in your parking lot would be the icing on the cake for many folks!

There's also the obvious: power your office with solar, if possible. Use recycled paper when you need to and avoid bottled water when you can serve tap water. I love the phrase "crafting your practice," because it implies an intentional process. As we've seen, the more intentional you are, the better your chances for success.

Finally, we've talked about the importance of where clients do their banking, but it's just as important for you as well. Are you banking with one of the big national banks that have dropped out of the Net-Zero Banking Alliance because of political pressure? Or one of the big banks that refuse to stop financing fossil fuels? Or are you working with a credit union that keeps the funds local to support your community? Or are you using a B Corp bank like Climate First Bank or Amalgamated Bank – banks that have a mission to be socially responsible, sustainable, and fight climate change? With the advent of online banking, there's no excuse anymore to continue using banks that aren't aligned with your values and mission.

ORGANIZATIONS

Being able to connect with others to both network and learn is important. Not surprisingly, responsible investing has a trade group that has been around for decades called the US SIF: The Sustainable Investment Forum. The Forum focuses on public policy, offers sustainable investing courses, provides industry research, and fosters collaboration and networking opportunities. I've attended their conferences, met with members of Congress, and advocated on Capitol Hill with their team. While not a requirement to be a member, it's a really good idea.

Several other organizations work with investors on topics such as shareholder advocacy, standardizations, and reporting:

- Ceres
- Interfaith Center on Corporate Responsibility (ICCR)
- United Nations Principles for Responsible Investment (UNPRI)
- Global Impact Investing Network (GIIN)
- Climate Action 100+
- The FAIRR Initiative
- Intentional Endowments Network
- Carbon Disclosure Project (CDP)

There are several other complementary organizations focused on the environment, social issues, and the like. Some are local, and some are national/international. While they are not industry organizations, teaming up with them to provide education, fundraising, or board service can be very advantageous as you grow your SRI practice. Examples of these might be the Sierra Club, Nature Conservancy, and Planned Parenthood, among others.

INDEPENDENT OR WORKING WITHIN A LARGER SRI FIRM OR A LARGER NON-SRI FIRM?

Finally, maybe one of the biggest questions you'll face is do you create your own SRI firm, or do you work within a larger organization? Each has its advantages and disadvantages; let's look at both.

You'll get the most flexibility by creating your own firm. When I launched Krull & Company in 2004, it was both the most exciting and scariest time of my life. There was so much to do – create a marketing plan and materials, reach out to clients about the new firm and prepare account transfer paperwork, and get my tech stack set up – among many other things. I had 100% of the responsibility but also the flexibility to set things up exactly how I wanted them. Did I get everything right? Of course not, but I learned a lot along the way, and I think it helped me to become a better businessperson and entrepreneur. Ultimately, if you are willing to put in the work, the extra hours, and shoulder all the responsibility, starting your own firm will be the most rewarding long-term option.

Your second option is to join a large non-SRI firm and become the SRI specialist. Joining (or remaining if you're already an advisor) an established firm enables you to focus only on your prospects and clients and implementing a sustainable investing program. The firm will take care of operations, compliance, and most of the marketing for you. It's up to you to distinguish yourself as the SRI expert. In speaking with colleagues who have decided on this route, the downside is that often the firm doesn't support SRI portfolios, so you might feel like an island in a sea of traditional investment advisors.

Finally, if you're willing to team up with other like-minded folks, joining an SRI firm might be the best of both worlds. SRI firms are typically smaller, so you can have a bigger impact, but they also have operational and compliance teams in place so you can focus on helping clients instead of running a business. An established SRI firm will also likely have a range of sustainable investment models already constructed for you, with track records and professional money managers making investment decisions.

You'll also get an established brand name and a marketing plan to help you get up and running quickly. While there isn't as much competition in the SRI space as there is in traditional investments, having a recognized brand can be advantageous. Joining an established SRI firm will help you scale up quicker and more efficiently. Shameless plug: Earth Equity is always looking to add quality, experienced financial advisors who want to make a difference and help clients align their investments with their values.

CONCLUSION

However, you choose to make your transition, make sure to take your time, be intentional, and craft the situation that is right for you. You don't want to throw yourself into a new role only to realize soon after that it's not right for you, or that you don't have the flexibility you want, or that there's too much responsibility. I wish you the best in your process!

CHAPTER FIFTEEN

DEALING WITH THE POLITICS OF SRI

OVERVIEW

This chapter dives into the political debate over responsible investing. I know the rule that politics and business don't mix, but the responsible investing industry didn't start this fight – those who felt threatened by it did. They have turned the investing style into a political punching bag over the past few years. We're going to look at why this has happened, how to avoid the political aspects of the investment style, and how to come out ahead in the conversation.

WOKE INVESTING AND DISINFORMATION

Larry Fink is one of the most recognized figures in the investment world. As CEO of Blackrock, his firm is responsible for managing over $11.5 trillion dollars of client funds – the largest in the world. Obviously, Larry isn't a stupid guy, and he sees the writing on the wall when it comes to climate change.

In 2020, he wrote a letter to CEOs calling for a fundamental reshaping of finance. In the letter, he states that "climate risk is investment risk," and that "as a fiduciary, our responsibility is to help clients navigate this transition. Our investment conviction is that sustainability and climate-integrated portfolios can provide better risk-adjusted returns to investors. And with the impact of sustainability on investment returns increasing, we believe that sustainable investing is the strongest foundation for client portfolios going forward."[1] This was a ground shaking statement coming from someone at the top of the investment management industry.

At the time, I was excited to see such a bold statement coming from this huge asset manager. The tide was starting to turn. However, there was one aspect of the letter that was not well received by the fossil fuel industry: the call for an energy transition. He said, "Over the next few years, one of the most important questions we will face is the scale and scope of government action on climate change, which will generally define the speed with which we move to a low-carbon economy. . . . Every government, company, and shareholder must confront climate change." The legacy fossil fuel industry took this statement as a threat to their livelihoods and began their work to undermine and discredit the sustainable and responsible investment movement.

---

[1] Black Rock, 2020 Black Rock Client Letter, https://www.blackrock.com/corporate/investor-relations/2020-blackrock-client-letter.

According to the Environmental Protection Agency, "The largest source of greenhouse gas emissions from human activities in the United States is from burning fossil fuels for electricity, heat, and transportation."[2] The need to move off fossil fuels as quickly as possible to reduce our carbon emissions is a known fact. Many advisors, including myself, believe it is unwise to invest in fossil fuel companies for the sheer reason that I'd be hard-pressed to find another sector with as much risk and potential liability.

The fossil fuel industry has actively participated in a disinformation campaign regarding the impact of their products. A Congressional Joint Staff report from April 2024 states, "Documents demonstrate for the first time that fossil fuel companies internally do not dispute that they have understood since at least the 1960s that burning fossil fuels causes climate change and then worked for decades to undermine public understanding of this fact and to deny the underlying science. Big Oil's deception campaign evolved from explicit denial of the basic science underlying climate change to deception, disinformation, and doublespeak."[3] If you look at the actions of the fossil fuel industry from a purely governance perspective, the risk and liability would be off the chart.

The products produced by the fossil fuel industry are driving humanity's existential crisis via climate change. There are more than enough both fundamental and moral reasons to divest from the sector. But what happens when people and their sources of revenue are threatened? They fight back no matter how wrong they are.

Now, it's no secret that corporations play a huge role in deciding and dictating legislative and regulatory policy. In many cases, it's a revolving door for regulators between government jobs and corporate jobs without much of

---

[2] US Environmental Protection Agency, "Sources of Greenhouse Gas Emissions," https://www.epa.gov/ghgemissions/sources-greenhouse-gas-emissions.
[3] US Senate Budget Committee, "The Cost of Fossil Fuel Dependence: Economic and Budgetary Costs for American Taxpayers," https://www.budget.senate.gov/imo/media/doc/fossil_fuel_report1.pdf.

a line in between. And, since the 2010 Citizens United decision in the Supreme Court, corporations have had an even bigger role as they can now contribute unlimited amounts to political campaigns. You should be able to figure out what happened next: the fossil fuel industry began to use their funded politicians to fire up the rhetoric and introduce anti-ESG legislation.

As an aside, I'll never understand the vehement opposition to transitioning to a cleaner, more sustainable energy system (outside of the fossil fuel industry). I understand that there may be skepticism about climate change and its causes despite all evidence to the contrary, but the downsides to a sustainable economy are minimal, and the upsides are extraordinary. Here is my favorite cartoon depicting my thoughts on the subject:

Source: Joel Pett/TCA

An investigation by the independent think tank InfluenceMap found that in February 2021, "the West Virginia Coal Association sent a draft of an anti-ESG bill, which appeared to be drafted by Alliance Resource

Partners, (the second largest coal producer in the eastern US) to West Virginia Delegate Zack Maynard, who subsequently introduced the legislation HB 3084."[4]

The report further shows that in the following month,

> The lobbyist from Alliance Resource Partners emailed the head of West Virginia Pensions and Retirement Committee, writing that HB 3084 is "part of a multi-state initiative to counter back against corporate cancel culture specifically ESG." He also attached a white paper, titled "Energy Discrimination: A Threat to Capitalism, Prosperity, & Flourishing" which was authored for the Texas Public Policy Foundation's Life: Powered initiative by Bud Brigham, an oil/gas, minerals, and frac sand executive who has served on the National Petroleum Council. In the white paper, which characterizes ESG investing as a campaign to "bully business into divesting from fossil fuels," Brigham writes that "the climate catastrophist view is based on questionable science," and "fossil fuels have helped America become a world leader in many areas, including environmental quality." The report sources were acquired through the Freedom of Information Act and have been verified.

This backroom process of creating and implementing legislation has led to anti-ESG laws in several states, including Texas, Oklahoma, Missouri, and Florida, among others. In May 2022, former vice president Mike Pence got in on the action as well, complaining that "Woke Capitalism" threatened economic freedom and that the shift was "entirely manufactured by a handful of very large and powerful Wall Street financiers promoting left-wing environmental, social and governance goals (ESG), and ignoring the interests of businesses and their employees."[5]

---

[4] InfluenceMap, "New Analysis: Fossil Fuel Industry Indirectly and Directly Driving Anti-ESG Political Movement," https://influencemap.org/pressrelease/New-Analysis-Fossil-Fuel-Industry-Indirectly-and-Directly-Driving-Anti-ESG-Political-Movement-22497.
[5] Mike Pence, "Only Republicans Can Stop the ESG Madness," *Wall Street Journal*, May 25, 2022, https://www.wsj.com/articles/only-republicans-can-stop-the-esg-madness-woke-musk-consumer-demand-free-speech-corporate-america-11653574189.

It's this basic lack of understanding regarding how ESG works that makes their argument so dangerous. As you have seen throughout this book, ESG is simply a set of metrics detailing the risks a company faces. When executed properly, this additional due diligence should create a portfolio with less systemic risk and more opportunities for long-term growth. Unfortunately, the emotional manipulation that politicians and self-serving businesspeople use ignores the reality of the situation.

The ironic part about all of this is that Blackrock took the brunt of the ESG backlash. You've seen in Chapter 5 my breakdown of the most popular ESG fund that the company manages, the iShares ESG Aware MSCI USA ETF. This fund is anything but sustainable, doesn't divest from fossil fuels, and owns companies like McDonald's and Northrop Grumman. But, because Larry Fink was writing letters suggesting that climate change is going to change our economic systems, the company was targeted.

Media outlets bought into the ESG disinformation campaign just like the politicians who were paid for by the fossil fuel industry. Headlines like "The March of Folly Over ESG Investing"[6] in the *Wall Street Journal* and "Investors Pull Billions from Sustainable Funds Amid Political Heat"[7] in the *New York Times* paint a less than glowing picture of the industry. But oftentimes these articles neglect to put the source of the story into context. I know this because I was interviewed by Bloomberg on this issue. However, a flashy headline makes the story easier to sell.

As I said earlier, all this pressure has led to anti-ESG legislation, especially in Republican-dominated states. This rush to create anti-free market legislation has ended up costing states potentially billions of dollars. Daniel Garrett of the Wharton School and Ivan Ivanov of the Federal Reserve

---

[6] The Editorial Board, "The March of Folly Over ESG Investing," *Wall Street Journal*, https://www.wsj.com/opinion/the-march-of-folly-over-esg-investing-emotions-politics-profit-override-sound-principles-1faa95dc.

[7] "ESG Funds Face Significant Withdrawals Amid Controversy," *New York Times*, January 19, 2024, https://www.nytimes.com/2024/01/19/business/esg-funds-withdrawals.html.

Bank of Chicago produced a paper in June of 2022 called "Gas, Guns, and Governments Financial Costs of Anti-ESG Policies." In the paper, they say, "In 2021 Texas prohibited municipalities from hiring banks with certain ESG policies, leading to the abrupt exit of five large municipal bond underwriters. Issuers with historical relationships with the barred underwriters face higher uncertainty and borrowing costs after enactment of the laws, amounting to $300–$500 million in additional interest on $31.8 billion borrowed. These effects are consistent with deterioration in underwriter competition and loss of relationship-specific assets."[8] The political points scored by the anti-ESG bill in Texas will end up costing taxpayers hundreds of millions of dollars.

Many of these laws have been challenged in court, and some, such as Oklahoma and Missouri, have been blocked. And it's likely that we'll see more as time goes on. The reality of the situation is that anti-ESG laws are anti-free market. It's really quite simple: if you don't want to invest using ESG principles, don't hire an investment manager who uses ESG metrics as part of their due diligence process. The irony of free market politicians choosing to legislate against free market principles is not lost on me and shouldn't be lost on you. Follow the money, and you'll find their motivation.

It's unfortunate that this political pressure has had a negative impact on ESG investing in general. Larry Fink has stopped writing about climate reshaping finance. Even though there are more responsible mutual funds and ETFs available than ever, many have removed *ESG* from their names to appease the skeptics and politicians. Corporations are transitioning their ESG and diversity, equity, and inclusion initiatives and renaming and/ or reframing them. I guess it's all part of the evolution of a new concept, and we must believe that responsible investing will be better on the other side.

---

[8] Daniel G. Garrett and Ivan T. Ivanov, "Gas, Guns, and Governments: Financial Costs of Anti-ESG Policies," March 11, 2024, https://ssrn.com/abstract=4123366.

Unfortunately, when it comes to climate change and the solutions that are needed, time is of the essence.

IN PRACTICE

Your job is to remove the politics as much as possible from your practice. Unfortunately, sometimes we're faced with rules and legislation that we have no control over, and we need to remain compliant. But if you structure your SRI practice in a way that focuses on opportunities for the new, cleaner, and more resource-efficient economy, you will do both your clients and you a service.

Focus on the changing economy: the growth of clean energy generation, battery technologies, and grid upgrades. Know that smart investments in infrastructure will lead to better outcomes from a resilience and adaptation perspective. And understand the important role that efficiency plays – in information technology, real estate and green building, and for resources like water. Stress the fact that sustainable investing is ultimately the very definition of growth investing – investing in innovation and innovators who will have an impact on the future.

Your job is to stay positive, but also realistic. Sustainable investing is growth investing, which isn't always in vogue. There will be times when value investing outperforms, and that is okay as long as you take the long view. After the 2020 surge in asset growth and outperformance, the market shifted to a more value-focused investment style from 2021 and into 2023. Growth investments underperformed, which meant that so did sustainable investments. The headlines trumpeted the ESG underperformance without putting the results in context. Journalists focused on raw performance without regard for investment cycles and styles. The anti-ESG crowd celebrated and amplified this disinformation. Remember, sustainable investing is investing in the next economy – it is long-term investing.

UNDERSTAND THE CRITICISMS

We've discussed it previously in the book, but it is important to understand the criticisms of sustainable investing, and especially ESG. The people who criticize ESG because they believe the practice is "woke investing" don't understand the definition. I've encountered this multiple times as I explain that ESG risk isn't the risk the company poses on the environment, social issues, or governance. It is the risk *on* the company from environmental, social, and governance issues. While this may seem like semantics, it is anything but. When you're gauging the risk on a company, you're engaging in enhanced due diligence – the more risk data, the better. It is quantifiable.

Another criticism is the lack of standardization when it comes to ESG analysis. The metrics and scoring system that Sustainalytics uses in its rating process may be very different than what MSCI or Ethos uses. This does create vast disparities in rankings for both companies and industries. While as SRI professionals, we may be able to parse out the differences between the different rating companies, the retail investor may not be able to. And certainly not the anti-ESG crowd who decries the process as a sham.

You can minimize this criticism by conducting your due diligence to understand the main players in the ESG rating world and how their systems and algorithms work. You may not be able to convince someone who doesn't want to be convinced, but you will be able to better explain the differences, and why you have chosen the company that you have as your data provider.

BE A THOUGHT LEADER

Working in sustainable investing gives you ample opportunity to be a thought leader. You are not a garden variety investment advisor, but a specialist who brings a unique perspective to the investing and financial planning experience. Use this to your advantage from a client service and marketing perspective. Very few other advisors are going to have the same insights that you do, which gives you a competitive advantage.

CHAPTER SIXTEEN

THE WRAP-UP

My intention in writing this book was to provide you with the tools that are necessary to grow an investment practice focusing on sustainable investing, or to transition from your current traditional financial advisor practice to a sustainable one. I hope I succeeded.

I love telling the story about starting the firm in my home back in Roanoke, Virginia. How grateful I was that most of my clients from Merrill Lynch took a leap of faith and followed me into the new endeavor. How it was a struggle to put together a truly sustainable portfolio back in the day because the investment options simply didn't exist yet. I think about clients who have been with me from the start. I think about clients who aren't with us anymore who held a special place in my heart: Jack, Eric, Maurice, Bryce, and others. The thing that makes this career, that really is a lifestyle, so rewarding is knowing the impact that we can have on peoples' lives. Knowing how we can bring together their values along with their investments in a way that benefits everyone. It truly is a win-win.

An important aspect of being a sustainable investment advisor is knowing the history of the discipline and that you're carrying on a proud tradition. From early church leaders to the tree-hugging hippies of the 1970s to today's sophisticated sustainable, resilient, and innovative investment advisors, we all share a common theme to do well by doing good. As with all things, though, innovation in the industry will continue to advance – we can never rest on our laurels. When I think about just the past five years, the advancements in transparency and reporting, the proliferation of climate solutions providers and our ability to invest in them, and the widespread interest by the investing public, I'm very hopeful.

By now, you should be able to clearly explain the difference between environmental, social, and governance (ESG) and sustainable investing. I love the term *less bad* investing and use it every chance I get. I've said it a lot in the book, but I'll say it again: retail investors want to own solutions to our greatest challenges. You can now give them what they want. And there are lots of people to help when you consider all the demographics and statistics. 84% of overall investors are very or somewhat interested in sustainable investing; 99% of Gen Z, 97% of millennials, 86% of Gen X, and even 72% of baby boomers![1] The opportunity is most definitely there.

Help your clients to break away from the big, fossil fuel financing, profit-driven banks. Find trusted banks and bankers who abide by the Global Alliance for Banking on Values principles, who are part of the solution, not a part of the problem. Remember that there is a lot of inertia when it comes to switching banks – their goal is to provide customers with several services to make the relationship more "sticky" and difficult to leave. But continuing to support these banks is the equivalent of continuing to invest in Chevron. It's time to move on.

Be vigilant about greenwashing. The due diligence necessary to rise above the mediocrity of generic ESG funds takes work, but it's ultimately worth it, as you are better able to provide clients with the investments and impact they desire. When you see ExxonMobil or McDonald's or Lockheed

---

[1] Morgan Stanley Institute for Sustainable Investing, "Sustainable Signals: Understanding Individual Investors' Interests and Priorities."

Martin in a responsible fund, you now know to say "next," and move onto the next possibility. You know to look under the hood and see what the holdings are, because ultimately, it's the holdings that determine what's sustainable and what isn't.

Take your fiduciary duty seriously. I truly believe that by integrating ESG risk data; by investing in sustainability, resilience, and innovation; and by understanding our clients desire to have an impact, we are fulfilling our fiduciary duty. We take pride in doing what is in our clients' best interest, and it's a great feeling to know that sense of responsibility. As I said, take it seriously.

You now have the tools to create your own sustainable portfolio to use with your clients. You know how to source mutual funds and exchange-traded funds that own solutions providers, and how to avoid those ESG funds that are simply less bad. You understand the crossover trap, and how to position thematic funds next to core funds. And you know how to grade the portfolio using third-party tools.

One of the hardest parts of the job is creating an individual stock portfolio, but you also now have the tools to start that process. From creating your universe to scoring companies to putting it all together, if it fits your business model, you can offer your clients a chance to individually own some of the companies making a difference.

You understand the importance of integrating climate risk into your financial plans, and what a difference that will likely make in our changed climate world. Insurance, retirement location, investments, and so many other aspects of the plan may be complicated as the impacts hit home. You can make a huge difference in your clients' lives by making this a priority.

Most of the working population have a huge interest in sustainable investing, yet their 401(k)s and other retirement plans likely don't have a sustainable investing option. The opportunity to provide a solution to this supply and demand disparity could be a big opportunity for you if you have an interest in retirement plans.

And you now have some ideas to craft your own sustainable investment practice, from communications and software to the details that clients notice, like e-statements and avoiding plastic water bottles and the like. You should know how to deal with the political attacks that have arisen as responsible investing has gained momentum. The ability to communicate the importance of sustainable, resilient, and innovative investing to the public, prospects, and clients will give you a leg up on those who don't understand the nature of the practice.

As we end, I'd like to hear from you. Give me your feedback on how we can make future editions of the book better. I'd also like to offer you my services if it makes sense to you and your practice. From consulting on making the transition to a sustainable business model, to licensing our sustainable, Earth Equity SMA portfolios (we offer direct contracts with RIAs, as well as being on several turnkey asset management platforms (TAMPS) including SMArtX) to use with your clients, I would love the opportunity to help you move forward. Or, if you're an experienced advisor, I'd love to talk with you about becoming a part of Earth Equity as we build out our nationwide presence.

Thank you for investing your time and attention in learning more about sustainable, resilient, and innovative investing. I wish you the best in your journey!

ACKNOWLEDGMENTS

This book has truly been a labor of love. I appreciate everyone who has contributed to the success of Earth Equity Advisors over the years, including our wonderful clients, teammates, colleagues, friends, and family. If you're not listed, it's not because I don't appreciate you – it's because at 55 years old, the memory ain't what it used to be.

I want to start out by thanking my amazing wife, Dr. Melissa Booth. The journey has not been an easy one to create and grow a business from scratch, but your undying support and belief in me have kept me going for over 20 years. Your wisdom about all thing's science, sustainability, environmental, and more have been a guiding light for me, and you never cease to amaze me with your insight and ability to spot trends before anyone else does. You truly are a futurist if there ever was one. Thank you for everything!

I also want to thank David Crawford, founder of Rainwater Management Systems, for including me on a visit to meet William McDonough back in 2003. That visit with Bill made a huge impact on my decision to start Krull & Company. And thanks to Bill for his time that day and all the leadership he has shown in the field of sustainability and circular economy over the decades.

I learned the importance of a hard day's work and what it meant to have a strong work ethic from my parents, Harold and Betty Krull. Neither finished high school, and both worked hourly jobs for most of their lives. They had wisdom that comes from the struggles of a blue-collar existence. They were savers and knew the value of a dollar. They always wanted the best for me, and I am forever grateful.

I discovered my appreciation for the outdoors from my brother, Bill Witkopf. He was a hunter and, back in the 1970s, an environmentalist. The time I spent hiking with him and the things he taught me during my formative years are still with me today as I sit at our lake cabin, in the North Carolina woods, writing this sentence.

Neill Yelverton and Kerry Keihn have been with Earth Equity for the entirety of our push to grow the firm. They have been invaluable teammates, each bringing something different and complementary to the table. We make a great team!

I've worked with my publicist and PR professional, Abbie Sheridan with Greenrose Communications, since 2017. She has been able to take our little firm and get us big exposure. I like to say that she's been able to help us "punch above our weight class" by getting me in the *Wall Street Journal*, the *New York Times*, *Barron's*, *Bloomberg*, *Money Magazine*, Michael Kitces's *Financial Advisor Success* Podcast, Reuters TV, and so many others. She's a rock star!

Thanks to my editor, Judith Newlin, who reached out to me what seems like forever ago, in the middle of 2022, telling me that she enjoyed the short-form writing I was doing for our blog, and my other media appearances. She asked if I was interested in writing a book about sustainable investing. Obviously, I was! Since then, we've changed publishers, been through a hurricane that created a delay in publication, and experienced the fun that is putting the final touches on a book. Thank you for your vision and for seeing the opportunity.

Thanks to Stephen Szymanski, who helped me get my interview at Merrill Lynch back in 1998. I sold Steve an Apple computer back when I was working in consumer electronics, and he subsequently became my Merrill financial advisor, who generously took on my small account and then made the call to the Roanoke Merrill Lynch office. You got the ball rolling – thank you!

In December 2022, Earth Equity was acquired by Prime Capital Financial. The intention of the acquisition was to help us create scale and reach a wider audience with our sustainable portfolios. Thanks to Glenn Spencer for seeing the opportunity in Earth Equity, and especially to John Seibolt, who has transitioned through the integration process from a colleague to a friend.

Finally, I want to thank our amazing Earth Equity clients – the list continues to grow every day. From those who followed me from Merrill Lynch to BB&T to Krull & Company, to the newest folks who are coming on board with a desire to align your investments with your values – you are ultimately the driver of everything we do. Everything that is written in this book has been learned through the experience of working with you, investing for you, and listening to you. I am forever grateful!

RESOURCES

T his is by no means an exhaustive list, but it should serve to help you as you go through your process to become a sustainable financial advisor.

ASSOCIATIONS AND INDUSTRY INFORMATION

US SIF: The Sustainable Investment Forum – https://www.ussif.org

CFA Institute Sustainable Investing Programs – https://www.cfainstitute.org/programs/sustainable-investing

Ceres – https://www.ceres.org

Interfaith Center on Corporate Responsibility (ICCR) – https://www.iccr.org

United Nations Principles for Responsible Investment (UNPRI) – https://www.unpri.org

United Nations Sustainable Development Goals – https://sdgs.un.org/goals

Global Impact Investing Network (GIIN) – https://thegiin.org

Climate Action 100+ – https://www.climateaction100.org

The FAIRR Initiative – https://www.fairr.org

Intentional Endowments Network – https://www.intentionalendowments.org

Carbon Disclosure Project (CDP) – https://www.cdp.net/

SASB Standards – https://sasb.ifrs.org

As You Sow – https://www.asyousow.org

Cradle to Cradle Product Innovation Institute – https://c2ccertified.org

INVESTMENT FIRMS AND BANKS

Earth Equity Advisors – https://www.earthequity.com

Green Alpha Advisors – https://greenalphaadvisors.com

Vert Asset Management – https://vertfunds.com

Calvert Impact – https://calvertimpact.org

Calvert – https://www.calvert.com

Green Century Funds – https://www.greencentury.com

Community Capital Management – https://www.ccminvests.com

Impax Asset Management – https://impaxam.com

Trillium Asset Management – https://www.trilliuminvest.com

Parnassus Investments – https://www.parnassus.com

Brown Advisory – https://www.brownadvisory.com/

Adasina Social Impact – https://www.adasinaetf.com

Domini – https://domini.com

Boston Trust Walden – https://www.bostontrustwalden.com

Greenbacker Capital – https://greenbackercapital.com

Alante Capital – https://www.alantecapital.com

Meridiam – https://www.meridiam.com

Citizen Mint – https://citizenmint.com
Climate First Bank – https://www.climatefirstbank.com
Amalgamated Bank – https://www.amalgamatedbank.com
Self-Help Credit Union – https://www.self-help.org
CNote – https://www.mycnote.com

OTHER RESOURCES

Morningstar Direct – https://www.morningstar.com/business/brands/data-analytics/products/direct
YourStake – https://www.yourstake.org
Sustainalytics – https://www.sustainalytics.com
CSR Hub – https://www.csrhub.com
Clarity AI – https://clarity.ai
Fossil Free Funds – https://fossilfreefunds.org
Other xxx-Free Funds Guides from As You Sow – https://www.asyousow.org/invest-your-values/
Nitrogen (Riskalyze) – https://nitrogenwealth.com
SMArtX – https://www.smartxadvisory.com
Morgan Stanley Institute for Sustainable Investing – https://www.morganstanley.com/what-we-do/institute-for-sustainable-investing
Green America – https://www.greenamerica.org
Trellis – https://trellis.net

DISCLOSURES

This document does not constitute advice or a recommendation or offer to sell or a solicitation to deal in any security or financial product. It is provided for information purposes only and on the understanding that the recipient has sufficient knowledge and experience to be able to understand and make their own evaluation of the proposals and services described herein, any risks associated therewith and any related legal, tax, accounting, or other material considerations. To the extent that the reader has any questions regarding the applicability of any specific issue discussed to their specific portfolio or situation, prospective investors are encouraged to contact Peter Krull or consult with the professional advisor of their choosing.

There is no guarantee that the investment objectives will be achieved. Moreover, the past performance is not a guarantee or indicator of future results.

Certain information contained herein has been obtained from third-party sources and such information has not been independently verified. No representation, warranty, or undertaking, expressed or implied, is given to the accuracy or completeness of such information by Peter Krull or any other person. While such sources are believed to be reliable, Peter Krull does not assume any responsibility for the accuracy or completeness of such information. Peter Krull does not undertake any obligation to update the information contained herein as of any future date.

Except where otherwise indicated, the information contained in this presentation is based on matters as they exist as of the date of preparation of such material and not as of the date of distribution or any future date. Recipients should not rely on this material in making any future investment decision.

Any indices and other financial benchmarks shown are provided for illustrative purposes only, are unmanaged, reflect reinvestment of income and dividends, and do not reflect the impact of advisory fees. Investors cannot invest directly in an index. Comparisons to indexes have limitations because indexes have volatility and other material characteristics that may differ from a particular hedge fund. For example, a hedge fund may typically hold substantially fewer securities than are contained in an index.

Certain information contained herein constitutes "forward-looking statements," which can be identified by the use of forward-looking terminology such as may, will, should, expect, anticipate, project, estimate, intend, continue, *or* believe, *or the negatives thereof or other variations thereon or comparable terminology. Due to various risks and uncertainties, actual events, results, or actual performance may differ materially from those reflected or contemplated in such forward-looking statements. Nothing contained herein may be relied on as a guarantee, promise, assurance, or a representation as to the future.*

INDEX